DARK SKY, DEEP WATER

Norman L R Franks

GRUB STREET · LONDON

Published by Grub Street,
The Basement,
10 Chivalry Road,
London SW11 1HT

First published by Grub Street in hardback 1997
This edition first published 1999

A catalogue record is available on request from the British Library.

ISBN 1-902304-37-3

Typeset by Pearl Graphics, Hemel Hempstead

Printed and bound in Great Britain by
Biddles Ltd, Guildford and King's Lynn

Front cover image depicts a Leigh Light Wellington coming into attack. It was
painted by J S Bailie who himself was a former Wellington and Baltimore pilot who
served in the Middle East in WWII

ACKNOWLEDGEMENTS

There are a number of people who have given considerable help to this
project and to each of them I acknowledge my grateful thanks: Robert
M Coppock, Naval Historical Branch, MoD; Frans Beckers; Harry
Hutson; Maureen Fahey; Dr Bob Yarston; Chris Goss; Mrs E J
Brame/Ken Hunt; Staff of the US Navy Historical Foundation,
Washington DC; Roberto Cesaretti of the Rivista Marittima, Rome;
Mario Buracchia, of the Stato Maggiore Della Marine Ufficio Storico,
Rome; Jeff Murphy, 36 Squadron Assn; Keith Rennles and Dennis
Feary.

CONTENTS

Acknowledgements   ii

Introduction   iv

CHAPTER 1	The *Luigi Torelli* and the Leigh Light	1
CHAPTER 2	U 373 – 12th Time Unlucky	13
CHAPTER 3	Happy Birthday Wolf!	27
CHAPTER 4	Battles in the Bay	37
CHAPTER 5	Fighting Back	55
CHAPTER 6	Shot Down	72
CHAPTER 7	Eleven Days in a Dinghy	91
CHAPTER 8	US Navy Cats and Libs	106
CHAPTER 9	Into the Teeth of Flak	129
CHAPTER 10	Catalinas in the Indian Ocean	142
CHAPTER 11	Operation Swamp	157
CHAPTER 12	U 415	170
CHAPTER 13	Mosquito Bites	184
CHAPTER 14	Mosquito Mayhem	197

Epilogue   210

Index of Personnel   216

INTRODUCTION

RAF Coastal Command's anti-U boat war was a progression of measures and counter-measures as each side endeavoured to stay one jump ahead of the other.

At the start of the war, Coastal Command was not prepared for a war on the scale that quickly developed, due in part to the peacetime assumption that German naval forces could be contained provided a good watch was kept on Germany's limited North Sea coast and the sea lanes from the Baltic between Denmark, Sweden and Norway, more usually known as the Kattegat and Skagerrak.

The fall of France changed all this overnight. Suddenly the Germans had access to French ports that looked out across the Bay of Biscay, from Brest down to Lorient, La Pallice, St Nazaire and Bordeaux. This opened up a whole new area to police for Coastal Command. Once U boats exited their North German ports, especially Kiel, and sailed out into the Atlantic, either between Scotland and Iceland or even Iceland and Greenland, they need no longer return to Germany but could, and did, head to a Biscay port. Here they could be re-supplied, repaired or serviced as necessary and with their crews rested, would continue attacking Allied shipping, either in the Atlantic, off the length of the American coast, off Africa or even round the Cape of Good Hope and into the Indian Ocean.

Of the many problems faced by Coastal Command once this happened, three stand out. Firstly, its aircraft were limited in both numbers and range. Of those it had, only the four-engined Short Sunderland flying boat had anything like the range to patrol out into the Atlantic. Coastal's shorter-range aeroplanes, such as the Armstrong-Whitworth Whitley and Avro Anson, were twin-engined, as were the antiquated Saro London and Supermarine Stranraer biplane flying boats. All the latter were little more than adequate but were soon outclassed in what they were asked to achieve.

Once things became a little more organised, Coastal, a poor second-class after the needs of Bomber Command, began to receive Vickers Wellingtons and American Lockheed Hudsons, while another US aircraft, the Consolidated Catalina, began to appear in 1941. This latter type also provided the necessary range to assist the Sunderland in the Atlantic or even to patrol the far reaches north of Scotland and off the Norwegian coast. Even so, for the first years of the war there was still a gap in mid-Atlantic, that couldn't be reached by aircraft from either the British Isles, Iceland, West Africa or Canada – and later America. This gap only closed much later with the advent of the Consolidated B24 Liberator in both US and RAF squadrons, the Boeing B17 Flying Fortress, and by using the Azores as a base and providing escort aircraft carriers with Atlantic convoys.

By far the most versatile aircraft in the early years of the war was the Wellington. Already a successful (for the period) bomber once it was stopped from operating in daylight, the Wellington was a success in virtually every role in which it was used, and Coastal Command came to rely on it to a great extent in the mid-war years.

Another problem was in locating the U boats. In the early days the only way was to spot them at sea, either on the surface, or, if extremely fortunate, to spot their periscopes, provided of course a U boat captain just happened to raise his periscope just as (a) an aircraft was in visual range, and (b) one of the aeroplane's crew happened to be looking at the right spot of water. And there is no comparison to viewing a duck on the Serpentine in Hyde Park; the North Sea, the Irish Sea, the Atlantic, etc, are vast, undulating areas of water, never still even on the calmest of days, with waves and white-caps in the thousands. With the coming of ASV radar however, these chance sightings were improved.

The third problem became apparent whenever a crew were lucky enough to spot either a surfaced boat or a periscope. Not only had they to be, or to quickly get themselves, in a good position to attack, they had no real weapon with which to attack. As the war began they only had bombs and hitting a ship or a U-boat with a bomb was literally a very hit and miss affair. It was only when the RAF developed the depth charge as used by the Royal Navy on their anti-submarine ships, in such a way that they could be carried and dropped from the air, that the RAF had finally the chance of killing a U boat by air attack. Fortunately, it was not necessary to 'hit' the submarine with the depth charge, just get at least one near enough for the concussion to split open the sub's hull. Dropping them still needed skill and a good aim, but as was found, there was much variation in how an exploding depth charge, or depth charges, could affect a submarine. Some-times an excellent attack and perfect 'straddle' with four, six or eight depth charges did little more than rattle the boat's crockery, while another time a single depth charge that seemed to miss totally, did the trick and the boat plunged to the sea bed never to be seen again.

If Coastal Command had its problems, so too did the German U boat service. While it could operate more efficiently from its captured French ports, this in turn gave Coastal Command a convenient area in which to find sub-marines. U boats had to cross the Bay to begin operations and had to re-cross it once they had to return home, with either its torpedoes or its fuel and supplies spent.

U boats had also to surface to recharge their batteries so they had hopefully to judge their return across the Bay at night in order to recharge and to suck in fresh air, and because a U boat could travel faster on the sea rather than beneath it. By 1942 aircraft carried good air-to-surface radar (ASV – Air to Surface Vessel) and so could not only have a better chance of finding surfaced U boats by day and in all weathers, but could also find them at night. However, finding them at night was only half the problem. The way that was solved is described in Chapter One.

The other chapters in this book cover other interesting glimpses of the anti-U boat war and not all are concerned with sinking them. U boats could be just as dangerous when cornered. Finding and attacking them was fraught with danger as we shall read, but equally, the submariners who served their country in U boats lived and fought a war not to everyone's taste. It was cramped and dangerous, in a hostile environment. The North Atlantic was no sea-side at the best of times and in winter there are few less hospitable places to be than in a metal cigar-shaped vessel in a cold grey sea. Danger not only came from Allied ships and aircraft, but underwater obstructions, mines, or mechanical failures and so on. And if one had to abandon ship in mid-Atlantic, or even in the Bay of Biscay, it was pure chance if rescue came. The chances of anyone purposely putting out to pick you up were remote, and even if they did, they had to be quick. Unless lucky enough to be in a dinghy or on a raft, exposure killed just as surely as a bullet, but not as quickly.

In bringing these stories to you I have had the generous help of a number of men who were involved on both sides of the coin, men from Coastal Command and from the U boats themselves. From Coastal Command:

Flight Lieutenant

A F H Barber	202 Sqdn	L M 'Bill' Medcalf	36 Sqdn
Al Bishop DFC	423 Sqdn RCAF	Art Mountford	423 Sqdn RCAF
Ralph Blanchard	248 Sqdn	John O'Kane DFM	502 Sqdn
Flight Lieutenant Ken		Norman H Pearce	265 Sqdn
V S Caligari DFM	265 Sqdn	Alan D Peters	248 Sqdn
Don Conacher	10 Sqdn RAAF	George R Robertson	58 Sqdn
Harold Corbin CGM	248 Sqdn	Dr J S 'Jock' Rolland	461 Sqdn RAAF
Des Curtis DFC	618/248 Sqdn	J J Scott	58 Sqdn
John Davenport DFC	502 Sqdn	Charlie R Tomalin	248 Sqdn
George Done	461 Sqdn RAAF	G M 'Paddy' Watson	461 Sqdn RAAF
Les Doughty DFM	248 Sqdn	Maurice J Webb DFM	248 Sqdn
Len Eccles	265 Sqdn	Murray Wettlaufer	423 Sqdn RCAF
Air Commodore		George Williams CBE	608 & 36 Sqdns
J H Greswell			
CBE DSO DFC	172 & 179 Sqdns	And from the U boats:	
Aubrey H Hilliard	618/248 Sqdn	Admiral Girolamo	
Ron N Holton	36 Sqdn	Fantoni	*Luigi Torelli*
Jim B Hoyle	618/248 Sqdn	Fred Geils	U 373
Peter Jensen	461 Sqdn RAAF	Dr Johannes Glaser	U 373
C D 'Cap' Kramis	502 Sqdn	Günther Heinrich	U 960
Tom Layson	36 Sqdn	Günter Rautenberg	U 415
Stanley Layzell	36 Sqdn	Helmut Rochinski	U 461
Dudley Marrows		Johannes Rudolph	U 155
DSO DFC	461 Sqdn RAAF	Karl Wahnig	U 802
Tom Masters DFC	36 Sqdn	Rudi Wieser	U 763

CHAPTER ONE

THE *LUIGI TORELLI*
AND THE LEIGH LIGHT

German U boats crossing the Bay of Biscay, either inbound or outbound, generally made the dash at night and on the surface. Unless
it was a good and bright moonlit night, any aircraft which located
them on radar would have a difficult job attacking them. Firstly
they had to see a target to identify, in case the radar had picked up
a French or Spanish fishing boat, a lifeboat, or even an oil drum. If
found to be a submarine the aircraft crew, unless they found themselves with time and in a good attacking position, would invariably
have to circle and make another approach, by which time either the
U boat had dived beneath the waves, or if she remained on the
surface, the boat's gun-crews would be waiting for them. As the
attacking aircraft needed to be as near 50 feet above the sea as possible
in order to be effective with its depth charges, letting down over a
black sea on a dark night was more than a little hazardous and un-
nerving for pilot and crew alike.

Like most problems it wasn't difficult to solve, someone just had
to do it. The person who did was Wing Commander Humphrey de
Verd Leigh DFC, a former pilot and now an Admin Officer. Leigh
(aged 44 in July 1941), the son of a vicar, was a Surrey man and
before WW1 had been an engineering pupil with Vickers Ltd at
Weybridge. Joining the Royal Naval Air Service in WW1 he had seen
active service in Mesopotamia at the beginning of 1916 and later
aboard the carrier HMS *Ben-my-Chree* from Port Said. In 1917-18
he was on HMS *Empress*, a former cross-Channel steamer converted
to an aircraft carrier. Awarded the DFC in 1918, he had become a
Major by September of that year and was at the RAF Seaplane
Station, Dundee. Although granted a permanent commission in
August 1919, he was put on the unemployed list in November.

Leigh's idea was as obvious as an usherette trying to locate a seat
in a darkened cinema – shine a torch. An aircraft carrying a torch,

or in reality a large searchlight, was not new. In 1941 Douglas Havoc aircraft had been fitted with a searchlight and a huge bank of batteries in order to light-up German night bombers, so that one or two accompanying Hurricane fighters could shoot it down. This idea was, however, great on paper and pitiful in operation and was soon (although not soon enough for those so employed) rejected.

By 1942, however, the airborne searchlight, now a more sophisticated apparatus which could be used in conjunction with ASV radar, was back in favour with Coastal Command. Once a crew picked up a radar contact at night and the pilot had been brought into an attacking approach by his radar operator, the light could be switched on at an appropriate distance (usually somewhere between half-mile to a mile), and if it was indeed a U boat and in a good position from which to attack, the approach could be continued. This left the U-boat captain the same two choices of diving or fighting back, but less time to make a decision.

It had to be an horrendous situation for a man on a U boat's conning tower to find himself. One can imagine it. Halfway across the Bay in the middle of the night. It's raining cats and dogs and the wind is howling. Water is seeping down his neck, somehow getting it between his waterproof coat and hat. He is hoping to be relieved so he can go below and get warm. They are just a couple of hours away from being at their home port where they can relax, have that long awaited hot bath, some decent food, see that French girl who is a waitress at the local café. Sleep in a decent bed for eight hours at least, with no sea-watches for perhaps some weeks. Possibly even some home leave, a trip to Paris or a chance at a shore job for some months. Or even . . . . The mind has begun to wander momentarily.

Suddenly the dark night explodes into day. A bright dazzling light seems to stream towards and at him from the near distance. At the same time he becomes aware of engine noises, increasingly loud. He shuts his eyes against the glare but his mind is racing. There is no wondering what this is, he knows only too well. It is a British aeroplane, coming in fast and low, its bomb-doors open. He knows too that even before he can speak, several canister-like objects will tumble from that bomb-bay, and if on target will splash about his submarine in just seconds. His racing mind also tells him that there is a good chance that he has just these last few seconds to live. And even if he survives the explosions, the water and the concussions, his boat may begin to fill with sea water putting him and anyone else who is lucky enough to survive, into a cold sea with little chance of rescue or survival. It was a gut-wrenching, bowel-churning moment for even the hardiest of submariners.

*   *   *

Over the first couple of years of the war, RAF Coastal Command had killed comparatively few U boats (it didn't even have an effective weapon to attack them even if they were found), but by 1942 it had slightly better aircraft, a means of finding them on the surface, and a weapon with which to attack them. From now on, the aircraft versus U boat war would take on new dimensions. The two things Coastal Command needed at this stage was a good long-range aeroplane, and the ability to 'see' U boats in the dark. The first was now coming into service, the American B24 Consolidated Liberator. The second was Wing Commander Leigh's new airborne searchlight.

Being an airman with the RNAS and RAF who had hunted German submarines in the First World War, he had returned to the RAF in 1939, serving at Coastal Command HQ. His idea of fitting a search-light in the un-used ventral gun position of a Vickers Wellington was taken up by Coastal's C-in-C, Air Marshal Frederick Bowhill. Installation trials were conducted over 1941 at the Coastal Command Development Unit (CCDU) at Carew Cheriton, the first Wellington (P9223) carrying a 22″ Naval carbon arc searchlight with a four degree diverging beam that was lowered from the aircraft's belly by gravity although it had to be retracted by a hand-powered hydraulic pump. The two pilots during the trials were Flying Officer A W Southall and Pilot Officer F Blackmore.

With the trials proving successful, the first production Wellingtons, the Mark VIII, were delivered to 1417 Flight at RAF Chivenor, commanded by Squadron Leader J H Greswell, who had joined the RAF in 1935. Following a tour with 217 Squadron, he had also been sent to CCDU. Jeaff Greswell recalls:

> One of our biggest priority tasks was to devise an effective way of illuminating a surfaced U boat prior to attack at night. U boats particularly on passage through the Bay of Biscay, evaded attack by our aircraft, by remaining submerged by day and surfacing only at night to recharge batteries. After fruitless attempts to use flares of various kinds, the prototype Wellington P9223, fitted with Leigh Light, was delivered to CCDU for trials.

One difficulty found was that once a target had been located on the ASV radar, and the Light switched on, the beam was gently raised until the U boat was illuminated. This was a dangerous moment for if the pilot looked out whilst the beam was still moving, searching out the target, he could very quickly become disorientated with a good chance of hitting the sea. Thus the pilot needed to fly on instruments only until the target was in view. This became the Golden Rule for pilots operating Leigh Light aircraft.

In April 1942, 1417 Flight was raised to squadron status with the arrival of Wing Commander J B Russell, and it became 172 Squadron. For the next two months intensive training took place until the night of 3/4 June, the date of the first operational sorties. However, things had not been easy, as Jeaff Greswell remembers:

> One of the first production aircraft, and crew, was lost when it flew into the cliffs at Hartland Point [North Cornwall] in bad weather during training. By the end of May we had five aircraft and trained crews. Proof of the effectiveness of the system was urgent and despite the small number of aircraft available, HQCC ordered the first operational sorties to take place on the night of 3 June 1942. A petrol bowser damaged the wing of one Wellington, with the result that only four were fit to fly that night.

The four crews assigned to patrol over the Bay this night were those of Jimmy Russell, Greswell, Southall (later DSO DFC) and Blackmore. Heading out from Chivenor, they flew to Bishop's Rock, located off the Scilly Isles, a popular and essential Coastal Command check-point for most of the war; they then fanned out across the known transit areas used by U boats, flying south towards the northern coast of Spain.

Squadron Leader Greswell was flying Wellington 'F' (ES986), his crew consisting of Pilot Officer A W R Triggs RAAF, second pilot, Pilot Officer S J Pooley, navigator, while his three WOP/AGs who each took turns on the radar, radio and rear turret, were Sergeants E A Walker, E Roberts and D W Archibald. To actually find a U boat was comparatively rare at the best of times; some crews flew whole tours without even sighting a periscope. Therefore, to locate one, at night, and on the Squadron's first operational sorties was good luck, perhaps tempered only by the fact that Coastal knew where U boats should be, and any around on this night would be feeling fairly safe in the darkness.

On 25 May 1942, two Italian submarines, the *Luigi Torelli*, commanded by tenente di vascello Count Augusto Migliorini, and the *Morosini*, left Bordeaux and sailed down the Gironde to arrive at the auxiliary base of La Pallice where they would make final preparations for their war cruises. The Marconi Class *Luigi Torelli* had been built at Spezia and launched in January 1940, going into service in May.

Both Count Migliorini and *Morosini*'s tenente di vascello D'Allessandro were expert submariners and their crews had been well trained. With final preparations completed, the two boats left La

Pallice on the afternoon of 2 June – delayed by one day due to bad weather – and set out into the Bay, their destination being the seas off the Bahamas and Puerto Rico. After a few miles, the boats separated and each went its own way.

Count Migliorini took his *Torelli* south-west after reaching an area opposite the Gironde. At 0300 hours (GMT) on 3 June, he set a course of 264 degrees, alternating between sailing on the surface and sailing submerged. She was back on the surface on the night of 3/4 June and at 0127 hours GMT (0227 Axis time), in position 44.33N 06.46W, 70 miles to the north of Gijon (Spain), night suddenly became day! Those Italians on the boat's bridge saw a powerful searchlight. Seconds later an aircraft flew over them, turned off its searchlight and disappeared into the darkness. Jeaff Greswell recalls:

> We made contact with the *Torelli* on the return leg of our patrol having fixed our position by radar and a lighthouse on the Spanish coast.
>
> My radar operator, using the forward aerials, reported a contact 5½ miles to port. Using the standard attack procedure, the Leigh Light was lit at ¾-mile range at 250 feet, but failed to pick up the target dead ahead in the beam as we had hoped. However, both Pilot Officer Alan Triggs and myself spotted a large U boat disappearing under our port wing, but which at that moment was impossible for us to attack.
>
> I quickly realised what had happened. The barometric pressure set on the altimeter some 400 miles away at Chivenor was such that, when indicating 250 feet, we were actually flying nearer 400 feet when the Light was switched on, so the beam had overshot the target. Cursing our misfortune, I reset the altimeter reading and climbed away. We had reached a height of about 500 feet, turning, when I was amazed to see the U boat start firing coloured flares into the sky, giving me a perfect reference point towards which to start homing on for a second approach.

The navigation officer aboard the *Torelli* was Girolamo Fantoni, later to become a post-war Admiral in the Italian Navy, who takes up the story from the Italian side:

> On the bridge of the *Torelli* [the watch] tried to analyse the situation. The low-level fly past, without an attack, led to the thought that it might have been a German aircraft; in any event the Commander manned the two machine guns, cleared the bridge of guard personnel, and prepared to crash-dive. Being unaware of the existence of radio location, and in particular, airborne

radar, it was thought that the sighting by the aircraft was made by chance, due to the phosphorescence from our broad wake; consequently the Commander limited his actions to reducing speed to lessen the visibility of the wake, thus making it impossible for the aircraft to repeat the chance night sighting.

Whilst the few men on the bridge were going down into the conning tower, the aircraft turned again into the attack, but this time without mistake. At a range of a mile, at 250 feet, the Light was switched on and lit up the submarine. Fire was opened up by the gunners, and the aircraft released its four depth charges which exploded on each side of the boat, under the hull.

Jeaff Greswell:

This time, the procedure worked perfectly. The Leigh Light illuminated the U boat, and I attacked from the starboard beam, straddling the vessel with four depth charges. The submarine was severely damaged. After the attack we shadowed the damaged boat and carried out two runs over it to enable the rear gunner to strafe it. I reached PLE (Prudent Limit of Endurance) about 30 minutes later and set course for base.

Girolamo Fantoni:

The submarine started to shake in an incredible way. The Commander, last but one to leave the bridge, began to descend into the tower to give the order to dive, when the violent jolts sheared off the closing hook from the small door to the bridge which, as a result, closed itself, and the Bosun, the last to descend, was trapped on the bridge. In a few seconds, the diesel engines, still running, sucked all the air from the cabins, creating a strong depression, which impeded the ability to hear. The engines then stopped by themselves due to the lack of air. An unaccustomed silence and the pitch darkness dominated the scene inside the submarine which floated motionless and bow heavy – no noise, no voices, no light.

When finally air was restored in the boat, and the depression relieved, immediate action was taken to attend to the serious damage. To improve buoyancy, the Commander pumped air into the ballast tanks containing fuel, dumping the fuel overboard into the sea. A fire in the vicinity of the forward batteries, which was emitting thick smoke and chlorine gas, had to be isolated by closing the watertight doors to all forward compartments, including the radio station. Many of the ship's stations were damaged, and because there was no electrical power, the rudder and the steering compass were not working. The ammunition store, which was close to the fire, had to be flooded, after having withdrawn some ammunition for the gun. The Bosun, who had been left on the bridge, stated that the aircraft had carried out two more runs, firing machine guns haphazardly.

Having got the boat moving again, the Commander decided to head for the Spanish coast, navigating by the stars on a southerly course and steering by the hand-controlled rudder. In the distance more lights from the searchlight could be seen, but from time to time banks of fog gave some relief to the crew.

Jeaff Greswell:

On the return leg of our patrol, I successfully carried out a perfect homing and Leigh Light attack on an east-bound U boat (with rear turret machine-gun fire, having no depth charges left).

The other three aircraft did not share in our good fortune, but we had proved conclusively that the attack procedure would work. My subsequent interview with the C-in-C next day gave him the ammunition he needed to boost production of the Leigh Light Wellingtons, and to demand urgent action to install the American AYD radio altimeter (0 to 400 feet). On my second patrol, on 6 June, we again homed onto a U boat but once again my altimeter error resulted in an attack not being possible, and the U boat had crash-dived before a second approach could be made.

We carried Torpex-filled 250 lb depth charges with fuses designed to explode at a depth of 25 feet, so why was the *Torelli* not sunk when a straddle was achieved? The fact is that the fuses were defective, the explosions occurring well below 25 feet. It was not until early 1943 that the 'serious fault' was remedied. It seems certain that was the reason why 172 Squadron damaged, instead of sinking, so many U boats between June 1942 and May 1943 – eight out of a total of ten attacked.

The other boat attacked by Jeaff Greswell on the night of 3/4 June had to be the *Morosini*, simply because there were no other submarines in the Bay that night. The *Morosini* of course was undamaged by the Wellington's gunfire, but it is remarkable that the only two boats in the Bay should be found and attacked by this one Wellington, not only using a Leigh Light for the first time, but the Torpex depth charge. The *Morosini* did not return to its base from this patrol, being lost later with all hands to unknown causes, on her way back to Bordeaux.

Although severely damaged, the *Luigi Torelli* had survived, but these attacks by Jeaff Greswell and his crew were only the start of her adventures. All thoughts of continuing the war cruise to the Caribbean area had now ended. The fire aboard the boat was put out and power was used from the diesel engines rather than the batteries. Finally the rudder was repaired and the gyro compass put in place as the magnetic compass, without calibration, was definitely of no use.

Entering a thick fog bank off Cape Penas, inching along, the crew failed to realise a malfunction with the gyro compass, and the boat ran aground at high tide on rocks overlooking the headland. A strong undertow caused more damage to the hull, but in the evening, with some assistance from the Spanish, the *Torelli* was refloated and sheltered near the small port of Aviles where she was taken and berthed alongside a sandbank.

The crew began work on the hull to make it seaworthy. Holes were plugged with quick-drying cement and the buoyancy was restored, although precariously, by isolating the bow compartments, keeping the watertight doors closed, while pumping in air with the compressors. All the while, British aircraft repeatedly flew over the port.

The Spanish authorities were asked if the boat could remain in harbour in order to carry out all repairs but by 6 June, orders had come from Madrid to the local Naval Commander, that under international law, the boat would have to be interned if still in port at midnight. The Italian crew, therefore, had no choice but to sail from Aviles, which they did just half an hour short of the Spanish deadline. They had to leave some of their equipment ashore and the boat could only sail on the surface, being unable to submerge.

Obviously the task was to return to Bordeaux but it was going to be a slow and arduous process. The boat had no compass now and had to stay close to the Spanish coast. By dawn the next morning, they were in the vicinity of Santander, but the RAF knew perfectly well that a damaged submarine was about and were on the look out for her. Two Sunderlands from 10 RAAF Squadron located her at 0712 hours on the 7th.

The first, W3994 'X', piloted by Pilot Officer T A Egerton RAAF, with Pilot Officer M S Mainprize RAAF as his first pilot found the *Torelli* with four small boats nearby, and came in for an attack. The boat manoeuvred and fired back with the deck gun and the two 13mm machine guns, while other crewmen opened fire with sub-machine guns and even rifles. One enthusiastic sailor even suggested to Count Migliorini that being so low, the Sunderland might be knocked down if they raised their periscope! Unfortunately, the deck gun's shells were fused for use against ships, not aircraft. A stick of depth charges rained down, one large explosion being observed by the Australian crew alongside the boat's stern.

On the run-in the front gunner had opened fire, taken up by the rear gunner as they flew over, and members of both the deck gun and those manning guns on the conning tower were hit and wounded.

The exploding depth charges lifted the boat's stern out of the water but other than wounding crewmen from the gunfire, there was no serious damage. With no more depth charges, Egerton continued to strafe the boat, but gunfire from the *Torelli* also scored hits on the Sunderland, and two of its crew were wounded by shrapnel. Meantime, Egerton had had his radio operator home in the second Sunderland, captained by Flight Lieutenant E StC Yeomans RAAF ('A' W4019).

Yeomans and crew had been searching off Cape Mayor and had actually seen Egerton's Sunderland attacking. Coming in low and fast, the second Sunderland too received a hail of gunfire, bullets slashing into the flying-boat's tail. Once more depth charges fell about the crippled submarine and more damage was inflicted upon the Sunderland as it flew over. The *Torelli* however, was flooded almost up to the bridge but remained afloat stern-heavy, despite a heavy list. The rudder was also found to be jammed to one side. Ten men had also been hurled into the sea. The two Sunderlands, now unable to do further damage to the boat, both damaged themselves, with wounded on board and fuel starting to run low, turned for home. An Arado seaplane also appeared and made an attack on Yeoman's machine, but was driven off by the Sunderland's gunners.

Torelli's Commander ordered the deck-gun dismantled to help counter the list. One of the boat's machine guns was lost overboard and the other had been damaged, so effectively the boat was now defenceless. The stern compartment was flooded and became cut off and the compressor had to be shut down, therefore no more air could be pumped into the disaster areas.

The men in the water were rescued and after a quarter of an hour the boat's mechanics succeeded in getting the engines going again, using them to steer. Once more they had to seek the safety of a Spanish port and crept towards Santander which was just a few miles off. The boat limped into harbour shortly before midday, her crew lining up and her battle flag flying. In the outer reaches of the harbour, Migliorini spotted a sand-bank and ordered the boat beached to stop it sinking altogether. Nine wounded seamen were taken to the local military hospital while the rest of the crew were transferred to a hotel and reclothed into 'civvies'.

Two days later, on 9 June 1942, at high tide, the submarine's hull was filled with compressed air, the boat refloated and put into dry dock. With so much damage, the boat could no longer attempt a sea journey back to her French port and so it would only be a matter of time before she was interned. Meanwhile, although diplomatic activity was going on in the background, Migliorini continued to try to get his boat into a state that would permit them a return to Bordeaux.

Men and equipment arrived from Bordeaux to help, and about 20 of the crew, no longer required, returned to Bordeaux by road. Holes in the hull and ballast tanks were repaired by soldering flanges to them, although this meant that the boat would no longer be able to submerge, but could sail on the surface. Engines were repaired and the rudder fixed, but with the batteries having been destroyed, the boat's electrical generator was connected directly to the diesel engines. The destroyed radio room was also repaired and even updated.

The local Naval Commander was under strict orders not to let the boat sail without direct orders from Madrid, but once repairs had been effected, the boat was taken from dry dock and floated to a wet dock, but in a location where she could not leave without assistance. To be on the safe side, the Spanish Commander wanted some vital part of the boat to be dismantled but Migliorini prevaricated, and also said that as his fuel tanks were empty, he couldn't sail in any event. However, what the Spanish inspectors had missed was that one of the water tanks contained about a dozen tonnes of fuel. Over the previous few weeks, the wounded sailors were gradually discharged from hospital and had returned to the boat.

It was now July and there was intense diplomatic activity between Rome, Madrid and London as to the fate of the *Torelli*. Spain wished to be completely neutral, although London believed Spanish fishermen often assisted German and Italian submarines or even that German seamen used Spanish fishing boats to this end[1]. London wanted the boat interned under international law, while Italy accused the British of violations to neutrality laws and fighting inside Spanish territorial waters. Rome also insisted that as the boat was now fit to sail, she should be allowed to do so. As the days went by, the matter rose to the level of General Franco himself following intervention by the Italian Foreign Minister, and son-in-law to Mussolini, Count Galeazzo Ciano.

---

[1] Whether by choice or arrangement, U boats often surfaced at night in the midst of Spanish tunney fishing boats where they would recharge their batteries. On one occasion an RAF crew homed in on radar, and lit-up no fewer than 26 fishing boats in one night. This same pilot on another night illuminated one of several fishing boats only to have one seemingly fire at his aircraft. This turned out to come from a surfaced U boat alongside the Spaniard, which had crash-dived before the Wellington could come round for an attack.

Migliorini was ignoring most of the diplomatic exchanges and fully aware that the port Commander would prevent his departure, began to plot a plan of escape. On 4 July the boat was ready to leave dry dock, but the move did not actually come about until the 14th. At around 5 pm that evening, the dock was flooded and the *Torelli* began to be towed to a mooring location at the rear of the harbour. Ominously this was watched by the British Consul from the dockside. A Spanish gunboat, the *San Martin* was also stationed near the port exit, while the port's second-in-command was often seen in the area in a motor-boat, and a Spanish engineer was assigned to the submarine by the port Commander. Migliorini knew that he had to make a break before being tied up at the rear of the port, and while being manoeuvred by two tugs, asked that a 360-degree turn be permitted in order to check, by the sun, the magnetic deviation of the compass. (This, of course, was unnecessary as the magnetic compass was still totally unserviceable.)

To help the turn, Migliorini requested, and received permission to, release the tug from the bow, and then he ordered the engines to be started. The Spanish second-in-command, alarmed at this, leapt aboard the sub, but it was too late. Migliorini had succeeded in getting his boat's stern facing the harbour and his bows the exit. The Bosun, armed and ready, cut the stern tug's rope with an axe, the engines put into gear and the boat headed for the exit, leaving the gunboat unprepared for any sort of action other than a much belated and slow attempt to chase.

As soon as could be arranged, the two Spanish officers were put into a fishing boat and then the *Torelli* was headed for the French coast. There was still some hours of daylight, but no Allied opposition showed up. Again navigating by the sun and then by the stars, the submarine met up with a minesweeper escort off the French coast just before dawn, was escorted through the minefield, re-entered the Gironde at 2000 hours on 15 July and was safely in Bordeaux.

Thus the *Luigi Torelli* went into history as the first submarine attacked and damaged by the RAF's use of a Leigh Light, and the saga of her escape from Spain has also to be unique, especially considering the damage that had been inflicted upon her by one Wellington and two Sunderlands. Augusto Migliorini received the Medaglio di Bronso di Valor Militare.

However, it was not the end of her story. In 1943 she became a transport boat for taking precious materials to the Far East. Sailing to the Far East and following Italy's surrender, she was taken over by the Germans, operating out of Singapore as the submarine UIT 25. Once Germany too surrendered in May 1945, she became I 504 in the Japanese Navy until falling into American hands at the end of the Pacific war. She had been sent to Japan to have her engines overhauled. They finally scuttled her off Kobe, Japan, in August 1946.

Jeaff Greswell won the DFC for his actions on 3/4 June. In November 1942, he was sent to sell the Leigh Light concept to the US Army Air Corps and the US Navy. Upon his return to the UK he commanded 179 Squadron in June 1943, also equipped with Leigh Light Wellingtons, operating from Gibraltar. He received the DSO in 1944 and retired from the RAF in 1968 as an Air Commodore CB CBE. He emphasises:

> The primary aim of 172 Squadron's Ops on the night of 3/4 June 1942 was to test the Leigh Light system under operational conditions over the Bay of Biscay. My two attacks on a moonless night, proved that it worked. For the first time, RAF Coastal Command had the capability to sink U boats by night as well as by day. The almost disastrous result of the false reading of height on the altimeter which prevented the depth charges' release on the first approach to attack led to urgent action to instal radar altimeters.
>
> Concerning the Torpex depth charges [as opposed to the previous Amatol and then Minol-filled weapons], I vividly recall Wing Commander Leigh's concern that these new weapons should be supplied for use on our first patrols on 3 June. They arrived just in time. Therefore, I believe I was one of the first to make an attack with Torpex depth charges.

CHAPTER TWO

U 373 – 12TH TIME UNLUCKY

Some U boats led charmed lives while others were lost or simply disappeared on their first voyages. Bad luck, mechanical defects, or being in the wrong place at the wrong time easily led to disaster. By 1943 Allied aircraft were causing more and more problems for the German submarines, not only in the Bay of Biscay but out into the grey Atlantic.

However, the U boat crews were also and increasingly, causing problems for aircraft. An attacking land or seaplane was generally a big target and provided the U boat's gunners kept cool they had a more than even chance of hitting the aircraft which could result in either it being shot down, or making its pilot misjudge the moment he released his deadly depth charges. Of course, there were also many occasions when the aircraft, despite being hit, came steadily on, sometimes on fire, and was still able to release its ordinance before plunging into the waves. We shall read of such occurences in later chapters. Indeed, some episodes will clearly show just how dangerous it was to attack a surfaced U boat from the air.

373 was built by the Howaldtswerke AG at Kiel, as a type VIIC and commissioned on 22 May 1941. Her first commander was 26-year-old Oberleutnant, but soon promoted to Kapitänleutnant, Paul Karl Loeser and he was assigned to the 3rd U boat Flotilla. Loeser had been a watch officer (WO) on U 33 before the war, then IIWO with U 43, IWO on U 108 and finally in command of U 30. U 373, while commanded by Loeser, had an emblem of a lion rampant painted on its conning tower.

After her period of working-up, U 373 sailed to Trondheim and left this port on 4 September for the North Atlantic. Eight days later she came in contact with convoy SC42 (SC was the code for a convoy from Great Britain to the USA) but lost it in fog. U 373 then became part of Gruppe Brandenburg operating south-east of Cape Farewell but had no success and finally sailed into Brest on 2 October.

At the end of the month, she sailed as part of Gruppe Störtebecker off the west coast of Spain but again had little success and entered Lorient on 21 November. On Christmas Day 1941, U 373 sailed again, this time escorting the German blockade-runner the *Elsa Essberger* from 4 January. Exactly a week later (the 11th) she was attacked by an aircraft that dropped four bombs and machine-gunned her, suffering slight damage. The position of the attack was 4409/1006 (German BF7548), off the north-west coast of Spain. After an aborted convoy operation, U 373 was recalled to La Pallice where she docked on 15 January.

The aircraft was reported as a Hampden-type, but was in fact a four-engined Liberator from 224 Squadron, captained by Flight Lieutenant P J Cundy, already an experienced Coastal pilot, having flown with 53 and 120 Squadrons already in this war.

With repairs completed, U 373's next sailing came on the first day of March, this time heading right across the Atlantic to operate off the east coast of the United States. On this war cruise she scored her first successes by sinking the Greek freighter *Mount Lycabertus* of 4,292 BRT (British Registered Tonnage) on the 17th and the British freighter *Thursobank* of 5,575 BRT, on the 22nd. She arrived back at La Pallice on 17 April.

Her fifth war cruise began on 18 May, moving to St Nazaire to load 15 mines, then heading for the Delaware Bay the next day. She laid her deadly cargo on 11 June and on the 24th the American tug *John R Williams* of 396 BRT sank after hitting one of the mines. Meantime, U 373 failed to sink two freighters on 14 and 15 June, although she reported a hit on the second one. Two days later she headed for home but at 0130 hours on 6 July she was surprised by a British aircraft in position 4509/0558.

As fate would have it, this was a Wellington of 172 Squadron, the pilot being non other than Flight Lieutenant A W Southall, who had been one of the pilots flying the first Leigh Light sorties in company with Jeaff Greswell just over a month earlier. The crew of 'D', a Mark VIII Wellington was:

FL A W Southall	Pilot	Sgt W R Thomas	WOP/AG
PO F C Elisha	2nd pilot	Sgt W Cook	WOP/AG
FO D MacGregor	Navigator	Sgt E C Goodman	WOP/AG

Still operating out of Chivenor, north Devon, the aircraft's radar had picked up a contact at 0115 hours, eight miles to starboard, and in turning, Southall had spotted a surfaced U boat in position noted as 4518/0613 at 0123. The Wellington was at 500 feet, the submarine one mile ahead. Southall attacked with four 269 lb depth charges, set at 25 feet, released from 100 feet and estimated a straddle 20 yards ahead of the boat's bows. As the Wellington raced over the boat, its rear gunner opened fire with a brief burst seeing a sudden but brief bright flame but nothing afterwards. Southall came back and circled the area for half an hour but the boat had gone.

U 373 reported the attack by a Leigh Light Wellington which had dropped four 'bombs' and some machine-gun fire but there had been no damage to the boat. Two days later Loeser brought her into La Pallice, where she stayed for almost a month, heading back to sea for her sixth cruise on 6 August. Five days out she was attacked again by an aircraft, this time a Short Sunderland flying boat of 10 RAAF Squadron. U 373 gave her position as being 4451/1305, the time as 1705 hours (German time).

Sunderland 'U' (W3986) of 10 Squadron, from Mount Batten, was flying at 1,500 feet above some scattered 2/10ths cumulus cloud at 1554 hours GMT. The pilot, Flight Lieutenant S R C Wood spotted a glint of sunshine reflecting from a polished surface at sea level some 21 miles away! The Sunderland's radar was on but there was no indication of an object.[1] Wood, curious, altered course to investigate and closing in identified the object as a U boat while still some way off. Wood pulled the flying boat into some cloud, not letting down and emerging until he was about six miles from the submarine, then commenced a dive from up-sun. At three miles the alert watch crew on U 373 saw the Sunderland and the boat crash-dived. Wood ordered a stop-watch record and reaching the spot, dropped two depth charges 200 yards ahead of the swirl of water left by the diving boat and on her estimated track. According to the watch the boat had gone down one minute and five seconds earlier. Nothing further was seen and U 373 later reported the attack, estimating only one bomb being dropped, which only caused some light damage, so Wood and crew had not been far off target. Perhaps if he had dropped more depth charges . . . . .?! Wood's crew consisted of:

FL S R C Wood RAAF	Pilot	Sgt Price	1st WOP
FO Meidecke	2nd pilot	AC Walker	2nd WOP
PO Mackenzie	3rd pilot	LAC Moore	Rigger
FO Austin RAAF	Navigator	Sgt Dewhurst	Rear gunner
Sgt G F Horgan	Engineer	Cpl Perry	Armourer
Cpl C A Whitley	Fitter II		

---

[1] In order to keep ASV radar a secret from the Germans, aircraft were forbidden to overfly occupied territory or neutral Spain and if in difficulties should crash-land on the sea rather than on the Spanish mainland. In addition, the equipment became known as 'SE' – Special Equipment – in order to safeguard knowledge of its use.

Flight Lieutenant Wood, a peacetime solicitor from Caulfield, Victoria, New South Wales, had attacked and damged U 71 back on 5 June and he would go on to damage the Italian *Reginaldo Giuliani* on 1 September. He would later fly with 461 RAAF Squadron, receive the DFC and end the war as a Wing Commander. Sergeant Horgan had been in Yeoman's crew which had attacked and further damaged the *Luigi Torelli* off Santander on 7 June.

The slight damage inflicted on U 373 did not restrict her movements and Loeser continued to head out into the Atlantic, becoming a part of Gruppe Lohs on 18 August. In the vicinity of convoy ON122 (Britain to Halifax, Nova Scotia) she was attacked and depth-charged by a naval escort vessel but escaped damage. On the 29th she was supplied by the supply submarine U 462. On 20 September, trying to attack convoy SC100 (Britain to USA), U 373 fired three torpedoes at ships but scored no hits. HMCS *Rosthern*, a Canadian escort, depth-charged the sub, but again U 373 got away without damage. She returned to La Pallice on 4 October.

War cruise number seven began on 22 November 1942, becoming part of Gruppe Draufgänger on the 29th. On 7 December she was supplied by U 460 and although she was in contact with convoy HX218 (Halifax to Britain) on the 13th she was unable to make an attack. Three days later she was driven off before she could attack ships of ONS152 (slow convoy from Britain to Halifax). With Christmas and New Year spent at sea on her way home, she entered La Pallice on 3 January 1943 with nothing to show for her period at sea.

Hoping for better luck she commenced her eighth patrol on 25 February. Five days out she was attacked by what her watch crew said was a Whitley, in position 4657/1835. Her crew counted five explosions but the boat suffered no damage. Only one air attack upon a U boat was reported on this date, and only an American B24 Liberator of 1 Squadron USAAC made an attack in this area. Two days later U 373 became part of Gruppe Neuland and on the 11th she was sniffing around the edge of convoy HX228.

In the late morning, U 373 was on the surface closing in on the ships but air cover was being provided by a Liberator from 120 Squadron, operating from Aldergrove, Northern Ireland. Squadron Leader D J Isted, in Liberator III 'B' (FK214) had been airborne since 0213 hours. Around the convoy he was flying at 3,000 feet with 6/10ths cloud at 3,300 with visibility some 20 miles but less in frequent showers. At 1005, when some 20 miles from the convoy, he sighted a surfaced U boat ten miles away, in position 5200/2710, the 'SE' radar being off at the time. Desmond Isted dived, attacking the U boat from the starboard beam, as she was seen to begin a crash-dive. Releasing four depth charges from 60 feet while the conning tower and stern were still visible, the nearest D/C appeared to overshoot by about 40 feet, although later, the aircraft photograph seemed to indicate the nearest was closer to 120 feet away. Nothing else was seen, so Isted reported the attack to the Senior Naval Officer (SNO) leading the convoy escort ships and continued his patrol.

At 1222, again at 3,000 feet, 26 miles from the convoy, Isted found another U boat on the surface, but in reality it was U 373 again, trying desperately to catch the ships which had now inched away from his earlier position. The boat was seven miles from the Liberator, and Isted was already heading down towards her, but once again the sub's watchers had spotted the danger and a crash-dive was ordered. Isted attacked from the boat's port bow, releasing another two D/Cs from 60 feet, some 20 seconds after the boat disappeared. The nearest exploded about 300 feet ahead of the swirl and 20 feet to the starboard of a trail of oil, three miles long, which was leading from the edge of the swirl area. Again nothing further was seen. Whether U 373 was aware she was leaving an oil trail is not known.

Despite U 373 reporting two attacks by Sunderland aircraft, Isted and his Liberator was the only aircraft in the vicinity. No doubt in the haste to dive, the observers glimpsed the high-wing, deep fuselage and the four engines and quickly believed it was a flying boat coming for them. The first attack was recorded as being at 1007 hours, position 5139/2725, Isted's attack being timed at 1005 in position 5200/2710. Attack number two was reported as at 1220, position 5139/2715, Isted's time being 1222 in position 5205/2703. U 373 had noted three bomb explosions each time but listed no damage. Isted's crew were:

SL D J Isted	Pilot	FS R Bedford	WOP/AG
FO R A Crumpton	2nd pilot	FS T Timoney	WOP/AG
FS D J Appleton	Navigator	Sgt A Allwood	WOP/AG
Sgt A Richardson	Engineer		

Having survived these two air attacks and been kept down, Loeser was unable to close with the convoy and three days later became part of Gruppe Dränger, attacking convoy HX229 but on the 19th was again located, this time by the destroyer escorts who depth-charged her but again failed to score any damaging hits. Supplied by U 463 on 3 April, U 373 headed home, arriving on the 13th.

She was not so fortunate on her ninth cruise. Loaded with 12 mines her target was Port Lyautey, on the coast of French Morocco, sailing on 7 July. She would be in company with U 340, U 468 and U 757 while passing through the Bay of Biscay. By 24 July U 373 was in sector DH 1685, off Morocco and not far from Madeira and the Canary Islands. Operating in these waters was the escort carrier (Jeep

Carrier) USS *Santee*, watching out for U boats in transit to and from South Africa and the Cape, or operating off Freetown. A Grumman Avenger and F4F Wildcat team from the *Santee* located U 373 on this day, bombing and strafing the boat.

Leutnant Johannes Glaser, the boat's Executive Officer, remembers a Wildcat fighter aircraft strafing the boat and an Avenger torpedo plane which dropped an acoustic torpedo. The gun crew tried to ward off the air assault but with the death of two of their number and with seven others wounded, some of them critically, Loeser took her down. Glaser recalls:

> Fortunately the boat had a doctor on board, Ob.Ass.Arzt. Dr Thiele, who was able to operate on some of the severe cases. The boat had also been heavily damaged, only being able to cruise submerged at 20 metres, forcing Loeser to abort his mining mission. He returned to La Pallice, arriving on 16 August.
>
> We were extremely lucky to return from this patrol after a total of eight aircraft from the carrier and the USS *Bainbridge*, a destroyer escort, searched and hunted us for a period of more than eleven hours. The *Bainbridge* dropped two depth charges which damaged the auxiliary pump. We were then supposed to meet the *Milch Kuh*, U 461, but on the way to the rendezvous, this boat was sunk by aircraft. (See Chapter Six.)

Paul Karl Loeser now left U 373, command going to Oberleutnant, later Kapitänleutnant, Baron Detlef von Lehsten, aged 26, formally WO aboard U 584. The boat's emblem also changed, or to be correct, was added to, with two insignia of a stork carrying a child in its beak, placed either side of the existing Lion Rampant. He took the submarine out on her tenth war cruise on 6 October, 1943 for the Atlantic and during October and November was part of Gruppe Seigfried, then Gruppe Jahn, Gruppe Tirpitz and finally Gruppe Eisenhart. She had no successes and returned to her base on 26 November.

On New Year's Day 1944, at 1320 local time, U 373 again sailed for the Atlantic but two days later was caught on the surface at night in the Bay of Biscay by a Wellington of 612 Squadron. By coincidence, the pilot was Wing Commander J B Russell DSO, who had commanded 172 Squadron in 1942 and along with Greswell and Southall had flown those first Leigh Light sorties on 3/4 June 1942.

Flying Wellington 'L' (MP756) on a Percussion patrol, Flying Officer Bedford, on the ASV, picked up a radar contact at 800 feet, five miles, and homed Russell in on the surfaced boat which they illuminated after first having lost contact while making a turn, actually tracking over the sub, but unable to attack. The boat was in position 4613/0658 and Russell brought his Wellington round and the Light was operated at half a mile at 2030 hours. The boat was going down, however, but Russell dropped six D/Cs from 70 feet just three seconds after it disappeared. Being aimed 80 feet ahead of the swirl left by the diving boat, he estimated a good straddle.

Pulling up and round, Russell made a left hand turn and came back across the estimated track right between the two flame floats that denoted the line of the D/C's fall, Russell dropping a Marine Marker roughly mid-way between them. Sergeant George Underhill, in the rear turret, said he had seen at least three D/Cs explode, while the radio operater, Charles Brignall, thought it was four. Five minutes later radar contact was found again two miles away and they homed in. As the aircraft flew over AA fire came from the sea – the boat had resurfaced. Fred Geils, who had sailed in U 373 on her first nine war cruises, but who was not on this patrol having left upon being transferred to FdU-West (Führer der Unterseeboote, West) at Angers, has made a study of U 373 and in 'talking to some of his former ship-mates, relates:

U 373 released her escorts after having passed Point 'Pumpe' at the 50m (25-fathom) curve and then proceeded in a north-westerly direction. On 3 January her position at 2000 hours was in Naval Quadrant BF5745, and the seas were moderate (2-3) with a NNW wind of Force 3, cloudy skies (almost overcast), a light swell, with visibility fair, and 1,031 millibar air pressure.

At 2026 her Naxos radar monitoring device[1] picked up some irregular radar emissions which the operator on duty, Funk.Gfr. Meder, reported to the bridge. The bridge officer at that time was Watch Officer (IWO) Leutnant zur See Franke. Shortly afterwards the lookouts sighted an aircraft which Franke interpreted as being on a parallel course at 240 degrees. He decided to go all ahead full but stayed on top, preparing all flak guns (two twin-barrelled 2 cm, and one single-barrel 3.7 cm semi-automatic) to fire.

Leutnant Johannes Glaser was standing on the bridge as the attack began. As soon as the presence of aircraft had been detected, he released three Aphrodite balloons (a device that produced fake targets for aircraft radar). These may well have thrown Russell's radar

---

[1] A device for locating radar emissions from an aircraft's ASV radar which indicated the presence of an aircraft. Once the RAF realised the Germans had such a device, crews tended to switch the apparatus on and off from time to time.

operator off when he was trying to shadow U 373 outside flak range moments later.

Fred Geils continues:

> In the meantime, the CO had appeared on the bridge and ordered a crash-dive immediately. The time was 2030. While in the process of diving, four depth charges exploded close to the boat causing a water inrush via the stern tube which could not be contained. The boat could only be controlled (levelled off) after reaching a dangerous depth. All air-groups were hissing strongly and the main manifold (Haupt-Anblase-Verteiler) was stuck. Also, the rear diving planes were jammed at a 'hard-up' angle.
>
> With the boat sinking to A plus 70 (150 metres) and listing heavily aft the Captain decided to blow main ballast tanks by using the emergency manifold, and at A plus 20 (100 metres) he also ordered the blowing of tank V, fore. When reaching 20 metres, both electric motors short-circuited because of water inrush. A hell of a situation, I can tell you!
>
> U 373 popped to the surface like a cork and, being unable to dive, manned all flak guns and fended off L/612's subsequent strafing runs. However, what the crew didn't realise was that one depth charge from Russell's Wellington had hit the boat and got stuck between the upper deck walkway and the pressure hull, between the diesel exhaust openings and the stern of the boat, without exploding!

Having seen the U boat back on the surface and her opening fire with cannon and machine guns, the Wellington's rear gunner replied with 200 rounds although no hits were observed. Russell then began to shadow the boat at ranges of three to six miles for about an hour, at which time it was apparent from the radar bearings from the Marine Marker, that the boat's advance since the attack was about 75 degrees.

At 2140 homing procedures were commenced and at 2211 another attack was seen to be made by one of the aircraft which had been instructed to home-in. Just prior to this attack, some more flak was seen. A couple of minutes afterwards, Russell saw an orange glow on the water which persisted for about ten minutes, while the attacking aircraft made two strafing runs over the boat.

This new arrival was Liberator 'H' of 224 Squadron from St Eval, piloted by Flying Officer H Facey. As it came upon the scene shortly after 2200 hours, the navigator in the nose spotted a very pronounced wake and then a fully surfaced U boat at one mile ahead, in position 4602/0819. As the Liberator turned to secure a better approach, the boat began to fire, the Lib's mid-upper and beam guns replying. Coming in without the use of its Leigh Light, eight D/Cs went down from 200 feet but the rear gunner saw them overshoot. All the gunners in the aircraft and on the U boat exchanged fire as the Liberator swept across and they also observed the glow Russell was seeing, forward of the conning tower.

Officer Harold Facey came in again, meeting heavy flak fire as the boat made erratic course changes but at a reduced speed. At this point his radar operator was picking up three contacts, the first four miles off to port, another five miles dead astern and a third also at four miles to starboard. Meantime, the target boat had submerged, and only the Liberator's Marine Marker was visible. Facey circled the area for four hours but nothing else was seen. Oddly enough no other aircraft was seen either, although an hour after his attack they picked up one on radar but it was not seen visually.

In fact there were other U boats in the area, and in reality, although U 373 had been forced back onto the surface, Russell's crew had actually located a second boat, as Fred Geils records:

> Wing Commander Russell's crew apparently lost track of U 373 while he was trying to shadow her on radar rather than by sight. After a thorough research of all documents and talking to my former crew mates, it appears that U 373 was not attacked any-more after the strafing attack she had suffered. L/612 obviously shadowed U 629, (another type VIIC) Oberleutnant Hans-Helmuth Bugs, who somehow appeared on L/612's radar screen, because Bugs is the one who was attacked later by Liberator H/224 Squadron at 2204 hours.

(In the early hours of 4 January, U 629 was attacked again, this time by a Wellington XIV of 304 Polish Squadron and damaged.)

Russell's crew:

WC J B Russell DSO	Pilot
FO J T A May	2nd pilot
FL Skyrme	Obs(nav)
FS G H Underhill	WOP/AG
FS C V Brignall	WOP/AG
FO H M Bedford	WOP/AG

Baron von Lehsten brought his damaged U boat into Brest Harbour on 5 January. They had had a lucky escape. The boat had now survived eight air attacks and four depth-charge assaults by naval escort ships – a total now of 12 attacks upon her. However, there was some consternation upon coming into Brest when it was realised she had an unexploded depth charge on board and she had initially to clear the harbour until a bomb disposal team could disarm it.

She was out of action for some months and only forced to make her twelfth, and final, patrol the day after the Allies landed in Normandy. Every available U boat was needed to attack the invasion fleet, while Coastal Command did everything to block off the English Channel. They called it Operation Cork, which was literally to put a cork into the neck of the Channel between Southern Ireland and Cherbourg, the 'bung' penetrating right into the beach-head area.

However, as Johannes Glaser recalls, U 373 had left on the 6th, in company with other boats but when making a deep-diving test it turned out that several stuffing boxes at both propeller shafts were leaking, so the boat had to return to harbour. She was repaired and sailed at 2045 hours the next evening. He also confirms that as the boat was not fitted with a Schnorkel her operational area had been, or rather was supposed to have been, near Land's End, not the actual invasion area off the Seine Bight of Normandy.

It was a virtually impossible task for any U boat to get anywhere near the invasion beach area or the sea between it and the south coast of England. A number tried and were sunk or damaged, while numerous others didn't even get to the 'bottle neck' let alone the 'cork'.

U 373 attempted to carry out its mission and was in company with U 629, the same boat that had shared those attacks by 612 and 224 Squadrons in the first days of 1944. No fewer than 15 U boats left Brest once the invasion had been confirmed, with more coming out of the other Biscay ports. By now some boats had been fitted with the new Schnorkel tubes that allowed a boat to 'breathe' and to re-charge her batteries under water rather than coming to the surface, thus being more protected at night. However, to move quickly at night, as in daylight, boats needed to travel on the surface. Moreover, most of these boats were still non-Schnorkel equipped so these needed to surface to recharge as well as to travel more quickly.

During that first night aircraft made 22 sightings, and seven attacks were carried out, resulting in the loss of two boats with four others damaged; another was damaged in daylight. The next night, 7/8 June, the 36 boats now in the immediate area surfaced for another dash forward; Cork patrols were waiting for them. It would be a night when a new record was established, one crew sinking two U boats in a single patrol: U 373 and U 629.

Flying Officer K O Moore, from Vancouver, Canada, was 21 years old and a member of 224 Squadron, flying Liberators from St Eval.

'Kayo' Moore was interviewed after the night's events, and although partly a PR exercise, his words, and those of some of his crew, give good coverage of the event. Other than in press reports, they also appeared in a wartime book *Coastal Command Leads the Invasion* by SL M Wilson and FL A S L Robinson (Jarrolds Ltd). Shortly before take-off, Moore's squadron commander, Wing Commander W T McComb, said that there were '. . . bags of U boats around. You ought to sink two in an hour.' Moore replied with a grin, 'We'll sink two in half an hour to-night.' Liberator G-George took off at 2214 hours, their patrol area being between Ushant and the Scilly Isles. The next day he was telling reporters:

It was on the second lap of our beat that things began to liven up. Clearly silhouetted ahead of us, fully surfaced, was a U boat. I was the first to see it. As we approached we could see that the U boat crew had been taken by surprise. About eight German sailors on deck, apparently in utter confusion, were running like hell to man the guns. The U boat commander, however, made no attempt to order his vessel to crash-dive, and those manning the guns waited for us to close in.

Al Gibb, our front gunner, opened fire when we were within 1,000 yards and scored repeated hits on the conning tower and deck. Simultaneously, the U boat's crew opened fire on us. I took evasive action while Gibb continued to blaze away and then we tracked over the conning tower. The flak had been silenced during the last yards and as we released our depth charges, I saw one of the crew in the 'bandstand' double up and fall overboard into the water.

The U boat seemed to jump into the air and explode, splitting wide open. I made a steep turn. On the water we could see wreckage and large patches of oil. As we stooged around for another five minutes we saw black objects in the water, probably bodies.

The attack was timed at 0215 in position 4827/0547, near Ushant. Six depth charges had been used, dropped from about 50 feet, three being seen to fall either side of the submarine. Moore continued:

As we resumed patrol over the Channel, Mike Werbiski was busy at the wireless set sending out a flash report to advise Coastal Command that we had just made an attack. Don Greise came up and said, 'Come on, let's get two U boats.' I remember telling him to be patient because the night was still young.

Almost immediately, Warrant Officer McDowell, our Scottish

navigator, who at the time was adjusting his bomb-sight, shouted out a warning that he could see another U boat ahead, travelling fairly slowly. It was a small U boat and remained fully surfaced, making no attempt to avoid a fight.

Time was now 2240, the second boat in position 4810/0531. As K O Moore headed in, Al Gibb, still at the nose gun, commenced to fire towards the sub, Moore dropping down to 50 feet once again. They released their last six depth charges. Moore said:

> As we circled I saw the bow of the U boat rise twenty-five feet out of the water at a 75 degree angle and slide back into the sea. We made a third circuit over the spot where the U boat had vanished. Three dinghies were in the water with three or four German sailors in each. Then we went on with our patrol. The only one who showed any excitement was myself after the second attack when I exclaimed: 'My God! It's sunk!'

Moore had not needed to use his Leigh Light, but after the second kill he flew back over the spot with the Light on, seeing men in dinghies with others still in the water. According to the Germans, someone fired at them as the Liberator passed overhead. WO Werbiski was still at his radio and heard the excitement and asked what was happening. At first he thought everyone was pulling his leg about a second kill.

Fred Geils:

> Unfortunately no one aboard U 629 survived Operation 'Landwirt', although I am convinced they had a merciful death . . . . . G/224 returned after the attack, turned on its searchlight, and strafed the three dinghies with floating survivors, killing Bootsmannsmaat Nielson. Johannes Glaser, the executive officer in U 373 at the time, swam next to Nielsen when the strafing occurred.[1]

Johannes Glaser remembers leaving Brest and at 0150 on the morning of the 8th was in Marine Quadrant BF5211, Course 180 degrees. Suddenly a shadow ahead. On approaching this it turned out to be a sailing vessel, the *Jean Baptiste*, skippered by Captain Joseph

---

[1] Unhappily it was not unheard of for survivors to be shot-up in the water, although thankfully it was rare, or at least very few reported doing so – officially. In most cases it was no more than excited enthusiasm, the adrenalin pumping hard.

Hascoet. The radar monitoring operator aboard U 373 mistakenly believed that the radar impulses he was seeing stemmed from the fishing vessel and reported it to the Kommandant on the bridge. When the look-outs spotted the vessel throwing something over the side, it was further suspected that the vessel was working for the French Resistance, and the Kommandant ordered his gunners to open fire.

Fortunately no one aboard the fishing boat was hit and as the 3.7 cm gun became jammed, Lehsten probably realised his action was only endangering his boat by advertising its presence, and that his real objectives were elsewhere. He stopped the firing and moved away.

At 0240 hours the aircraft attack came – suddenly – with an approach from the down-moon side. The aircraft was already at low level and the boat tried desperately to evade the D/Cs by turning hard a'starboard, and opening up with her 2 cm and 3.7 cm guns. The boat received many hits by the strafing aircraft on the conning tower, but thanks to the armoured steel plates that were added to the bulwark prior to this patrol, none of the hits penetrated.

But the depth charges were another matter. Because they fell so close to the stern they caused severe damage to the aft torpedo room and the heavy inrush of water caused the boat's deck to be awash up to the rear of the conning tower. Lehsten ordered abandon ship although the 3.7 gun crew were still firing at the aircraft while standing ankle deep in water, which had rushed up the lower platform.

Quickly the boat reached an angle of over 45 degrees and was about to slide back into the water. When the order to stop the diesels was carried out, the last buoyancy was lost and she went down over the stern, taking with her the engineering officer, Leutnant Korger, the Diesel Obermaschinist, CPO Lorbeer, and Masch.Ob.Gefr Oehring, a stoker. In the meantime, the crew had put some rafts and dinghies into the water and tried to stay together.

Johannes Glaser found himself in the water, with men around him. He thought a second aircraft had come in and strafed them, but it was the Liberator coming back, using the flame floats dropped with the D/Cs as a point of reference. Nielsen was hit and killed right next to him. In all there were four casualties amongst the crew, the remaining 44 surviving. They were rescued by the same French fishing vessel, the *Jean Baptiste*, that they had tried to shoot up a short time earlier. Their skipper had seen the emergency flares fired by the men in the dinghies. He motored to the scene and took the men aboard, returning them to France the same day.

'Kayo' Moore received the Distinguished Service Order while DFCs went to Johnston McDowell and Peter Foster, plus a DFM for John Hamer. The crew:

FL K O Moore RCAF	Pilot
FO J M Ketcheson RCAF	2nd pilot
WO T J McDowell	Navigator
PO A P Gibb RCAF	2nd nav
Sgt J Hamer	Engineer
WO D H Greise RCAF	MU/gnr
WO E Davison RCAF	WOP/AG
WO W P Foster	WOP/AG
WO W N Werbiski RCAF	WOP/AG
FS I C Webb	Rear gunner

CHAPTER THREE

HAPPY BIRTHDAY WOLF!

U 607 was built at the Blohm and Voss works in Hamburg as a type VIIC and commissioned on 29 January 1942. Her first commander was Kapitänleutnant Ernst Mengerson. He was 29 and before the war had served as IWO aboard U 54. Since then he had commanded U 18, U 143 and U 101. Her first officer was Oberleutnant Wolf Jeschonnek, aged 22, half brother of Luftwaffe Generaloberst Hans Jeschonnek, who was Chief of the German Air Staff, and twice the age of brother Wolf. Wolf had previously served in minesweepers and aboard the *Schlesien*.

Final fitting out of the boat occurred in Kiel and by July all was ready. Sailing on the 9th she called at Kristiansand then headed out into the North Atlantic. On the 25th she joined Gruppe Wolf, south of Iceland and the next day was in a position to attack the outbound convoy to Halifax, ON113, torpedoing the British ship *Empire Rainbow* of 6,942 BRT, which she shared with U 704. On 30 July she was supplied by U 461 and the following day became part of Gruppe Steinbrink which was changed to Gruppe Pirat on 1 August.

On the 4th U 607 attacked convoy ON115, picking out a straggler which had previously been hit and damaged by U 553; they finished off the Belgian freighter *Belgian Soldier* of 7,167 BRT. Three days later she was not so lucky, firing five torpedoes on another straggling freighter from convoy SC94, but ending with a severe depth charging by convoy escorts which caused some light damage. Heading for France she docked at St Nazaire, which would be her home port, on the 16th.

It was back to the North Atlantic on 8 September 1942, part of Gruppe Pfeil and then Gruppe Blitz. Her crew remembered sunbathing south-west of the Azores. On 25 September she sighted convoy SC104. Before any real attack could be made, escort vessels were after her and she was heavily depth charged. With some slight damage she was driven off.

Now part of Gruppe Tiger, U 607 was supplied by U 117 on 4 October and then joined Gruppe Wotan. On 14 October she attacked convoy SC104 and sunk the Greek ship *Nellie* of 4,825 BRT. Yet again escort ships located her and she was again heavily depth charged. D/Cs exploded around her at a depth of 150 feet and again at 400 feet. Water entered the diesel room with such velocity that instruments struck by it were smashed and flattened. U 607 sank to around 600 feet before the plunge could be checked.

The boat was brought to the surface and it was fortunate that it was still night, which enabled her to slip away. However, an argument had broken out between Mengerson and his engineering officer, which would later lead to the latter's court martial and imprisonment. The boat limped to safety and running repairs were carried out which enabled the crew to start back to St Nazaire. However, on the 20th she was spotted at 1408 hours in position 4715/1455 by Coastal Command.

A Sunderland of 10 RAAF Squadron reported a sighting of two U boats at 1310 hours in position 4652/1955, although this may have been /1455, a bad 4 taken for a 9. The Sunderland pilot was the same Flight Lieutenant S R C Wood RAAF who had attacked U 373 on 11 August (see Chapter Two), and the Italian *Reginaldo Giuliani* on 1 September. Wood turned his Sunderland (W3986 'U') to gain a position up-sun and was lucky enough to find a cloud bank which shielded him from the eyes of the boat's watch crew. The ASV had not been switched on either, so the boat's Naxos equipment would not have been able to help warn them of the Sunderland's near presence.

Sam Wood had been at 8,000 feet but he gradually let down and when he was finally below the cloud the boats' watch crews saw him. The farthest U boat crash-dived as Wood was still three miles off, and the nearest began to do so ten seconds later. The Sunderland was quickly over the spot of the latter's position and released five depth charges (the sixth refused to release) from 50 feet some 30 seconds after the boat had gone down. They were aimed at an area 120 yards ahead of the swirl and at right angles to the boat's estimated track. Ten seconds after the explosions, the circling Sunderland crew saw a large air bubble and several smaller ones at the edge of a patch of scum, but nothing more substantial was observed and after 12 minutes, Wood flew away. His full crew is not listed in the Squadron records, just the three pilots and navigator:

FL S R C Wood DFC RAAF	Pilot
PO N C Gerrard RAAF	2nd pilot
PO Collett	3rd pilot
PO Austin	Navigator

The log of U 607 only noted three explosions following the attack by a Lerwick-type aircraft, which caused no damage. Three days later U 607 docked at St Nazaire.

Mengerson's command took some weeks to repair but it allowed the crew Christmas and New Year ashore, for their third war cruise did not begin until 2 January 1943. As part of Gruppe Falke and then Gruppe Haudegen, she found a drifting wreck on 26 January. The Norwegian tanker *Kollbjörg*, sailing with convoy HX223, had broken in two during a heavy storm and the fore-part was still afloat. Two torpedoes were used to sink it.

On 15 February U 607 attacked and sank a large American tanker, the *Atlantic Sun* of 11,355 BRT, off Newfoundland. A week later the boat was re-fuelled by the supply boat U 460 and in early March she missed a freighter with four torpedoes. She returned to base on the 9th. This was Mengerson's last patrol in U 607. He was given a shore appointment and Wolf Jeschonnek, the first officer, was given command.

With Jeschonnek in charge, U 607 left port for her fourth war cruise on 24 April. Just four days out, at 1025 hours on the morning of the 28th, a deadly Leigh Light bathed them in its beam. There were several aircraft out over the Bay and it is not absolutely certain which one found them. Favourite was the crew of Wellington 'Q' of 172 Squadron captained by Sergeant D W Bertram flying in the Derange area.[1]

Bertram had been airborne since 2145 hours and was at 1,200 feet. Radar picked up a contact 6½ miles to port and he took the Wellington down towards it. At ¾ of a mile the Light was switched on but at first the sea remained empty. Another search and the boat was picked out at 0118 hours in position 4512/1148, but the boat opened fire, hitting the Wimpy and damaging its hydraulics. Bertram took evasive action and his rear gunner opened fire as they flew over, but they were not able to drop their depth charges, and then the boat crash-dived. Sergeant Bertram's crew were:

Sgt D W Bertram	Pilot	Sgt W S Liddell	WOP/AG
Sgt J F Mundy	2nd pilot	Sgt C A Wheeler	WOP/AG
FS T K Cooper	Navigator	Sgt J J McAndrews	WOP/AG

Reporting a Leigh Light attack which they had driven off with flak

---

[1] Certain areas of the Bay were given code names by Coastal Command, such as Derange, Percussion, Musketry or Seaslug. While each remained approximately the same, they did alter in size from time to time.

fire (the boat's gunners thought they had shot-out the Light but obviously the Wellington's operator had turned it off once the aircraft was hit), Jeschonnek continued across the Bay and became part of Gruppe Drossel off the west coast of Spain on the 30th. On 7 May she picked up convoy SL125 (West Africa to Britain) but missed a ship with four torpedoes and then she was subjected to gunfire and depth charges from escort ships but escaped without damage. She was luckier on the 15th, three torpedoes slamming into the Eire registered freighter *Irish Oak* of 5,589 BRT which sank. This event took place 850 miles west of Ushant and *Irish Oak* was of course a neutral ship. Jeschonnek should have seen the name painted clearly on her sides as well as the Eire flag at her mast.

The next day U 607 was re-supplied by U 525 and a few days later she became part of Gruppe Mosel but saw no further action, returning home on 2 June. Just over a month later, on 10 July, Wolf Jeschonnek sallied forth on cruise number five, with orders to drop eight mines off the harbour of Kingston, Jamaica, in the Caribbean.

Three boats sailed in company, U 607, U 445 and U 613. This was during the period which saw much action over the Bay of Biscay. Not just routine actions but real battles, for Admiral Karl Dönitz, the 52-year-old head of the German U boat Service had given orders that any boats attacked by aircraft should remain on the surface and fight back. Many had done so before this edict, either because the captains had thought this the best way of defence, or they had had no time to crash-dive.

It had to be tempting to crash-dive in any event at the sight of an aircraft heading for them, but while they remained vulnerable to the approaching aircraft, this same aircraft was usually a pretty large target provided the U boat gunners could keep cool and aim effectively. Dönitz had seen casualties rise in recent months, especially now that his boats no longer had the protection of darkness when crossing the Bay, because Coastal Command were shining bright lights at them. At Headquarters, Coastal Command, the air leaders welcomed this change of tactic, for it gave their RAF crews a better chance of making a successful attack. And while they knew too that it put these same crews in more danger, the loss of an aircraft and crew was good arithmetic if it caused the loss of a U boat. This seems cold and calculating, but was no less of a fact.

By July 1943, the developing tactics used by U boats demanded that if the boats were to remain on the surface, always assuming there was no time to get well beneath the waves before an aircraft could attack, they should now sail in mini-convoys of between three and five vessels. In this way, any RAF aircraft that was able to surprise them would come under their combined defensive fires, and as only one boat could be attacked at one time, cross-fire from the others should prove effective, or may at least deter the attacker. Some boats, including U 607, had had their conning tower modified to take heavier AA armament, in her case a quadruple 20 mm gun.

However, for every tactic there was usually a counter-tactic thought up sooner or later, and Coastal Command, sizing up the situation, gave orders that whenever possible, following the discovery of a convoy of U boats, the initial aircraft should not attack (unless the pilot could see an effective way of doing so without too much danger), but stand off and call up other aircraft. There was always a number of Coastal aircraft operating over the Bay, and it would not take too long for one or two supporting aircraft to be homed-in to the U boat's location.

This in turn led to a real ding-dong battle, for the Germans also tried to counter the RAF's tactics by sending out long-range Ju88C twin-engined fighters, a Gruppe from KG40 (V Gruppe) being based near the French coast for just this purpose. In turn the RAF began operating over the Bay with Beaufighter and Mosquito fighters, flying 'Instep' patrols in order to counter these Ju88 incursions. Meantime, the Royal Navy operated small groups of sloops and destroyers on the outer reaches of the Bay, ready to sweep up any boats that escaped the RAF net, or to rush in and support any engagements started by the RAF anti-submarine aircraft. This was just the situation in mid-July as U 607 and her two companions were heading out.

U 607 left St Nazaire at 0730 on 10 July. The ship's crew were not totally fit, having suffered a mild form of dysentry a few days earlier which had effected most of them, including Wolf Jeschonnek. The two boats were led by Oberleutnant Rupprecht Graf von Treuberg, in U 445, followed by U 607. A minesweeper took station each side of the convoy, which was preceded by a 4,000-ton Sperrbrecher (blockade runner or armed merchantship used for escort). At Buoy 1, four and a half hours out, the surface ships turned back and the U boats submerged at 2300 hours. They surfaced at 1400 to recharge batteries and were joined by Kapitänleutnant Helmut Köppe with his U 613 from La Pallice.

The 11th and 12th were uneventful and at one minute past midnight on the 13th, a bottle of champagne was opened and a toast drunk by the officers in celebration of Wolf Jeschonnek's 24th birthday. The average age of the crew was just 21½, the oldest man being 31. It was not going to be an auspicious day however, but it would be memorable.

At 0755 hours the boats surfaced and took up an arrowhead

formation, with U 613, being guard boat for the day, leading. Almost immediately an RAF Halifax was sighted astern and soon afterwards a Sunderland ahead. U 607 turned away from the Halifax in order to present as narrow a target as possible but this increased the distance between her and the two other boats.

Layout Halifax 'O' (HR691) of 58 Squadron had been airborne at 0228 hours to fly a Musketry patrol, captained by Flying Officer A R D Clutterbuck. Shortly after 0700 they began to observe things as their flight log notes:

> 0703   4320/0905 sighted scores of fishing vessels of various sizes, none larger than trawler type – nets out – all within 20 miles of the coast.
>
> 0710   Whilst patrolling just outside territorial waters and passing Cape Prior, three red balls of fire fired and burst 200 yards from aircraft – warning shots, and altered course away from the coast.
>
> 0758   Attacked and destroyed a U boat, position 4509/0954.

Sunderland 'N-Nuts' of 228 Squadron (JM708) piloted by Flying Officer R D Hanbury had been airborne since 0304 hours, also on a Musketry patrol. Their flight log records:

> 0753   Position 4502/0914, sighted three fully surfaced U boats.
>
> 0756   Circled U boats at 100 feet, Halifax aircraft approached on course 200 degrees and also circled boats. MTB[1]: "Am over three enemy submarines in position 4502/0914."
>
> 0810   MTB: "Enemy submarines previously reported were sighted on surface on course 206 degrees, 13 knots."
>
> 0820   MTB: "U boats circling on surface."
>
> 0825   R/T message from Halifax – "We have only petrol remaining for ten minutes." Also further considerable amount of conversation with Halifax. Subsequently, when one U boat had been isolated from the others, attack took place.
>
> 0838   Attacked U boat with seven depth charges.

The U boats had begun taking evasive action as the two aircraft circled. The outside U boat (U 607) and the nearest to the Halifax continually drew away, keeping its stern to the aircraft. Flak fire was pretty accurate as Clutterbuck gently switched back and forth and when he finally got in touch with the Sunderland crew, Clutterbuck

---

[1] MTB – Message to Base; MFB – Message from Base.

said that he was going to fly on a reciprocal course. He then turned and commenced circling the boats in an anti-clockwise direction and succeeded in splitting the German's fire. The starboard U boat then broke away and began to submerge.

U 607 was now totally separated from the other two boats, one of which was going down. Only a few minutes had elapsed from the sighting of the aircraft, and Jeschonnek and his officer on the bridge were so confident that the combined fire of all boats would keep off the aircraft that they both lit cigarettes and waited for the aircraft to come within gun range. Not that he had any reason to appear so calm. He was apparently of a superstitious turn of mind and had had a premonition of disaster; the loss of his favourite cap overboard the previous day, a cap he had worn on all his previous cruises, and which he had regarded as a personal talisman, had not helped.

His gunners began to fire as the aircraft got to within a 1,000 yards but both the single 20 mm guns jammed although the 20 mm quad kept going. However, now fully aware that he was some way from the other two boats, Jeschonnek turned to try and rejoin.

Hanbury saw his chance and took his Sunderland down to attack, dropping seven depth charges from 50 feet. It was estimated that three fell close to the port side aft of the conning tower and three close to the starboard side forward. Two of the crew saw the conning tower blown into the air, a large portion of the bow went forward, stood on end over the vertical then slid into the sea. The remainder of the boat rocked violently, capsized and sank. During the attack the Sunderland's front gun had fired, and the German crew later reported that bullets had pierced the quad-gun's shield and killed the gun's crew. Immediately afterwards the boat had broken its back.

Meantime, Clutterbuck, seeing one of the other boats going down, dived to attack it, and dropped eight depth charges from 50 feet five seconds after the boat had disappeared. They straddled the boat's track ahead of the swirl, two exploding on or near the boat, others undershooting.

U 607 had indeed broken in half. Several men had been blown into the water and a few had managed to escape from below before the two halves went down. An estimated 20 men had been topsides: Jeschonnek and his first and third officers and the coxswain; three men had been on the quad gun plus a supply man, and three men on each of the single 20 mm guns; the gunnery officer, Leutnant Gassauer, one seaman to clear away empty cartridge cases, two seamen hoisting ammunition, plus the port and starboard lookouts. Several were killed and as none was wearing life vests, others were subsequently drowned.

From the Sunderland, large pieces of wreckage could be seen and about 25 men were spotted in the water. Hanbury came in low and dropped a dinghy near what appeared to be the main group of survivors and seven men managed to scramble aboard, four officers and three seamen. Meantime, the third U boat had also submerged. The Sunderland's flight log continued:

0900 Ordered homing procedure.
0923 Marine Marker dropped.
0935 Observed dinghy inflated and six men aboard.
0957 MTB: "Have dropped dinghy, remaining six survivors on board."
0959 MFB: "Remain over U boat and await surface vessel now on way."

Clutterbuck had already left being low on fuel. At 0920 another Sunderland arrived and seventeen minutes later, another Halifax but this soon left due to PLE. Yet another Sunderland arrived, but as the time was now progressing, and the aircraft had now been in the area for some while, anxious eyes began to look towards the distant French coast in case German aircraft appeared. And at 1142 an aircraft thought to be a Ju88 was seen high overhead, but it did not come down.

The surface craft were now half an hour away, and Hanbury decided he must leave soon, switching on his ASV to see how close the Navy was. His PLE was reached but it was not until 1307 that he finally set course for base. He had been in the vicinity of the attack, and the dinghy, for almost five hours. This was about 150 miles north of Spain, and some 350 from France.

Reader 'Hank' Hanbury, a former Imperial Airways flying boat pilot, won the DFC for this day's work, while Allister McFarlane, who had manned the front gun, was given the DFM. The crew list was:

FO R D Hanbury	Pilot	FS B Lacey	
PO T Pearson		FS E House	
PO K W Knights		FS N Wilson	
FS A Beal	Navigator	Sgt A McFarlane	WOP/AG
FS G D Williames		Sgt F Akers	
Sgt L H Kirby			

Clutterbuck – he was always known as just plain Clutterbuck – also received the DFC. Flying Officer A R Burns had been his co-pilot and it had been him who had first spotted the three boats. The crew consisted of:

FO A R D Clutterbuck	Pilot	Sgt J D Rice	WOP/AG
FO A R Burns	2nd pilot	Sgt W W A Cole	WOP/AG
Sgt M G McDougall	Navigator	Sgt T J N James	WOP/AG
Sgt L J Dale	Engineer	Sgt F Ladd	WOP/AG

At around noon, the corvettes of the Royal Navy's Second Support Group were seen nearing the area and they passed close to the dinghy but did not stop. Obviously the Navy, still very much aware that there were two more U boats somewhere in the vicinity, were far more concerned with finding them than in picking up German survivors. As the Navy commander later stated: 'With the prospect of a kill in front of me I could not spare a ship to pick them up and perforce left them to a contemplation of nature while the hunt was on.'

As the day wore on, the survivors no doubt thought they had had it, a situation which was not improved even when the dejected party spotted five Ju88s flying in formation at around 10,000 feet. They went right over the dinghy seemingly unaware of its existence and flew away. However, the Navy had not forgotten them and Hanbury's endeavours were not wasted. In the early hours of the next day, HMS *Wren* returned to the area and located the dinghy at 0400 hours. A whaler was lowered and when it had approached the men, they were asked for the number of their U boat. This they refused to give and the whaler immediately put about with a shout of: 'No number, no rescue.' The German captain quickly decided to divulge the number and he called the whaler back. Five minutes later the survivors were aboard and safe at last. They were:

Oberleutnant zur See Wolf Jeschonnek (captain)
Leutnant zur See Egon Horsemann (first lieutenant)
Leutnant zur See Friedrich Gassauer (gunnery officer)
Oberfähnrich zur See Gerhard Teschke (senior midshipman)
Matrosenobergefreiter Karl Lanedziewitz (able seaman)
Maschinenobergefreiter Viktor Jantzen (stoker, 1st class)
Matrose I Günther Unterhollenberg (ordinary seaman)

The boat's complement had been 51, comprising seven officers, three chief petty officers, 12 leading hands and 29 other ratings. This was above the norm as there had been a supernumerary engineering officer aboard, who was due to take the place of the existing engineering officer at the end of this patrol. Also two Flakspezialisten (flak-gun specialists) and one ordnance artificer, for the new AA defences that were aboard, plus a surgeon lieutenant, deemed necessary now that boats were being ordered to stay on the surface and fight back, a course of action that suggested casualties. None of these men had survived, and the engineering officer had been the 31 year old, a popular and efficient man who had risen from the lower deck.

Less than a month after Wolf Jeschonnek was sunk, rescued and taken prisoner, his half-brother Hans, the Luftwaffe Generaloberst, committed suicide. He was continually being held scapegoat for problems with the defence of Germany and the final straw had come following the Allied air attack upon the German experimental rocket base at Peenemunde on the night of 17/18 August 1943. Given a verbal dressing down by Hitler himself, and then another by Hermann Göring, Jeschonnek shot himself.

Whilst being questioned after capture, Wolf told his interrogators that he believed that sending U boats across the dangerous Bay area in groups would continue but this would only work if the Luftwaffe were able to give them adequate air cover. He also thought that making three passages in and out of the Bay was worth a Ritterkreuz (Knight's Cross of the Iron Cross, the coveted decoration worn at the throat). Unfortunately Wolf Jeschonnek did not receive a Ritterkreuz, and his birthday only brought the loss of his command and most of his men. However, he did survive. One might even say that this was his second 'birthday'.

Although both U 445 and U 613 effected an escape from the aircraft and the ships of the Second Support Group, only the former was destined to return to its home port. U 613 was lost ten days later, the 23rd, sunk by American ships and carrier-borne aircraft while still on her way to lay mines off Jacksonville, Florida. South of the Azores she was found by these ships and aircraft that were escorting convoy UGS12 (military convoy from the US to Casablanca).

Oddly enough, Graf von Treuberg's U 445 was attacked and damaged by another 58 Squadron Halifax on 2 January 1944. She was eventually lost to the frigate HMS *Louis* on 24 August 1944.

CHAPTER FOUR

BATTLES IN THE BAY

Before the month of July was out there were other episodes involving U boats that continued practicing the doctrine of staying up to fight, two of them involving boats that were supply vessels. The first of these occurred on the 24th.

U 459 was built at Kiel by the Deutsche Werke AG, and commissioned on 15 November 1941. She was a type XIV submarine designed to be used as a tanker, taking fuel out into the Atlantic to resupply boats that were then able to remain out of port, rather than come home and run the gauntlet through the Bay. U 459 could carry 750 tons of fuel, a good deal of provisions and six spare torpedoes. She had no torpedo tubes herself so could not attack shipping but had defensive 2 cm and 3.7 cm guns. Six of these supply boats were built but all were sunk within a short time. They were very heavy and the submerge time took too long. These, and other similar boats that supplied not only fuel, oil, food and additional torpedoes, were known as 'Milch Cows' and it was as important to sink them as it was normal attack U boats, which without them, would be forced to abandon their war cruises and return home.

The commander of U 459 was Korvettenkapitän Georg von Wilamowitz-Möllendorff. Born in November 1893 he was, at 48, the oldest U boat commander to see active duty in WW2. Affectionately known to his crew as 'Wild Mowitz', his was the first tanker boat in service. Its conning tower emblem was an elephant beneath two palm trees.

Assigned to the 10th U boat Flotilla, she sailed on her first mission from Kiel on 21 March 1942 for the North Atlantic and made history on 19 April by supplying U 108, the first boat supplied at sea by a U-tanker. From then until 5 May she resupplied a further 13 boats. Operating then from St Nazaire she sailed from this port on 6 June and supplied fuel to 17 boats before returning on 19 July.

Nine boats were refuelled on her third patrol, between 22

September and 4 November, which had begun on 18 August, this time to the South Atlantic. On 4 September she came across a lifeboat from the American steamer SS *California* which had been sunk by an Italian submarine. Wilamowitz-Möllendorff surfaced and gave the occupants assistance although it was against orders and policy to take people on board. However, his identity was later established due to a survivor remembering the boat's emblem.

This cruise was followed by her fourth patrol between 20 December and 7 March 1943 to the Central Atlantic, supplying six boats. This time she returned to Bordeaux where she was prepared for her fifth cruise which began on 21 April. At first all went well, no fewer than 21 U boats being supplied between 1 and 26 May; however, she was attacked by two aircraft at noon on 30 May. Bombs were dropped on her and her gunners claimed hits on both attackers, but she sustained only light damage.

Despite recording that her attackers were two 'Lancaster type' aircraft, it would seem the aircraft were firstly a Whitley and then a Liberator. Whitley 'N' (Z9440) from No.10 OTU (a Bomber Command OTU attached to 19 Group of Coastal Command to bolster the number of aircraft over the Bay at this period) had taken off at 0940 and it sent an SOS at 1220, reporting engine trouble. However, the 'trouble' seems to have been caused by U 459's gunners.

Also closing in on the reported submarine was Liberator 'G' from 224 Squadron. At 1222 hours the captain sighted depth-charge pools still foaming, four to five miles off and turned towards them, then spotted the U boat circling to starboard, position 4440/1030. The U boat reported its position at this time as 4533/1054. As the Lib headed in a Whitley was seen one to two miles away, flying east, presumably having just delivered the attack which had caused the D/C pools. The Lib dived to attack the U boat from astern, meeting intense and accurate flak but six D/Cs were sent down. A second attack, also in the face of heavy flak fire lobbed down three D/Cs which overshot, while a third attack could only be made with machine-gun fire. The Lib was hit in these attacks, and the pilot immediately headed away, although once clear, it was found that the damage had been only slight. Undoubtedly the U boat crew believed both aircraft had been hit and shot down. In fact the Whitley did not return. The attacking crews were:

Whitley:

Sgt L Slade	Pilot	Sgt G F Dimmock
Sgt W J Wood		PO R A Russell
Sgt W F Wicks		Sgt G W Vines

Liberator:
FL M J Elworthy   Pilot – rest of crew unknown.

However, U 459 was almost home and docked safely on 3 June.

This time she was in port a while longer than usual, but on 22 July she was off once more. However, Ultra intercepts had picked up that certain escort vessels were being assigned to her upon departure, so Coastal Command were informed to be on the lookout.

Sailing at 0930 hours she waited at the mouth of the Gironde overnight and was joined by U 117 (Hans Neumann) and then by U 461 (Wolf Stiebler). However, U 461 was found to have a leak in Diving Tank 6 and had to return to harbour. One by one the other two submarines set sail, escorted by two destroyers, four minesweepers and a Sperrbrecher. This escort parted company shortly after midnight of the 23/24th. The boat was then found to have been sabotaged. The air quick release valve failed to close properly and it was discovered that someone had cleverly inserted a thick piece of copper wire round part of the valve seating. It was removed and the boat continued her cruise.

Two days out of Bordeaux, at 1750 hours, she was picked up on the radar set of Wellington 'Q' of 172 Squadron, captained by Flying Officer W H T Jennings. The contact was six miles to starboard, Jennings taking his aircraft into cloud. Coming out he saw the U boat on the surface which was obviously going to stay up and fight.

Jennings came down to 100 feet and headed in but at 350 yards away the Wellington caught the full force of the U boat's guns. Both pilots may have been hit, perhaps even killed outright but the Wellington ploughed straight on and crashed into its intended target. Only the rear gunner, Sergeant A A Turner, who knew nothing of the last seconds, survived.

The chief officer of U 459 was Oberleutnant zur See Karl Kämper, aged 32 years. He had been a merchant navy officer, serving in the liner *Columbus*. In 1981 he wrote an account of the action which in part records:

> On the tower was the Commander, myself as officer of the watch, one petty officer and three or four sailors. We kept a sharp lookout, especially for aircraft, knowing only too well the danger of our situation. After a short time, I think it was only 15 or 20 minutes later, the first aircraft, a white painted Wellington bomber, was seen to starboard, abeam, not very far away. I gave the aircraft alarm signal, which meant not to submerge but to man all anti-aircraft guns.

The Wellington immediately turned for the attack, coming down to a low height. We fired with six 2 cm gun barrels. Apparently the Wellington was badly hit; it lost too much height and nearly crashed into our boat, that is to say, it half crashed on the boat and half into the sea. The left wing tore open our after deck while the middle part crashed against the breastworks of the conning tower, taking with it nearly all our anti-aircraft weapons and all the men who had manned them, leaving only our 3.7 cm gun on the foredeck. Then it plunged into the sea not far from our boat.

However, the Wellington had dropped some water bombs [depth charges], two of them lying on our deck. A man cried "Captain there is a bomb!" The Commander yelled, "Drop it overboard," which two men did. The bomb exploded under our stern, damaged our rudder and one screw (we had two engines) and water got into the stern room.

Crewmen were able to close the rear bulkhead door but the boat was badly damaged. We could no longer sail other than in a circle and we had almost no anti-aircraft weapons. Not long afterwards, I guess about a quarter of an hour, the next Wellington appeared and attacked immediately with bombs and gunfire. Being now unable to complete our task nor return to the French coast, the Commander gave the order to abandon ship and to open the valves to make the boat sink. Our Commander went down with her.

The second Wellington continued to attack as long as our boat was on the surface, then flew in circles around the crew who were now drifting in the sea with life-belts. We could see one man from the first Wellington's crew drifting in a small dinghy about a mile from us. Then the second Wellington dropped some smoke bombs.

In the meantime we had gathered ourselves together. The weather was fine, the sun still shining, air and water warm, sea calm with no wind. I counted the men and could see that we had lost about one third of the crew, including the Commander and the Chief Engineer.

As there were smoke bombs burning around us, we hoped for rescue and rescue came late in the night after we had been in the sea for about ten hours. We were picked up by a Polish destroyer that was operating with an English flotilla. We were treated very correctly by the Polish crew and three days later, landed at Plymouth, as prisoners of war for four years.

We had had on board the U boat a load of yellow rubber rescue boats [dinghies?] each of which was folded in a small packet and had a little compressed air bottle. Originally these were intended for the Luftwaffe, but at the time U boat crews were also issued with them, one between two men. Between attacks by the first Wellington and the second, we had taken all these rubber boats on deck and operated the air bottles, so that they were lying on deck ready for use. When the second Wellington attacked all the boats were destroyed by gunfire.

There had been a few moments of panic aboard U 459. The switchboards in the electric motor room had caught fire and the diesels were jolted from their bases. The CO was reluctant to abandon ship, trying to decide whether they could make base on the surface. He ordered a message to base requesting air cover but also ordered that 30 rubber dinghies be placed on deck as a precaution. Gradually the fires below were got under control, but the arrival of the second Wellington ended all hopes of a trip home.

As the aircraft came in, some of the crew attempted to man the 3.7 mm deck gun but were hit by gunfire from the Wellington. After the attack, the men left were ordered into the water and several saw the CO on the bridge, saluting them before disappearing into the conning tower hatch to complete the scuttling. They believed he made no attempt to save himself.

Sergeant A A Turner, the rear gunner of the downed Wellington, a man who had played for Charlton Athletic Football Club pre-war, and who had already been in crews that had damaged two U boats, had found himself in the sea after the crash. Lucky for him the aircraft dinghy had released on impact and inflated quite near him, allowing him to get aboard. It had been upside down but being virtually un-injured, he was easily able to right it. As he lay there he could see the German crew quite clearly on the deck of the boat, smoke pouring from the rear. Debris was all around. The following report was later produced from Flight Sergeant Turner's recollections:

At approximately 1715 hours, Q/172 was at the bottom of its patrol and about to turn onto the short westerly leg when an SE indication was obtained at six miles to starboard. Aircraft was at 1,000 feet in cloud. Aircraft broke at five miles and a U boat was seen on the surface which the Captain announced looked as if it was going to fight it out. The Captain decided to go straight into the attack and did so in a dive coming down to 100 feet when 1,000 yards from the U boat. Flight Sergeant Turner then saw pieces of fuselage being shot away by AA fire.

The attack was pressed but Flight Sergeant Turner had no knowledge of when the depth charges were released or how they fell since his only recollection is of an explosion in the aircraft. The next thing he knew was being under water and kicking away something with his feet. He then came to the surface. He was able, after kicking off his flying boots, to swim to a dinghy which he saw beyond two fires on the water, marking the wreckage of the aircraft. He saw one body in the water which may have been the second pilot.

Having reached the dinghy which was upside down, he clambered on and saw the U boat with the crew on deck. It was circling slowly and had black smoke pouring from the stern. He removed his coat and Mae West to wave at them but it was apparently out of control and came no nearer. He then succeeded in righting the dinghy, losing his coat and Mae West in the process.

The dinghy rations had disappeared but there was a bellows, knife and leak stoppers. Shortly afterwards, V/547 made its attack on the U boat and after depth charges had exploded the U boat was seen no more. Flight Sergeant Turner remained in the dinghy for nine hours and at 0230 hours on 25 July, was picked up by a destroyer which heard his shouts and spotted him. He was put ashore at Plymouth on the morning of the 26th. He suffered only superficial injuries.

Jennings' crew consisted of:

FO W H T Jennings	Pilot	FO J Johnson	WOP/AG
FO J G McCormack	2nd pilot	FS L Harrop	WOP/AG
FS J W Buxton	Navigator	Sgt A A Turner	WOP/AG

The second Wellington was aircraft 'V' of 547 Squadron; operating from Davidstow Moor on a Musketry 3 patrol, they had been airborne at 1425 hours. Their flight log indicated:

1756 Sighted U boat dead ahead on the surface, position 4602/1038.

1759 MTB: "Am over enemy submarine, position 4557/1038, on surface, course 270 degrees."

1759 Attacked U boat.

1801 Aircraft dinghy, one survivor. Dropped aircraft cushion and supplies. Possibly recovered by survivor. Dropped Marine Marker 1½ miles from about 20 dinghies containing survivors from U boat which were joined.

1820 MTB: "Have attacked U boat with depth charges – sunk."

1900 MTB: "Am over dinghy, one aircrew, position 4553/1038."

1932 MTB: "Am over 20 U boat survivors."

2009 MFB: "Return to base immediately."
2130 MTB: "ETA 2300 hours."
2246 Landed base.

The crew consisted of:

FO J Whyte	Pilot	FS R J Taylor
FO W J Dickson		FS A L Bathurst
FO A Fisher		FS L G Simpson

Turner and the U boat survivors were picked up by the Polish destroyer ORP *Orken*, part of Force W. The Germans comprised five officers, nine chief and petty officers and 27 men, from a total complement of seven officers, 12 chief and petty officers and 40 men (in all 59), thus two officers, three chief and petty officers and 13 men had died (total 18).

When interrogated, the survivors described their lost Commander as a cheerful man, a born leader and they felt it was quite in keeping with his character that he should choose to go down with his ship.

Before the month of July was out there was another, more famous fight between a small group of U boats and aircraft of Coastal Command. As we read above, U 461 had been part of the original group of boats which included U 459, sailing from Bordeaux on 22 July, which made rendezvous at the mouth of the Gironde, but she had had to return to port following the discovery of a leak in Diving Tank No.6. Apparently this had developed following the fouling of another ocean-going tanker during bad weather while at mooring in Bordeaux harbour.

With the leak fixed, U 461 left Bordeaux on 28 July, in company with U 462 (Kapitänleutnant Bruno Vöwe) and a third boat. However, this third vessel discovered a faulty clutch and returned to harbour, so the other two joined up with U 504 (Kapitänleutnant Wilhelm Luis, aged 27), outward bound from another base. I have covered the action of this group of U boats in my book *Conflict over the Bay* (Wm Kimber, 1985) but since then several other interesting accounts and information have filtered through which I feel need to be added.

The two boats U 460 and U 461, like U 459, were 'Milch Cows', boats sent out to resupply U boats already in the Atlantic with fuel, torpedoes and food. Both were type XIV submarines built at the Deutsche Works in Kiel (in the series of supply submarines U 459, 460, 461, 462, 463 and 464). The commander of U 461 was Korvetten-kapitän Wolf-Harro Stiebler, who was nearing his 36th birthday, and had served in U boats since pre-war. Stiebler was born in

Hannovorisch Munden, on 4 August 1907, attained his present rank on 1 June 1943 and had commanded U 461 since 22 April 1942.

U 461 operated from St Nazaire in August 1942 following her first patrol from Germany beginning in June. Cruising the South Atlantic she supplied several boats and had survived a heavy attack by a Sunderland in which deck boards were blown off, instrument glass was broken and depth gauges smashed.

Returning to St Nazaire in October, Stiebler took her out again the following month, again going to the South Atlantic, again supplying a number of boats before returning to base on 5 January 1943. On this mission she brought back the Master of the 5,136-ton *Teesbank* (Captain Lorains), picked up by the attacking U boat and then transferred to U 461 to bring back to German Navy HQ. In February U 461 returned to the old area, supplied more boats and again took delivery of a Master for prison camp, the time that of the 4,312-ton *Saint Margaret* (Captain D M S Davis). Again upon her return U 461 was attacked by an aircraft, using a Leigh Light, but did not sustain any damage, and she made port in early April. Cruise number five began later that month and was completed without too many problems.

For her part, U 462 had sailed on seven supply missions since the summer of 1942. Her commander, Bruno Vöwe, was 39 and had been in the Navy some time, and had transferred to the submarine service in 1935, prior to being commissioned. He had also been an instructor at the German U boat school.

Most of U 462's cruises had been completed without major mishap but on her sixth, starting in June 1943, she had been attacked and damaged by four Mosquito aircraft of 151 and 456 Squadrons, and had also suffered crew casualties, forcing her return to base. Sailing on her next mission, a Liberator of 224 Squadron had found and damaged her on 2 July about 80 miles north-west of Cape Ortegal which again forced her back to base. She was about to find out that it was not going to be a case of third time lucky.

With U 461 starting out on her sixth and final cruise, U 462 on her eighth and last, the three boats began with escorts of three Narvik class destroyers, one Sperrbrecher and at least six minesweepers, plus the occasional air cover by Ju88s. An hour before midnight of the 23rd, the escorts turned back and led by U 461 the three boats headed out across the Bay.

By morning they were on a course of 230 degrees, on the surface, and making around ten knots. At around 0930 hours, U 461's watch crew spotted a Sunderland but the flying boat kept its distance and out of range of any of the U boat's AA fire. As required by orders, the discovery of a formation of U boats had first to be reported and other supporting aircraft homed-in.

Before his death in May 1991, Wolf Stiebler recorded the following information. He had ordered that the boats cruise on the surface all night and rendezvous at a point in the Bay next morning. U 461 and U 507 made the rendezvous but U 462 was missing. They stayed on the surface as long as they dared and Stiebler was about to give orders to submerge when they saw flashes against the rising sun, which proved to be U 462 signalling with her searchlight.

They sailed back and discovered that U 462 had been submerged all night and her batteries needed recharging: using the searchlight had flattened them further. It was impossible for the boat to submerge so Stiebler had to make a decision. Knowing it was dangerous to remain on the surface he had to decide whether to remain up with her or to dive and leave her to her fate. Finally he felt compelled to stay with her, and soon afterwards, as if he had tempted fate, was spotted by the flying boat.

Nervously the three U boat commanders eyed the flying boat and half an hour later a second aircraft appeared. An hour passed, and a third aircraft arrived. U 461 was the centre boat with U 462 to starboard and U 504 to port. Despite Stiebler's note that it was a Sunderland that had first been seen, Coastal Command record that the first sighting was by the crew of a 53 Squadron Liberator, captained by Flying Officer W J Irving (BZ730 'O') who had been on a Musketry patrol since dawn. This aircraft gave a sighting report but noted the wrong area by 80 miles which soon led to the belief there were two U boat groups. The next aircraft to spot them was indeed a Sunderland, from 228 Squadron (JM679) piloted by Flying Officer S White. He called in the correct location (which at that moment indicated a second group), but suddenly a Ju88 turned up, forcing White to jettison his depth charges and head for cloud.

Shortly afterwards, a Catalina of 210 Squadron came on the scene, which was co-operating with the ships of Captain Walker's Second Support Group. After calling up 19 Group HQ, it flew to the ships to give them a visual message by Aldis lamp of the U boat location. This quickly sent the ships steaming to the spot. Stiebler too had radioed base, asking for Ju88 cover as they were being threatened by a number of aircraft, but a group of fighters nearby were running short of fuel and had to return home. Because of the amount of radio traffic between aircraft and England, picked up by the Germans, an order was sent to the boats for them to disperse and act independently, and presumably to dive if they could.

The next aircraft to appear was an American B24 of the 19th Squadron homing in on 228's call, which coincided with Flying Officer White's return, having lost the Ju88. So there were now three aircraft circling, 53's Lib, the American Lib and White's Sunderland. A fourth aircraft arrived, a 502 Squadron Halifax, piloted by Flying Officer W S Biggar, who decided to open the attack, and amidst flak, flew over and dropped three 600 lb bombs which overshot by 70-100 yards. The Halifax was holed in the starboard elevator.

A second 502 Squadron Halifax now appeared (aircraft 'S') flown by a Dutch pilot, Flying Officer A van Rossum, followed soon after-wards by a Sunderland (W6077 'U') of 461 Squadron RAAF, piloted by Flight Lieutenant D Marrows RAAF, flying a machine with rapidly drying fuel tanks. The latter crew had been ordered to the incorrect area by the initial sighting report, so that by the time the error had been realized, they were running short of fuel, as the navigator, Flying Officer J S 'Jock' Rolland RAAF was later to record:

> It has been written that our shortage of fuel was caused by excessive consumption. Not so! The engines were in no way thirsty and the pilot's cruise control was impeccable.
>
> It was caused by a rare 'boob' by the normally reliable 19 Group. Having reached PLE on patrol and set course for home, we received a message from Group giving the position of three surfaced U boats. On arriving at or near the position given, there was nothing to be seen but an empty Bay of Biscay.
>
> So, off on a square search for over an hour. We were just on the umpteenth and last possible leg when another message arrived apologising for having made an error of 1 degree latitude on the first position. By then, our reserves were practically nil, so the only thing to do was lay a track through the new position. If contact was established it allowed no more than ten minutes for action. If no contact, it was a case of 'Home James' and be very sparing with the horses.

Pilot Officer Peter Jensen, the Sunderland's First Wireless Operator, saw the three boats and the wall of flak they put up. As the nearby Liberator went in he quickly thought that with their single front gun there was no way his pilot was going to be able to attack. However, he had not reckoned with Dudley Marrows, and was dismayed to hear the Klaxon sound which heralded the depth charges being run out.

It was now just minutes short of noon. Marrows knew that if they were going to make an attack before their fuel state made it impossible it would have to be soon – or not at all. In company with van Rossum's Halifax, the two aircraft made independent attacks, thereby splitting the AA fire as the American Lib also edged in, taking some of the flak too. Van Rossum dropped single 600 lb bombs, while Marrows let go his depth charges which straddled U 461. Van Rossum scored a near miss near to U 462's stern and then smoke was seen coming from its conning tower as the boat began to circle, its rudder damaged. Meanwhile the American Liberator had been hit and limped away.

Wolf Stiebler later said that at the moment of attack he had attempted to turn the boat to port, being unable to turn to starboard owing to the short distance between him and U 462. He also saw U 462 sustain a near miss and her crew beginning to abandon ship. In that split second Marrows' depth charges exploded about his boat. They broke the U boat's back and part of Stiebler's clothing caught on something and he was dragged beneath the water for a considerable depth before he struggled free and bobbed to the surface.

While this was happening, the 53 Squadron Liberator (Irving) made a run-in but it was hit by flak and also had to limp away, eventually to land in Portugal. Gunfire from Marrows' Sunderland had also cut down some of the gunners manning the boat's quad 20 mm gun. A survivor later reported that machine-gun fire from the Sunderland was very accurate killing two leading members of the quad gun. The gunlayer of the port single 20 mm gun said he fired until the aircraft was 60 feet away and then his ammunition ran out. The survivors on the bridge were all suddenly in the water, Stiebler came to the surface, and two others scrambled from the conning tower hatch, but one later disappeared. The surviving one from inside the boat said there was a tremendous explosion and a wall of water rushed into the control room from forward, and he thought the bows had been blown off.

Last man off the doomed submarine was Matrosenobergefreiter (able seaman) Helmut Rochinski, aged 20. He recalls:

> During the battle I was in the conning tower as helmsman, so could not see the action. We had surfaced early in the morning – just after 0600 hours – and we were still blowing our diving tanks when a bridgewatch called, 'Aircraft, 180 degrees!' Within half an hour there were five aircraft reported.
>
> Because I was in the conning tower I could only hear what was happening on the bridge. Several attacks were made by the aircraft and there were casualties on the bridge. The first was Obersteuer-mann Klimaschewski, who was standing above the tower hatch. He was hit and fell. I caught him and then supported his head with my leather jacket but he died in my arms. Then the quadruple flak gun was out of the fight, and only the two single guns were still firing. Our freedom of movement to starboard was also limited as we were running in line abreast with the other submarines. U 462 was hit and then U 504 dived leaving U 461 alone.

Our captain sent down a message to be transmitted: 'Are in battle with five aircraft, request air support.' Several more attacks followed and one aircraft dropped its bombs very close and a terrible shock followed. Our captain asked about the state of the boat and moments later he ordered, 'Leave the boat.' That was the last command I passed down.

I climbed the ladder and reached the bridge. After me, nobody else got out; I was the last. I grabbed a hold on the periscope but was then swept away by the waves. U 461 sank very fast and the aircraft still circled over us for a long while. A Sunderland dropped a dinghy and we put some wounded men into it while the rest of us clung to its ropes.

After some hours there were British ships around us. The corvette U08-HMS *Woodpecker* picked us up. The wounded men were sent to the sick bay while we received dry clothing and food. After a few days we arrived in a British port; then sent to a POW camp.

U 462 had had her problems too. One gunner was killed by gunfire and a Leutnant was wounded in the face when the 3.7 cm deck gun had a premature. As well as a damaged rudder, the aft torpedo hatch had been buckled making it impossible for the boat to dive. The stern compartment was slowly flooding and there was water in the engine room. Until now all three U boats had kept up a concentrated barrage against the aircraft but ammunition was now running short. U 462 signalled base that U 461 had sunk and then Vöwe gave the order to prepare to scuttle. Before he did so, another air attack came and there was also a bomb from a high flying aircraft which may in fact have been the first of the shells arriving from the on-coming sloops of the Navy. As the boat began to settle, the aircraft crews saw shells splashing in the water around it. Oberleutnant Hans Krüger, the Leitenden Ingenieurs (senior engineering officer) on U 462 recorded his recollections of the action. He was 35 years old and had been in the Navy since 1926 and commissioned in 1941. Before joining U 462 prior to her commissioning he had been an instructor at the Naval School at Wesermunde:

When the first radar signals of aircraft were picked up we were charging our batteries after a long period under water. There was a Liberator keeping out of reach of our flak and diving was not possible. By 1015 there was a Sunderland too and then a Catalina.

U 461 was the first to be attacked by the three aircraft. All the boats were firing with all their guns. About 1100 hours the listening post reported: 'Fast surface craft are approaching.' Meanwhile the aircraft attacked us continually.

U 461 shot down an aircraft [!], then a Sunderland attacked and destroyed the boat with depth charges. At 1200 hours, British surface craft arrived and opened fire, shells bursting nearby. Our ammunition came to an end. The empty cartridges in the control room reached almost to our knees. Then a hit on the starboard aft. The pressure door to the stern area was damaged and there was water coming in. We tried to shore-up the door but this was no solution.

The boat swung out of line, turning in circles. With our final shots we gave U 504 the opportunity to dive undamaged, although eight hours later she too was sunk by depth charges. Meantime we were given the order to leave the boat. The whole crew, together with two badly wounded men, escaped before the boat was scuttled. Before our eyes she went down with her ensign flying. Crew member Sauer, seriously wounded, died in the dinghy. After eight hours we were picked up by the British ships to start four years in a POW camp.

In all, just three officers, two chief and petty officers and ten men survived from U 461, while U 462 only lost one able seaman. U 461's complement had been 60, U 462's 65.

While these actions had been going on, the five sloops of Walker's Group had been approaching. On board HMS *Woodpecker* was an RAF officer and an extract from his diary gives a vivid picture:

Friday 30 July: Went on the bridge at midnight. Left bridge at 4 am and had a few hours sleep. About 8.30 the fun really started. What a terrific day! A Sunderland and a Catalina were around and they signalled that no less than three U boats were on the surface about ten miles away ahead. The SNO in HMS *Kite* made the signal "General Chase". Off we went at full speed, line abreast – a grand sight – smooth blue sea and blue sky – all ratings and officers at actions stations.

Soon we saw the aircraft circling low and diving to drop depth charges. Two of the U boats were visible by this time and the Sunderland dropped a couple of depth charges plumb on either side of the conning tower of one of them. That broke the U boat's back and he disappeared pretty quickly, leaving some survivors and a raft in the water. Simultaneously, all our ships had opened fire with 4-inch [guns] on the second U boat [already sinking as a result of an attack by a Halifax]. He too left survivors who had to wait until U boat No.3 had been located and dealt with. Not unnaturally No.3 dived in some haste and we were now set the task of finding him beneath the surface. It was like great cats stalking an over-sized mouse.

Kite found him first and dropped a pattern of depth charges. Then *Woodpecker* set about him and dropped depth charges. *Kite* got a fix and with his direction we proceeded to lay a 'plaster' which is rather what the name denotes. *Wild Goose* repeated the dose, but while she was doing so, the first patches of oil were observed and soon it was coming up in great quantities – the sea stank of it. Wood and other wreckage came up too. This was about 3.30 pm.

We recovered various things. *Wren* found some German clothing. The evidence was decisive and the ships (which had been shielding one another during the action) reformed and made off to pick up survivors. The C-in-C Plymouth signalled "Well done". C-in-C Western Approaches sent, "Warmest congratulations."

Now for the survivors. We picked up 17, including the Captain and First Officer. The other ships picked up a further 50 or so altogether. Ours were in or clinging to a rubber float, shaped like a big rubber ring. Some were injured. One had a bullet in his stomach and a broken ankle. They were mostly shaking with cold and/or reaction from the experience. Several of them were truculent and some had never been in a U boat before – possibly never to sea before. Their lifebelts and equipment are excellent. Other survivors have been reported some miles away. We are making course for them. (Later): Prisoners have been disposed of and are reported happy. Two of our officers have to give up their bunks for the U boat officers (international law!). Two in the sick bay look rather mouldy.

The dinghy with six people has been picked up. They were Huns not RAF. They had a sail up. One report says that No.2 submarine contained an RAF officer who had been shot down and was picked up by the U boat. If so he went down with the U boat.

Reference to the dinghy and six men was of course Stiebler and his few survivors. Marrows and crew had dropped an RAF dinghy to them, which is why, at first, the approaching ship had thought they must be downed RAF crewmen. In the event, of course, there was no RAF man aboard any of the U boats; they had hardly had time to do anything, let alone rescue a downed RAF man.

A report from Captain Walker's Group also makes interesting reading, complementing the RAF liaison officer's diary:

. . . all was at peace until at 0714, 30 July, an H/F, D/F bearing 216 degrees was taken in *Wildgoose*. Course was thereupon altered to 216 degrees, but at 0757 a signal was intercepted from an aircraft reporting himself over three U boats in position 44 deg. 00 mins. North, 10 deg. 35 mins. West, followed by a second H/F, D/F bearing at 0804, 225 deg. from *Wildgoose*. At 0817, the Group now being on course 240 deg. an H/F, D/F bearing 244 deg., first class, was taken in *Kite* and from this time onwards reports poured in from aircraft circling various geographical positions. I kept the Group on course 240 deg. until 0927 when further H/F, D/F bearings caused me to alter slightly to 243 deg. speed 18 knots.

At 0947 what appeared to be a depth-charge explosion over the horizon was sighted fine on the port bow and HM Ships went into Action Stations as speed was increased to 18½ knots. Definite depth-charge explosions were seen ahead at 0955 and 1004, whereupon the General Chase was hoisted in *Kite*, a signal which is believed to have been flown on very few occasions since the days of Nelson. Subsequent events went to show that the hoisting of General Chase coincided with a state of general alarm among the enemy, who were sighted for the first time at 1005 right ahead. The enemy consisted of two 1,600 tons U boats and a third smaller U boat, the first two being supply ships and the third operational.

Fire was opened in *Kite* at the clearly visible U boat with A and B guns and very shortly afterwards the remainder of the Group chimed in. From the beginning to the end of this short Gunnery Action 121 rounds of 4-inch were fired, 56 by *Kite*, 37 by *Wren*, 16 by *Wildgoose* and 12 by *Woodcock*. At 1013 a hit on the enemy was observed in *Kite* at a range of 1,350 yards (hits were also claimed by *Wildgoose* and *Woodcock*), and almost at once a message – "U boats no more" was received from the aircraft circling the position, followed 1½ minutes later by a second signal from the same observer consisting of the single word: "Congratulations". Thus perished U 462 which was afterwards learned to have hastened its own end by scuttling when the crew could take it no longer. Its fellow U 461 had already been sunk by aircraft attack and this left the operational U boat only, to be destroyed.

By 1030 HM Ships were up at the position where the enemy had sunk for the last time; survivors packed tight in rubber dinghies were passed close to on the port side. Other wreckage and survivors were seen a mile or so further away and I later detached *Woodpecker* to pick up the more distant party, leaving the nearer party in the water and also in blissful ignorance of the harrowing moments through which they were about to live.

After passing the position I had ordered *Woodpecker*,

Wildgoose and *Woodcock* to form a square patrol, at the same time instructing *Wren* to join me, and at 1034, having obtained a contact a few minutes earlier, *Kite* fired a ten-charge pattern set to 300 and 150 feet. This attack was followed by an attack from *Wren* who fired a pattern at 1040 when she was in a position seven cables distant from *Kite* on my port quarter. When orders to fire *Kite*'s pattern were given, no one could foretell what effect it would have on the members of the Aryan bathing party who were but a short distance astern, with the whites of their eyes still clearly visible. It was a fateful moment although there was no question of a sword hanging over their heads; rather was their fate to be decided much lower down. However, all went well with them and after the depth charges had erupted, the Germans were still seen to be rocking gently on the bosom of the ocean, although doubtless, for the time being, concentrating heavily on the immediate future and taking no thought of the morrow.

From this time onwards contact was lost and regained inter-mittently until 1132 when *Kite* was once again in firm contact, firing her second ten-charge pattern set to 350 and 550 feet at 1049. I looked on these first three attacks as preliminary sparring. They showed me: (a) that the U boat had gone deep, (b) that it had taken swift avoiding action from the three normal asdic attacks, and was therefore no milch-cow, (c) that it was now necessary to get down to the job seriously. Accordingly I decided to apply the 'creeping attack' and instructed *Woodpecker* to come up on my port quarter, to proceed ahead, (not operating Asdics) and fire a 22-charge pattern set to 500 and 750 feet, directed by *Kite*. This was fired at 1258 after which a quantity of oil was seen to come to the surface. These tactics were followed in the next attack in which *Wildgoose* was used as a firing ship, carrying out her attack at 1342 having been directed onto the target and receiving her firing instructions from *Kite*.

After this attack contact faded among all the echoes from the depth-charge explosions, and at 1440 *Kite* proceeded to investigate the area of the attacks. Whalers were sent away from *Kite*, *Wildgoose* and *Woodpecker* to make a collection among the considerable quantity of wreckage brought to the surface. Trophies collected included the usual split wood, and clothing and some bacon.

I finished investigating the area at 1500 and the Group pro-ceeded back towards the dinghies which had been passed, and nearly depth charged, four and a half hours earlier. These were alongside at 1545 and with the remainder of the Group screening, *Kite* spent the next three quarters of an hour collecting up the survivors from U 462. This collection complete, HM Ships proceeded on course 258 degrees to pass through the position of the last series of attacks and on reaching the area the sea was found to be covered with oil to a great extent.

Walker sent the following message to C-in-C Plymouth and C-in-C Western Approaches at the Admiralty:

> Situation at 1900 B. Supply U Boat 'U 461' sunk by aircraft in position 45 33N, 10 47W at 1206, survivors in *Woodpecker*. Supply U boat 'U 462' sunk by gunfire of Second Support Group near same position at 1214, survivors in *Kite* and *Wren*. A third U boat, 750 tons sunk by depth-charge attacks of Second Support Group in position 45 33N, 10 56W at 1543, much wreckage, human remains and oil, no survivors.

Walker's wording of this signal seems to show that his ships were responsible for the second sinking but the submarine had already been mortally damaged by aircraft before he arrived.

Captains of the ships were: *Kite*, Captain F J Walker (Lt Cdr W F R Segrave); *Woodpecker*, Lt Cdr R E S Hugonin; *Wildgoose*, Lt Cdr D E G Wemyss; *Wren*, Lt Cdr R M Aubrey; *Woodcock*, Lt Cdr G Gwinnner.

A couple of weeks later, one of the officers aboard HMS *Woodpecker* sent a parcel to Dudley Marrows with the enclosed letter:

HMS *Woodpecker*
c/o GPO

18th August

Dear Marrows,
We salved a bit of what you left of a certain enemy concern, now liquidated. We had other things to do but while picking up the survivors (for some information we didn't want to wait for rather than for their own sweet selves), we grabbed a few bits which I am sending to you. Our amateur engraver has attended to the best bit and I am enclosing enough for you to chop up and give a piece to each of your crew if you want to.

I am also sending the Captain's 'Mae West' which you have the right to wear it seems to me. I don't know if you would consider it unlucky but it was lucky for its last owner except insomuch as he had to wear it at all!

It will interest your gunners to know that their shooting was good and among others they hit the AA gunner between the eyes.

Heartiest congratulations on a well pressed home attack combined with a straight aim, and on the co-incidence of the war. Be sure to come and see us if you ever get the chance.

Yours,

Studholme-Brownrigg

(Lieut RN)

The life jacket is now on exhibit in Australia and Wolf Stiebler later stated that it was British and must have come from one of the three captains captured by U 128 and transferred to U 461 in December 1942.

Dudley Marrows' crew:

FL D Marrows RAAF	Captain
PO P C Leigh RAAF	1st Pilot
FS P E Taplin RAAF	2nd Pilot
FO J S Rolland RAAF	Navigator
Sgt G M Watson RAF	Engineer
Sgt A N Pearce RAAF	Fitter
PO P T Jensen RAAF	1st WOP/AG
FS H H Morgan RAAF	2nd WOP/AG
Sgt D C Sidney RAAF	AG
Sgt R L Webster RAAF	3rd WOP/AG
Sgt F Bamber RAAF	Rigger
J Tainer	u/t

CHAPTER FIVE

FIGHTING BACK

Captain F J Walker's five sloops of the Second Support Group were to witness another aircraft versus U boat action two days later, the first day of August 1943. And so too did the RAF liaison officer diarist aboard HMS *Woodpecker*.

This time the U boat was U 454, a type VIIC submarine built at the Deutsche Werke AG, Kiel, and commissioned on 24 July 1941. Her commander was Kapitänleutnant Burkhard Häcklander, aged 27. He had previously served in destroyers and had seen action during the Norwegian campaign. U 454 became part of the 7th U boat Arctic Flotilla and beginning December, sailed on four war cruises in the Arctic. Her conning tower emblem was that of a Polar Bear on an iceflow holding a shield containing a ship's wheel.

Almost immediately she was successful. On 17 January 1942 she damaged the Russian armed trawler *RT-88* (1,088 BRT), then made attacks on the British convoy to North Russia, PQ8. Firing three torpedoes at 1846 hours, she sank the freighter *Harmatris* of 5,395 tons. Less than four hours later she sank the British escort destroyer HMS *Matabele* of 1,870 tons. By 20 January she was back in Kirkenes, Norway, and then went into Trondheim.

She was out from Trondheim on 3 March, part of Gruppe Aufnahme and then Gruppe Umhang. There was a short contact with another arctic convoy – PQ12 – but she was driven off and returned to Trondheim on the 15th. Nine days later she was out again, once more making contact with an arctic convoy, this time PQ13, but once more escort ships drove her off. Back in harbour by 2 April she began cruise number four on the 8th for a repeat performance. Contact made with convoys but driven off without being able to make attacks. By the end of the month U 454 was back at base, and in early May moved to Kiel for a refit.

On 4 July 1942 she sailed for the Atlantic as part of Gruppe Wolf but once more she had no luck. Although in contact with a convoy, she again found herself driven down, and later with Gruppe Pirat and then Gruppe Steinbrink, two further convoy contacts ended with pressure from escort ships, one of which – HMS *Dianthus* – damaged her on 7 August. Her new home was St Nazaire where she now had to run to for repairs.

Cruise six was no better. Leaving St Nazaire on 26 September an aircraft located her on the 30th. Lookouts identified a Sunderland, and indeed a Sunderland 'H' (DV960) of 461 Squadron RAAF from Hamworthy found her shortly before midday in position 4639/1555. Flying at 2,000 feet the U boat was spotted dead ahead just short of ten miles in excellent visibility. Closing to two miles, the Sunderland pilot began a diving approach along the boat's track but was seen and the sub began to crash-dive. Six depth charges rained down from 50 feet, exploding mostly between the conning tower and stern, the latter still just out of the water. Nothing further was seen although the flying boat circled for some minutes. Gunfire from both front and rear gunners scored possible hits but little else. U 454 suffered no damage and reported four depth-charge explosions. The Sunderland crew was:

PO H G Cooke RAAF	Pilot	FS W Milne DFM
PO H L Osborne RAAF		Sgt E A Fuller
Sgt N T Aldridge RNZAF		Sgt E F Burton
PO D H Kennedy RAAF		Sgt H R Ovens RAAF
Sgt A W Bunce		Sgt P Evans
Sgt E C E Miles		

Although U 454 was part of three Wolf Packs during October and November (Panther, Veilchen and Kreuzotter) the closest chance of success was against convoy ONS144 but her five torpedoes missed their targets. Bad luck cost her a crew member, a man being lost overboard during refuelling from U 117 on 8 November. By 7 December she was back in port.

Her crew were lucky enough to spend Christmas and New Year on land, the next cruise not beginning until 18 January 1943. Nine days later she became part of Gruppe Landsknecht off the west coast of Ireland. On 6 February she was located again by aircraft, this time Liberator W/120 Squadron operating out of Reykjavik. The aircraft was part of the escort flying round convoy SC118 which it had met at 10 am that morning. Just before noon the crew, flying over a calm sea, spotted a wake seven miles off and closing in saw it was a U boat; this was 31 miles from the convoy. The Sunderland dived and dropped six D/Cs as the boat dived but nothing was seen to indicate success for the RAF crew.

The Liberator turned towards the convoy to report but within a few minutes, still at 100 feet, and now 26 miles from the ships, the Lib's captain spotted another surfaced U boat one mile ahead, in position 5350/3020 (the U boat – U 454 – reporting this to be 5403/2935). The Lib attacked from the boat's port quarter as she crash-dived. The two remaining D/Cs went down as the stern was still visible, one entering the water each side of her. An oil patch appeared some 60 by 40 feet in diameter which indicated that the boat had at least been damaged, as indeed she had, but not enough for her to abort her mission.

Reporting to the convoy's SNO (Senior Naval Officer), two Navy corvettes were despatched to the area but they found nothing. The Navy assessment committee thought the boat would have suffered 'a severe shake-up'. The Lib crew consisted of:

FS J H Frewin	Pilot	Sgt F B Pincott	WOP/AG
Sgt H J Bennett	2nd pilot	Sgt D H Auld	WOP/AG
Sgt V B McKenzie	Navigator	Sgt G J Duckworth	WOP/AG
Sgt B J Bennett	Engineer		

Supplied by U 460 on 15 February, U 454 became part of Gruppe Ritter and on the 21st came into contact with convoy ON166. Two days later, while still trying to gain a firing position, she was spotted by the US Coast Guard cutter *Spencer*, severely depth-charged and damaged sufficiently for her to have to return home. Survivors from U 454 were later to tell their interrogators that they had sunk two independently routed (ie: not in convoys) merchantmen on this patrol. However, before she could make port she ran into heavy seas and lost one man overboard on 27 February. She arrived at St Nazaire on 8 March.

Her eighth patrol began on 17 April, operating with Gruppe Rheine and then Gruppe Elbe. On 12 May she contacted convoy SC129 (GB to USA), only to be driven off once more. She just hadn't been able to sustain the success of her very first war cruise. Supplied by U 459 she stayed out a little longer but was back in port by 23 May, this time La Pallice.

She had had to dock at La Pallice, as a 'guest boat' owing to a lack of space at St Nazaire. She sailed in company with U 706 on 29 July, lost contact with the other boat but met up again on 1 August. U 454 remained submerged during the night of 31 July, surfacing at 0830 the next morning but was forced to submerge immediately due to aircraft in the area. At 1100 hours another attempt at surfacing to re-charge batteries was made, but only 45 minutes later aircraft forced her to dive yet again. At 1400 she tried once more, but within five minutes aircraft made it necessary to submerge.

Things were now becoming serious. Trying to avoid the deadly Leigh Light aircraft during darkness was one thing, being then unable to surface in daylight to recharge batteries and replace the foul air was another. At 1640 U 454's crew came up for the last time. Almost at once their Naxos equipment picked up an incoming aircraft by its ASV signal. Within minutes a Sunderland came into view. As they watched, the Sunderland fired off two red flares, presumably to attract the attention of nearby surface ships, the presence of which the submarine had no knowledge. Unknown to them, Walker's sloops were just 5½ miles away, engaged in their own U boat hunt in company with a Catalina.

Sunderland B/10 RAAF Squadron was on a Musketry patrol, having left Mount Batten at 1001 hours, with Flight Lieutenant Ken Fry at the controls. A farmer in peacetime, he was just nine days short of his 30th birthday. They sighted the Navy's sloops and the Catalina and made to join them but they then spotted U 454 from 170 feet, two miles away. Before they could do much about it they were over the boat, Fry heaving the flying boat round in a tight turn to starboard and then heading for the submarine from its starboard quarter, preparing to drop a stick of six D/Cs from 50 feet. In the nose-gun position, the front gunner began to fire at the boat, as she was obviously going to stay up and fight. The Sunderland crew had no way of knowing that U 454 was in no position to submerge. The boat's gunners also began firing as the Sunderland thundered towards them.

The Second Support Group's report recorded:

> Another eventful day began just before 0900 on 1 August when a signal was intercepted from [an] aircraft reporting himself over a U boat in a position 045 deg. 50 mins. North, 009 deg. 40 mins. West. My latest movement had brought me close to this position and by 0900 the Second Support Group was away on course 345 degrees speed 15 knots, which was increased to 16 knots by 1000. At 1012 I altered course to 350 degrees and by 1022 the Group was crashing along at 17 knots on that course, through a rough sea and heavy short swell.
>
> During the time from 0900 onwards, nothing had been received from the aircraft although he had been instructed by Base to home my striking force to the position of the sighting and at 0936 he informed Base that he was returning owing to fuel shortage. It would have been better if this aircraft had dropped a marker on the position of her sighting, and had transmitted a homing signal before leaving the area. However, no contact was obtained but

I continued on this course until 1246 when a second Catalina, O for Oboe, reported a submarine 132 degs., 34 miles, whereupon course was altered to 180 degs., speed 17 knots.

Speed was increased to 18 knots at 1330 and the aircraft ahead of the Group was making every possible effort to ensure that I should find my way to the correct position. An hour later a smoke float, now burning very low, was alongside and a short distance away another, much more vigorous, which had been newly dropped at my request, by my attentive and efficient guide. After passing both smoke floats, course was altered to 270 degs. at Asdic sweeping speed, on the assumption that the enemy had been outward bound, and at 1440 a Sunderland aircraft was observed dropping depth charges on a bearing of 306 degs. To my deep regret the Sunderland was seen to crash into the sea very shortly after the depth charges exploded and it was subsequently learned that both pilots had been killed by gunfire from the U boat on which they had pressed home their attack. The death of the aircraft captain and the release of his depth charges must have been practically coincidental.

Course had been altered towards, when the depth-charge explosions were seen, and at 1516 survivors were sighted in the water. Their presence made it clear that the Second Support Group, after its rush to the scene, had arrived a few minutes too late to be in at the kill but it was some comfort at least to be in at the death, although, unfortunately HM Ships had not been able to hasten it in any way. The morale of the German survivors did not appear to be very high as although they had only been in the sea for a few minutes there was a tremendous amount of howling and squealing among them and two members of the 'master race' cried out continuously for twenty minutes before their turn came to be hauled aboard. They were uninjured but in an advanced state of panic.

It was learned that the U boat had been U 454 and by 1530 its captain and thirteen other prisoners were on board *Kite*, after which the Group resumed patrol on course 270 degs. at 12 knots.

The RAF diarist noted:

U boat reported at periscope depth some distance away. We alter course and pack on full speed ahead. Things are warming up and we forgo lunch and have a sandwich on the bridge. Catalina signals: 'No more endurance. Good hunting – cheerio!' However, two Sunderlands are around and as we approach we see a smoke float and one of the Sunderlands is evidently going to attack. She dived low and drops depth charges. Immediately after the attack she is in difficulties. She hits the water and there is an appalling explosion and we just catch sight of the Sunderland's tail before it sinks under the waves. No survivors from that, says the Captain and we shake our heads sadly. Then someone shouts: 'There's a dinghy!'

Wildgoose being nearest collects them.[1] They are six in number and some of them injured. The story goes that both pilots were killed by gunfire. The engines and fuel tanks were shot up by the U boat, but the important thing is that they sank the U boat. No doubt about that because our sister ship picks up about 20 Huns. We now have about 100 Germans on the five ships as another small contingent was picked up last night.

According to the survivors from the Sunderland, the depth charges had gone down as the aircraft was hit, three falling either side of the conning tower. The flying boat had been hit in the starboard inner engine and starboard main petrol tank, sending a flood of petrol onto the machine's bridge while the aircraft was still ¼ of a mile away. Flying over the U boat it carried on for a short while, then turned to port and ditched into a 15-20 foot swell across wind. Those that got out were picked up by HMS *Wren*.

The second Catalina had been aircraft S/4th US Squadron (479th Anti-submarine Group) from St Eval, also on Musketry patrol, captained by Lieutenant Irwin. Their log records:

1032   Intercepted message, U boat in position 4550/0920.
1125   Found Escort Group 'Fisher' 4535/1000 – SNO told aircraft
       to search 350 degrees, 15 miles.
1442   Position 4749/0944, intercepted message – sighted U boat
       at 4542/1024.

The Sunderland crew:

FL K G Fry RAAF	Captain	Sgt F O Petterson	2nd engineer
FO H R Budd RAAF	1st pilot	FS B E Cook	WOP/AG
FO J M Curtis RAAF	2nd pilot	FS R G Welfare	WOP/AG
FO J H Portus RAAF	Navigator	Sgt J E Fryer	Fitter IIA
PO A M Welch RAAF	Nav u/t	Sgt J Haslam	Armourer
Sgt H B Lydeamore	1st engineer	Sgt D I Conacher	Air gunner

The survivors were Portus, Petterson, Cook, Welfare, Jack Haslam

---

[1] Flying boat survivors say HMS *Wren*.

and Don Conacher. They managed to scramble onto the starboard mainplane of the Sunderland which they found floating on the sea, using it as a raft for the half an hour it took for the sloop to reach them. Apart from Häcklander, the only other U boat officer to survive had been the second lieutenant, Gerhard Braun, not yet 21. In all 14 survived (two officers, 2 petty officers and ten ratings); 33 went down with the boat.

Despite Walker's report, neither of the two pilots flying the Sunderland were in fact killed in the attack, although the second pilot was wounded. Don Conacher, who for many years would be the Honorary Secretary of the Sunderland Squadrons Branch of the RAAF Association (NSW Division), recalls the dramatic events of 1 August 1943:

> Up until the end of July 1943 our crew had progressed through more than 30 operational flights, anti-submarine patrols and convoy escorts.
>
> After take-off at 1000 hours on 1 August, we proceeded to a rendezvous with the 2nd Escort Group on a patrol over north-west of Cape Finisterre. At about 1400 hours a U boat was sighted, I think by our captain, Bob Fry, who was piloting at the time. I was in the tail turret and at the sighting I felt a surge of adrenalin and as Bob made a steep diving turn towards the U boat, I caught a brief glimpse of it. As he straightened out for his bombing run I heard Bob say, 'I'll get the bastard if it is the last thing I do.'
>
> The U boat opened fire with three 20 mm cannon and Tubby Fryer in the nose turret opened fire with our ineffective .303 Vickers GO drum-fed machine gun. I could feel and hear hits on us and as the depth charges were dropped I prepared to open fire as we passed over but my fire seemed to be very ineffective, either the turret or the hydraulic lines had been damaged. As the water and spray subsided I saw the U boat break in two and sink.
>
> The plane flew on for some time, could not gain height and the motors were sounding very rough. I was told to vacate the turret and prepare to ditch and as I started towards the bridge I saw a large hole in the fuselage near the tail. As I started up the ladder to the bridge, Pete Petterson asked me to bring up any Mae Wests in the wardroom which I did; having been in the turret I had mine on.
>
> When I got to the bridge level I saw a large hole in the starboard main fuel tank, which Pete Petterson had tried to plug with his Mae-West. The fuel was blowing everywhere and everything was saturated in petrol; I don't know why we did not catch fire.
>
> To me, Bob Fry seemed OK, but not Bob Budd in the second

seat, who seemed to be in a lot of pain. I did not see Max Curtis – he should have been at the radar set. John Portus and Arthur Welch were removing the astrodome and stowing it; all the NCOs of the crew seemed OK. Phil Cook and Ron Welfare were at the wireless set, Pete Petterson and Bert Lydeamore were at the engineer's panel, Tubby Fryer and I were just behind the main spar with the dinghies. As the plane came down for landing it was obvious we were in for a rough landing as the swell was very big.

As we touched down and Bob Fry cut the engines and jumped out of the pilot's seat, water was rushing up through the forward hatch between the pilots; obviously the hull had been holed by cannon fire. Before Tubby and I could move the dinghies, we were hit by a swirling maelstrom of water which tossed me about. I was aware the plane was sinking and I was going down with it. I felt certain I was about to die and I wondered how my mother would receive the news. The water around me was very dark and then I had a feeling that I was going up not down, and the water above me was becoming lighter. As I broke the surface some of the crew were clambering up a broken wing, floating on the sea.

When I tried to swim to the wing I found my right ankle seemed broken and decided not to get on the wing. When I tried to activate the CO_2 bottle on my Mae West, nothing happened, although it still supported me. I was not very high in the water, so when a 'Gibson Girl' emergency radio floated by, I fastened onto it.

Nobody got out after me but my hopes rose for a brief time when I saw an American leather flying jacket floating by, but it was empty. Perhaps if more of the crew had been wearing their Mae Wests, more might have survived. After our experience, all crews were instructed to wear them when flying and when I returned to the Squadron, I suggested Mae Wests have a pocket stitched to them to carry an Australian quart water bottle.

I was aware that the boys on the wing and I were drifting apart and Phil Cook called out to me, 'Hang on Don, a ship is coming.' We continued to drift apart and because of the very rough sea I lost sight of them. However, I was cheered up by the appearance of an RAF Liberator which made several low circuits around me and I could see some of the crew waving.

I then became aware of the approaching ship which soon towered over me, and I was thrown a lifebuoy on a rope so I let go the dinghy-radio and slipped into it and was hauled aboard and carried down to the sick bay where I was stripped and wrapped in blankets. I was bloody cold and the ship's doctor gave me a whisky to warm me, but all it did was to make me spew up all the salt water I had swallowed, but it made me feel a whole lot better.

Soon afterwards, two more of the crew were brought into sick bay, Ron Welfare, radio operator, who also had a broken ankle, and John Portus, our navigator, whose feet were badly cut. The others were examined, given warm clothes and left sick bay. At this time I was amazed at the appearance of Flight Lieutenant John Jewell. He was our Squadron Navigation Officer and well known to me. I said, 'What the hell are you doing here?', and was told he was on exchange duty with HMS *Wren*. He spoke to us all for a while and asked about the lost crew members. After more medical attention we were settled down for the night which proved a long and painful one for me.

Next day was a busy one for the doctor. John's feet were re-dressed, Ron's ankle and mine were set in plaster casts – quite an achievement without X-rays – and a wound on my left leg was cleaned up. We were told that survivors from the U boat we had sunk had been rescued by HMS *Kite*. We did see one member of another U boat who had been rescued by *Wren* when he came into the sick bay for medical attention, escorted by a German-speaking Chief Petty Officer. He asked the CPO who we were and was told we were some Australian airmen. He then asked the CPO to tell us he hoped we recovered from our injuries, which created quite an impression with me.

After two days, John's feet had improved and he left us for more comfortable quarters. My ankle was causing me a lot of pain and swelling. The doctor said he would prefer to leave it until we reached Plymouth where it could be X-rayed. We reached Plymouth on the fourth day and tied up at the Naval Dock where we were taken ashore. The U boat prisoners were also led off – blindfolded. Ron and I were taken into what seemed to be a sick bay on the dock and put into bed. To our surprise two armed army privates followed us in and took guard at our bedsides. They understood we were Germans and could not be convinced we were Australian airmen. Two Naval nurses then came in and told them who we were. Soon an ambulance arrived and took us to the Naval Hospital.

X-rays showed my ankle was badly broken; the talus bone was shattered and the whole thing continued to swell until it eventually burst open and could not be replastered, so it was put into a wooden splint box, which made it impossible to be moved to the shelter during air raids, and I was told my recovery would be a long one.

I was in hospital for many weeks and finally discharged with a very poor prognosis, that my ankle would remain permanently stiff. This prognosis did not satisfy the Medical Officer of No. 10 Squadron, Squadron Leader Shortridge, who arranged for me to be sent to No.2 Aircrew Convalescent Depot in Hoylake, Cheshire, where I underwent protracted and involved physiotherapy until the end of the year, when I finally returned to the Squadron.

The new Commanding Officer, Wing Commander Ron Gillies, who I had flown with, appointed me to the Training Section. Unlike my crew mates, I was retained on the Squadron. Commissioned in January 1944 and resumed flying duties in February. After completing the necessary special courses I was made Squadron Gunnery Officer in December and I was in another sub-attack, my third, in that month. I was still flying at the end of the war.

Just three days after the events of 1 August 1943, another Sunderland crew (mostly Canadian) found itself in a similar situation, this time, however, it was not over the Bay of Biscay, but south of Iceland. Another difference was that whereas U 454 had been an experienced boat, being on her eighth patrol, U 489 was on her first.

Built at the Kiel Deutsche Werke AG as a type XIV submarine, she had been commissioned on 8 March 1943 with command going to Oberleutnant zur See Adalbert Schmandt, aged 33. Schmandt had previously been a pre-war merchant seaman, then watch officer aboard U-B, the former captured HMS *Seal*, and later the ex-Dutch submarine UD 5. A 1,600-ton supply U boat, U 489's conning tower emblem was of a Rampant Bear drinking from a milk bottle. She had a complement of six officers, eight chief and petty officers and 40 men for a total of 54.

U 489 sailed from Kiel on 22 July, under orders from the 12th U boat Flotilla, and headed out into the North Atlantic. According to survivors her original destination had been Japan, but after a few days out she had received orders to proceed to her operational area south of Madagascar. Both seem a good distance for a new boat crew and perhaps in any event, the farthest they would go would be the Indian Ocean, which German U boats 'shared' with Japanese submarines. Wherever her destination might have been, it soon became academic.

Six days out she found and rescued three German Luftwaffe men, the crew of a Blohm & Voss Bv138 (its code noted as being K6+ BK) flying boat, which had been shot down by Beaufighters of 404 Squadron RCAF on the morning of the 28th. The Beaus had been part of the air cover to HMS *Belfast* and two destroyers. A Ju88 had been sighted, chased and driven off into cloud and then Navy radar had found another snooper, the SNO sending the Beaus off to intercept it. Shortly afterwards the Beaus found the Bv138 and Squadron Leader A L de la Haye/Flight Sergeant C A Smith (JM113 'P') made a head-on attack scoring hits on its engines. Another Beau (JL947 'D'), Flying Officer S S Shulemson/Sergeant A D Glasgow, followed this with a stern attack after which the machine burst into flames and glided onto the sea where it nosed over. One survivor was seen standing on the fuselage firing five-star distress signals. Another Bv138 was then seen and de la Haye shot this down too but no survivors were seen from this one. Later another flying boat was engaged and damaged.

Of course, there was no question of taking the three airmen back to friendly territory, they would just have to travel with the U boat to whatever its destination might be.

U 489 didn't even get off to a good start finding that for several days she was constantly having to dive because of the presence of aircraft and surface vessels during her passage through the Rosengarten – a U boat transit area north of Scotland and south of Iceland. This began to bring pressure regarding the recharge of batteries. Then on 3 August a Hudson of 269 Squadron flying from Reykjavik located her at 0732 hours south of Iceland.

The Hudson pilot closed in as the U boat began to circle. The Hudson circled too, then came in for an attack but intense flak fire forced it away. Just on 0800 hours the RAF crew tried again, dropping a 100 lb anti-submarine bomb from 3,500 feet which overshot the sub which was still blazing away. Another bomb five minutes later fell 30 yards from the boat's beam, and then the aircraft made a strafing run. The second bomb caused some damage; the forward battery hatch rubber joint had been ruptured and began to leak water. More importantly, the word was out that a U boat was in this locality. A dive presented problems, the boat going down to 656 feet before she could be controlled properly. From then on the crew knew their diving capacity was limited. The Hudson III crew in 'J', V9053, were:

FS E L J Brame	Pilot	Sgt Y T Borland	
FS W Styring		Sgt E Beaudry	WOP/AG

'Peter' Brame noted in his flying log book:

> A/S Patrol. Moorings. Attacked surfaced U boat for 50 minutes with A/S bombs and gunfire. Met fierce anti-aircraft fire up to 2,000 feet. Submerged after front gun attack.

(On 21 September Peter Brame and his crew attacked another submarine and fought this one for one hour and 27 minutes with bombs and D/Cs. This time return fire hit their Hudson in the wings, damaging an aileron; one hole in the mainplane was a foot in diameter. All three of his crew were Canadian; Edmund Beaudry, a particular friend, was later the best man at his wedding.)

Not long after this, U489 was forced to dive by approaching destroyers, which attacked with depth charges, but she escaped them and further damage, although strangely there is no report of any Naval vessels making an attack. Having to remain below, her batteries were once more in desperate need of recharging, forcing her to the surface on the morning of the 4th. Shortly after 0900 hours the crew of a Sunderland from 423 Squadron RCAF, operating from Castle Archdale (Lough Erne) spotted her on the surface from 4,000 feet, four or five miles away. No sooner had they identified a U boat than the mixed RCAF and RAF crew saw her begin to weave. They had no idea that she was reluctant to dive due to the state of her batteries or the damage she had sustained, all they were aware of was that the boat was obviously going to remain on the surface and make a fight of it. The Canadian pilot was Flying Officer A A Bishop, who had been with 423 Squadron since July 1942 just as it was forming. At first he flew as co-pilot but in January 1943 was made aircraft captain and given a crew of various spare members on the Squadron. In June 1943, Squadron Leader J R Sumner RCAF completed his tour and Al took over his crew. Al Bishop recalls:

> Around 0400 I and my crew took off from Castle Archdale, Northern Ireland, in Sunderland DD859 G-George on an anti-submarine patrol in the area between Iceland and the Hebrides. We had picked up this Sunderland brand new at Wig Bay [Stranraer] on 21 June 1943 and flew it to Castle Archdale. We carried out a few hours training on it and started operations on 23 June. From then until 4 August we logged two hundred operational hours on it – 14 Ops. We were the only crew that flew 'G' on operations.
>
> At around 0900 the sky was clear and there was little or no wind. The crew sighted a fully surfaced U boat which made no attempt to dive. During that period of the anti-submarine war some of the submarines had been staying on the surface to fight it out with attacking aircraft so we did not find this unusual. As we circled the U boat we soon saw that the only advantage we might have in an attack was to approach down sun.
>
> We proceeded with such an attack as we descended to sea level.

As we approached they started shooting with what appeared to be cannons with exploding shells, and machine guns. I took evasive action by undulating the aircraft. As I levelled out at 50 feet for the final bombing attack the shells started to hit the aircraft. Two of my crew at the front of the Sunderland returned fire with a .5 on a swivel mount and a .303 in the front turret. I was successful in tracking over the submarine and dropped a six depth charge stick straddling the U boat.

After the attack the crew advised me that there was a fierce fire in the galley and bomb-bay areas with flames coming upstairs. I discovered the starboard engines were running at full power and there was very little aileron control. This was apparently caused by a shell which had burst under my seat severing the exacter controls. I had to throttle back and shut the starboard engines and use the rudders to maintain what little control I had. I decided to attempt a landing and advised everyone. Of course, all this happened in just a few seconds.

Al Bishop's co-pilot was Flying Officer D M Wettlaufer RCAF. Murray Wettlaufer remembers:

About 200 miles south of Iceland we spotted a sub on the surface. The alarm was sounded, a first sighting report was despatched, and we prepared to attack. As we circled to approach from the rear, the sub turned in circles to keep its guns to bear on us. We found out later that this was a mother ship which supplied other subs with fuel, food, torpedoes, etc, and that its armament consisted of a 4.7" gun, four 20 mm cannons and numerous .5 machine guns.

Our method was to attack from 50 feet using evasive action on the way in but the last part of the run had to be straight and level. The pilot dropped the depth charges which could be selected in a string of eight or separated into a stick of six, saving two for later. Suddenly, all hell let loose.

Several hits were made on our aircraft and I distinctly remember the jagged holes in the metal floor under my feet and all the gauges spinning around and around. Our controls were shot away but Al Bishop was able to drop our D/Cs after which we staggered on and crashed into the sea. I was thrown through the perspex windshield and found myself swimming to avoid the burning oil and gasolene on the water. We had made direct hits and the sub was severely damaged. The U boat crew abandoned ship into rubber rafts some 100 yards from us.

We had some anxious moments because we were swimming in

the water aided only by our Mae Wests but they paid little attention to us. The submarine heeled up with its stern high in the air and we saw it slip out of sight to its grave. As it disappeared, a severe explosion was felt. The German crew was heard to shout: 'Zeig Heil, zeig heil.'

Flying Officer A E Mountford RCAF was also part of the Sunderland crew:

I was 1st WOP, working the radio from take-off. I finished my shift and was due to be off for an hour which meant cooking the flying rations. This I did not usually mind, but not this day. The rations turned out to be kippers. Being a Prairie Boy from Saskatchewan I was not keen about eating let alone cooking same. I made a deal with the RAF WOP on the radio. If he'd cook them, I'd work his radio shift; this was a fateful decision.

I was busy sending out SOS when we hit the ocean and I imagine he was in ditching position or fighting fires down below. As a result, mention kippers and I'll never forget.

As operational radio we had to send very few messages during radio silence. However, in an attack you get rather busy. We first homed in on the radar contact which turned out to be two RN destroyers (the same ones which would rescue us a few hours later). Later, with visibility better, we picked up another contact which was soon identified as a U boat. For me, business suddenly picked up!

A first sighting report, a position report, an attack report – then, SOS – position, SOS – position. As far as we know none of this was picked up. I suspect our trailing antenna was shot off early by the flak. While engaged with the above, I had a view of the submarine and also the pretty black gobs of Ack-Ack fire as we went in – 'quite relaxed'. We felt a hit. Bish advised us of a hit on the port wing area. Beside me was a circular inspection panel into the wing tanks area, so I opened the panel and observed a good fire around the tanks. This information I passed on to Bish and suggested we should get down before we blew. As we were not that far into our patrol, the tanks were still full, which probably saved us.

I recall how cool everyone was. I ended up with the radio wiring and loose equipment pinning me tight after we crashed but was fortunate to work myself free and escape through the astro hatch. By this time I was well below the water, and on reaching surface found myself surrounded by burning fuel. Surprisingly I was able to swim clear and team up with Murray Wettlaufer, who although he was badly wounded was wearing a Mae West. (While working radio a Mae West was too bulky in the small space we had, therefore I didn't have mine on.) With a seat cushion between us we swam as the sub came close, the German crew having got into their dinghies, then blew up and sank.

Al 'Bish' Bishop:

In trying to land we bounced and I had trouble controlling the aircraft. As we hit the water again, the left wing dropped a little and the left float caught in the water, cartwheeling us into the sea. I recall putting my right arm in front of my face and the next thing I knew I was under the water, then rising to the surface.

What was left of the aircraft was on fire, and there were flames on the water. I swam through a gap and as I did so I heard Sergeant Finn call: 'Skipper, can you give me a hand?' I swam towards him to discover that he had no Mae West and was obviously badly hurt. [Finn had a broken right arm.] He did not struggle, probably because of the injuries, and his extensive swimming experience. I grabbed hold of him with my right arm but could not see any of the others. After I saw the U boat go down, and some Germans on rafts, but making no attempt to help us, I recall little of the next fifty minutes. Finn was on my right arm which had been bruised in the crash and was getting sore and stiff. I attempted to change arms but every little movement caused him to scream with pain.

Those survivors that found themselves in the water, were soon aware of the U boat close by and at least one of them eyed a gun on the conning tower that seemed to be pointing in their direction.

Art Mountford, having struggled clear of the burning fuel, saw the blackened and badly injured face of Murray Wettlaufer. Together, they both encouraged each other to such good effect that they extricated themselves away from the flames until they were floating at a safe distance.

Flight Sergeant Richardson, who after having his front turret shot away, helped to fight the fire in the wardroom and galley, but later said he remembered nothing of his departure from the aircraft. Once clear of the flames he found that his Mae West had been punctured by flak but he found a piece of wood which kept him up until rescued – but only just in time – by the destroyer's whaler.

Murray Wettlaufer:

About 45 minutes later a British Town Class destroyer, HMS

Castletown arrived and launched a whaler and picked up about 50 Germans before they saw us. I was put in the bottom of the boat, rowed to the ship and lifted high in the air by a crane and deposited on deck. They took me to a lieutenant's cabin where I was given emergency treatment for my wounds and for the shock of being in that cold water. Five of our crew had been lost but only one body was recovered. The next day we arrived in Iceland where I was taken to the local military hospital where I spent my 21st birthday. After a week I was flown to England and hospitalized near London. After eight months of hospital and rehabilitation, I returned to Castle Archdale and operations.

Art Mountford:

I had passed out cold by the time we were rescued by a whaler from HMS *Castletown*. The Navy crew had a guy nick-named 'Cat's Eyes' on duty when we had first flown over the two ships. As the name implies, this chap kept an eye on us as we flew away, and later saw us dive down, followed by lots of smoke; they were on the way then, to our location.

They had written us off by then because of the burning aircraft, and at first concentrated on picking up the U boat survivors. Once I was picked up they saw my Canadian shoulder flashes and we were sent to the wardroom, instead of down below. I ended up in the RN surgeon's bunk. It was lucky for Wettlaufer and Finn they had been rescued by a destroyer with a surgeon on board. I was slightly injured and full of sea water. Every once in a while a couple of ratings would carry me to the head – nothing worked. I was too cold so put back to bed. I don't know how many trips I made but I do remember one of the sailors say: 'For Christ sakes Canada, ai'nt you ever going to pee!'

Al Bishop:

Having been in the water for some 50 minutes I was feeling pretty cold and once I hit the destroyer's wardroom I started to shiver so violently I could not talk. I went out on deck long enough to identify Sergeant Hadcroft's body and witness his burial at sea. Then the ship's doctor gave me something and put me in a bunk where I slept through to about 2 am the next morning. We were coming into Reykjavik Harbour.

We were put ashore and into the hospital. Art and I were walking, the rest on stretchers, so I did not get a chance to talk to any of the Germans. A week later Art and I went back to

Ireland in a Liberator – 13 August – and then went on a month's sick leave. I returned to flying on 19 September and resumed Ops on 2 October and ended the war as a Squadron Leader.

The Sunderland crew:

FO A A Bishop RCAF	Pilot
FO D M Wettlaufer RCAF	2nd pilot
PO H Parliament RCAF	Navigator
Sgt P McDonnell RAF	Engineer
Sgt H Gossip	Engineer
FO A E Mountford RCAF	1st WOP/AG
FS J S Kelly RAF	AG
Sgt F Hadcroft RAF	WOP
Sgt H E Finn RCAF	WOP/AG
FS J B Horsburgh RAF	WOP
FS J A V Richardson RAF	WOP

Of these Parliament, Gossip, McDonnell, Hadcroft and Horsburgh did not survive. Al Bishop received an Immediate Distinguished Flying Cross.

Upon interrogation, U 489's commander reported that one depth charge seemed to damage one of the boat's fuel tanks, as oil traces appeared. The boat was also down by the stern. He saw the Sunderland badly hit by fire from a 20 mm gun and crash. About ten minutes later the upper works of the destroyers were seen and it was then that one of the three scuttling charges which had previously been set, fired. However, the junior engineer officer stated that the boat was scuttled by opening the vents. After the order to abandon ship had been given, everyone except the senior engineering officer, Oberleutnant Hans Mude, was in the dinghies and heading away when there was a loud explosion in U 489. Most of the survivors believed this to have been caused by a depth charge which had lodged itself on deck but it may have been a scuttling charge. It wounded the senior engineering officer so badly that he died shortly afterwards, aboard the rescue vessel. The rest were collected by HMS *Castletown* and HMS *Orwell* within half an hour or so.

In all there had been six officers, eight chief and petty officers, plus 40 seamen. All survived except the mortally injured engineer, who was also buried at sea from the *Castletown*. The three rescued Luftwaffe men aboard also survived, although one had been injured. The officer ended up in a POW camp in England, while his two NCOs were sent to a camp in Canada, together with crew members of U 489.

CHAPTER SIX

SHOT DOWN

In chapter four we read of the encounter between U 461 and Sunderland 'U' of 461 Squadron. Only a few weeks later, Dudley Marrows and his crew were to meet the surface vessels of the 2nd Escort Group again but in very different circumstances.

One member of the crew not flying with Dudley Marrows by this stage was Paddy Watson, who had now transferred to the crew of Russ Baird as First Engineer. Paddy recalls a number of interesting stories during his time with 461 Squadron, one of the few Irishmen with this Australian outfit.

On 14 May 1943, I was detailed to fly, as First Engineer, with F/Lt Manger on a patrol involving convoy escort in an area about 300 miles to the west of Ireland. The direct route was to fly over Cork County and North Kerry. I had no idea where we were going, as only pilots and navigators attended briefings. Soon, green fields appeared below us and I wondered what was going on! The quickest way to cross the St George's Channel was by way of Cork and Kerry in the neutral Irish Free State, or Eire. This was 'officially' forbidden, of course, but in fact quite common. The Captain said: 'Paddy, we are flying over your country to reach a convoy, have you any knowledge of anti-aircraft guns around Cork?', to which I replied: 'I don't know if there are any guns in Cork city area, but there are probably some, so keep away. Dublin city is well defended and I have seen a Wellington bomber being fired at during one of my leaves home.' I continued: 'Most important, Skipper, is to keep well north of Brandon Mountain, near Dingle, Kerry, as it is 3,000 feet high and at least three Allied aircraft have hit it in recent months. I know because my father is in the local Home Guard in Tralee, and he has been called out on each report of a crash. One aircraft was a Sunderland – all died.' Then I added: 'Keep off this land,

Skipper, remember we are neutral!' Then, over the intercom came the voice of a crew-mate, saying: 'Paddy, I have just been to the 'heads' and it gave me much pleasure to pump the contents over your stinking country.' There was an uproar of laughter from all the crew, while I remonstrated with the remark: 'We have no business being here!' At a reunion in Perth in 1982, F/Lt Watts retold this story to all, remarking: 'That's why the grass is so green in Ireland.' In the mess at Pembroke Dock we kept a 'line book', which sadly disappeared after the war, but I do recall one which was included. It was as follows: 'Flying in thick cloud, Russ Baird, asked his second pilot, Johnny Dobson, to go down to the galley and try to see the sea, as they slowly descended. Suddenly, over the intercom Johnny called out, 'Skipper, I'm washing my hands!' As the only Irishman aircrew member in the Squadron, I came in for a bit of ragging. Typical was to head for a 'blip' in the Bay of Biscay only to find that there below us was a dirty little cargo boat with 'EIRE' written in big letters on its hull. The remarks were quite 'offensive'!

On 16 September 1943, Marrows and crew took off on a patrol to the Bay. The crew had changed slightly since the end of July and was now:

FL D Marrows DFC RAAF	Captain
FO P C Leigh RAAF	1st pilot
PO I V R Peatty RAAF	2nd pilot
PO W G Done RAAF	Navigator
Sgt J T Eshelby RAAF	Engineer
Sgt A N Pearce RAAF	Fitter
Sgt F Bamber RAAF	Rigger
PO P T Jensen RAAF	1st WOP/AG
Sgt R L Webster RAAF	2nd WOP/AG
Sgt P R Criddle RAAF	3rd WOP/AG
Sgt D C Sidney RAAF	Air gunner

Dudley Marrows recalls:

By this time there were a few changes in the crew. Navigator Jock Rolland had finished his tour and had been replaced by George Done; the second pilot was Ivor Peatty, and engineer Jack Eshelby, the third wireless operator was Dick Criddle. It was to be an eventful flight for all, but especially for the four new crew members. And there were to be two further coincidences. Firstly we were near the spot of our action against U 461 and secondly, when rescued it was by Captain Walker's group.

Again we were well south, on a very clear day, when 'specks' were sighted and reported, and all possible eyes strained to see/ verify. We were engaged at the time in manoeuvres to obtain wind direction and were on a westerly course which George Done wisely suggested we maintain – to reduce the endurance of the enemy aircraft if that was what they were.

It was Pete Jensen, our 1st WAG who first sighted the 'specks'. He was in the rear turret at the time – alert, correct search procedure and keen young eyes. Soon he reported five aircraft astern, so obviously they must be closing.

I decided to hold height and increase airspeed, for obviously we had been spotted, and there seemed to be some cloud miles away to the west, so there was some slight hope that we might make it. The aircraft were gaining. Soon Pete reported six not five EA and that they were gaining, so what to do; stay up where we were, go down to sea level, send signals to base that we were being attacked, jettison depth charges?

The aircraft were soon identified as Ju88s; I think their silhouette was imprinted on the mind of every crew member who flew in the Bay. Decisions were made and carried out, sending the signal, jettisoning the D/Cs and making ready. We had a new extra gun this time, a VGO which we installed in the 2nd pilot's window, from where he had a limited range of fire forward to starboard, loaded with all tracer for scare purposes.

[E/461 EK578, had been airborne at 0655. At 1630 hours Base Control received the following message from the Sunderland: 'Position 4632/ 1137 – Being attacked by enemy aircraft.' Then silence.]

By one of those odd coincidences, their former Flight Engineer, Paddy Watson, was nearby, flying with Russ Baird in W/461 (JM683). Paddy remembers:

I was crewing with Russ Baird as his First Engineer at the time. We had flown down to the area about 30 miles north of Corunna, Spain and were heading for home. This area was notorious for enemy attacks. Often we flew below cloud until we reached the coast, then the sun shone and we all got very alert. The Ju88s would be waiting above the clouds for us to appear.

Such was the situation when Dudley was attacked. I remember our wireless operator handing a report to Russ that he had intercepted a 'Mayday' call from another aircraft in the area. Suddenly, one of the pilots called over the intercom: 'Look, starboard 45 degrees, there are aircraft flying around a Sunderland about five miles distant!'

We all felt a great urge to go to its assistance, but there was nothing we could do, except report its position to Group HQ. It was our duty to return home, rather than hazard our aircraft and crew. So we headed due west, away from the action which was taking place and after half an hour turned for home. It was a very sad moment when I discovered it was Dudley, with whom I had been flying on so many operations. Later, back at Pembroke Dock, it was with great relief that we heard they had all been picked up.

Dudley Marrows continues his story:

I decided to maintain height as I had learned through my previous experiences that I could do a much more effective diving run if I had height below me. I was ready to loose height if any endeavour was made to attack us from below, but they never did; they did not need to!

George Done was in the astrodome, a position mid-upper, from which you have a commanding view in all directions other than below. He had the great responsibility of controlling evasive action, particularly vital for anything coming from astern where the pilot could not see. There seemed to be, from the time the Ju88s were first sighted, to when the action began, a rather long period of time which went by in seconds. Actually they only gained on us by our difference in speeds.

It soon became obvious that we were not going to be attacked one at a time – effective manoeuvres are possible against one – to turn in to and down just before the Ju88 gets in critical range – critical timing indeed, and George Done had the ability and did the job well – particularly so as he was a 'newcomer'. However, the Ju88 formation split into two, to the port and starboard, with obviously a control aircraft. Their tactics were new, to us at least; an aircraft from either side attacked at the same time, so no matter what manoeuvre I made (at George's timing) I had to place myself in a very vulnerable position from one of the Ju88s. There appeared nothing we could do but manoeuvre as effectively as possible, continuously, always endeavouring to turn into the nearest approaching Ju88. Having plenty of height this appeared to be effective for a while, but we soon suffered hits and lost valuable height.

One of the first hits reported to me was from Pete Jensen in the four-gun tail turret, our most effective weapon. He reported the turret inoperative; we assumed the hydraulic lines had been shot away. Permission was given Pete to vacate as he might have been of help elsewhere. He was lucky as the turret itself was badly hit just after he left it.

We believe that the extra guns we had in the galley (one VGO each side) and the 2nd pilot's VGO did give them something to think about as they appeared to avoid coming in from starboard ahead where a stream of tracers were going out. We were repeatedly hit, however, one sufficiently close to the wireless operator which put the set out of action and scattered splinters, cutting him facially. One gun of the two in the mid-upper turret jammed and 'Bubbles' Pearce had no opportunity to clear it. A shell exploded in the nose, adjacent to the front gunner and sorely wounded 'Pierre' Bamber, who was firing a single VGO from below the nose turret, which became inoperative – hydraulics again. Pierre contined to fire despite his wound. In the galley, 'Bunny' Sidney was badly scalded when a forgotten kettle of boiling water was spilt over him during the violent manoeuvring.

All this time damage was being done to the engines; first one lost power and then another, making it difficult, then impossible, to manoeuvre. The Ju88s were being most effective as a team, only stopping to briefly reorganise and then back in again.

We believed we damaged one aircraft sufficiently to make it break off, and that others were hit, however, they sure won the day. A flying boat pilot is very aware of the condition of the sea below him – wind, waves, swells. I had made up my mind, I believe sub-consciously, which way I would ditch if I could and had to.

We eventually reached the point whereby I could no longer maintain height, let alone manoeuvre defensively, so I had to ditch. The appropriate signal and preparation was made, thankfully in time, and I was fortunate enough to make a stall landing along the swell without any damage other than that the port side float collapsed.

The sea was very rough, certainly seemed to us, with quite big swells. The hull was leaking like a sieve, and we went through our abandon aircraft drill rather urgently. Just as I got onto the mainplane, one Ju88 made a pass, leaving a trail of bullet holes through the outer mainplane, but they did not attack after that. When it became apparent we were going to remain afloat for a little while, I went back down below, collecting whatever food-stuffs and drink there was left and collecting the third rubber dinghy from the tail section. The other two were already on the wing.

I decided to get into the dinghies in case the aircraft tipped with the port float gone and was afraid of the dinghies being ripped

by the jagged edges of the bullet holes. However, we lost the
rope of the small dinghy and Jimmy Leigh volunteered, and
promptly went in to get it, while we expedited the inflating and
launching of the other two, making sure they are not separated.
Alas, Jimmy's dinghy had been cut by shrapnel so he had to swim
back to join us in the other two.

We had a problem getting poor Pierre into the dinghy, being
wounded and not a strong swimmer. Fortunately I was, so was
able to help him. Then one of the main dinghies burst, probably
damaged by shrapnel. We tried to salvage what we could and
being in the other dinghy, I will never forget the looks on the
faces of those when they swam from the useless dinghy and held
on to the other one. They well knew, as we all knew, that eleven
men would overload one dinghy by an almost impossible degree
and increase air pressure, with the resultant worry as to whether
we would soon lose our sole dinghy through it bursting too.

Naturally we gave the OK for them to get in – eleven men,
one painfully wounded, sitting in the dinghy, legs inward, like
the petals of a closely petalled flower. Little waves were breaking
over us, we had wet bottoms, legs and soon uppers too.

We had a Bondi beach life saver with us, Bunny Sidney, who
organised the rigging up of a weather shield and the raising up
of it every time a wave was upon us. We did the usual things,
one of which was becoming violently seasick, and marshalling
what little equipment we had left. Pierre, with his injured leg and
side, suffered silently.

Naturally the night seemed long and cold, and cramped. Then
suddenly, an aircraft engine; but whose and would it find us? We
had had bad luck with our signalling equipment but we did use
the one remaining effective distress rocket if I remember right.
The aircraft was a Catalina, a Leigh Light-equipped machine. I
learnt afterwards that they picked us up on their radar. In any
case, they made an approach on us and there we were lit up by
a bloody wonderful great searchlight. The Catalina crew was
efficiently effective. They dropped markers, sent off appropriate
signals and signalled us that help was on the way. Some time
later it flew off, having reached its limit of endurance.

Shortly afterwards a Liberator arrived, but frustratingly had
difficulty in finding us at first. But the next event of significance
– great significance – was the sighting of the masts of a ship in
the distance.

Luckily, Walker's sloops were again way down south and by
no means were they in that area all the time. They had now
diverted well into Ju88 range to pick us up. Soon we were

stretching our cramped limbs on the deck of one of the ships. I recall Captain Walker addressing everyone over the loud speaker that we were the crew of U/461 which had sunk U 461 in their/ our joint battle. A resounding cheer went up from all the sloops, then it was hot baths, drinks, food, medical attention and bed.

Peter Jensen, First Wireless Operator and the man in the rear turret as the action began, remembers:

It was another T3 patrol and a first-light take-off. Then down to Spain, plenty of cloud (that meant life insurance) spirits were high. Uneventful coast crawl, then at Finisterre 'course for home', always a welcome sound over the intercom. But as we progressed, the cloud began to dissipate then finally disappeared; our high spirits also disappeared for we had a long way to go and all in tiger country.

I had been on the radio set since take-off and was relieved by Bob Webster. I went down into the galley having had nothing to eat since our aircrew breakfast. Pierre Bamber, our Rigger, had cooked a big dish of baked beans and there was still a lot left even though I was last to have lunch – so I ate the lot!

I looked at the roster and saw Bunny Sidney in the tail was due for a break (an hour was the limit in a turret as no-one can keep the concentration of searching for longer than that) so went down and relieved him. I commenced searching and before long located something dead astern, slightly above the horizon. It was, I estimated, 17 miles, and I reported to the Skipper and George Done hopped up to the astrodome but couldn't see anything. Gradually the dot became visible, then it split into two, then three, four, five and finally six dots were clearly visible astern.

Dudley looked for cloud but there wasn't any, so he opened the throttles and began to climb. Slowly but surely the dots got bigger and bigger, became aircraft and eventually I was able to identify them as what we knew they would be – Ju88s.

The Ju88s began to divide. Four started coming up on our starboard and two on our port. I noticed also that the leader on the starboard had a glass nose, obviously the fighter controller, this meant that they were not just a group of fighters looking for easy pickings but a well trained and experienced bunch. We prepared for battle. The D/Cs were run-out and jettisoned, Pierre went up to the .303 in the nose, the two galley guns were installed and manned by Bunny and Ivor Peatty, and Jimmy Leigh put out his scatter gun.

We checked everything over and over, guns, ammunition,

turrets, sights, as the Ju88s flew alongside about 1,000 yards out. We sized them up and they sized us up! I followed the four on the starboard side with my turret until they were gone from view, then I calculated that the first attack would come from the starboard and we would turn into it, and the attacker would break away from the starboard quarter, so I sat and waited.

I didn't have to wait long. I heard George over the intercom: 'They will start from starboard, Skip, ready to turn to starboard, ready to turn to starboard – GO!' A wild diving turn; I heard cannon shells raking the fuselage and there he was, as I predicted, receding into the starboard quarter, his engines puffing black smoke as he throttled back, a perfect, no-deflection shot, an air-gunner's dream. I said: 'Dead Junkers 88,' and lined up the turret – at least I tried to line it up but it was dead as a dodo, what luck! The hydraulic line to the turret had been severed in the first attack! By this time the others were attacking, the sky was full of white puff-balls from the self-destroying shells which had missed us, black crosses flashing across my line of vision, our aircraft twisting and turning to George's instructions from the astrodome. I had a small handle with which I could rotate the turret, so I did this as best I could and by firing the guns by hand I sprayed tracer around the sky every time I saw a black cross, but it was pretty hopeless.

Suddenly there was a lull, the 88s pulled back and took stock; it seemed the scatter gun had them a bit perplexed, something they hadn't struck before. George came on the intercom: 'All positions report'.

'Tail to Control, all guns stopped.'

'Mid-upper to Control, both guns stopped.'

'Nose to Control, all OK.'

'Thank God for that!' said George. Bubbles in the mid-upper then managed to get one gun cleared, then it was on again.

I lost all track of time; our aircraft was being thrown around like a Spitfire. My ammunition bins hadn't been designed for such treatment and they broke away from their mountings and the tops burst open with the force of the ammunition being thrown up, as a result the belts twisted and stopped the guns. I kept clearing them and turning the turret as best I could, hoping the 88s wouldn't realise the turret was u/s. Once they did they would begin stern attacks and that would be it.

The poor old kite started to show signs of wear; practically every attack we collected a few shells and bullets. We lost the port inner engine and poor Pierre in the nose collected a 20 mm shell that blew him and his gun back into the wardroom. It also put the nose turret out of action and Dick Criddle lifted Pierre on to a bunk and attempted to dress his wounds. However, it wasn't all one sided; fortunately Bubbles was able to keep his gun going and I saw one Ju88 smoking badly and losing height.

I never thought it possible a Sunderland could survive the evasive action Dudley put it through. My ammunition belts were squirming around like snakes and it soon got to the stage where I could not clear a gun. Then our port outer was hit. The klaxon went for ditching.

What a shambles! The hull was full of holes like a colander, oil everywhere from busted hydraulic lines, everything moveable was being tossed hither and yon, and a lot of fixtures and stowed equipment had broken loose and being tossed around too. I made my way down the catwalk being thrown from side to side, then up in the air, then down with a bump. I climbed up the steps at the mid-upper where Bubbles was still hammering away with his one gun. I remember being surprised he still had ammunition left but he was conserving his fire and making every shot count. The 88s were armoured like a Sherman tank but he was still beating off their attacks. By this time his was the only gun left operating out of the eleven we had started with.

I finally made it to the bridge. Bob Webster had lost half his nose – blood all over his face. He yelled at me he had screwed the key down. I looked at the gauges on the transmitter – it was dead. In my crash position I wondered why it was so draughty and noisy, and looking up, George had jettisoned the astrodome as it was also the escape hatch, and he was now head and shoulders out in the slip-stream calling instructions to Dudley. I don't know how he wasn't thrown out.

Finally even the Skipper had to admit defeat. We lost the starboard outer engine and no way could our wonderful 'E' hold height on one engine. The klaxon went again and Bubbles vacated his turret. Pierre was passed up to the top deck and we all jammed into our crash positions and held our heads, braced for a shock that didn't come. Dudley put it down as lightly as a moth on a petal but our port float was only hanging by one strut and it was wiped off, so the wing dug in and the kite heeled over with the nose dug in and the port wing went under water to the inner engine.

We went through the ditching procedures that we had practised so often. Nose gunner out first, then Pierre gently passed up through the hatch, a couple more, then all the gear. One by one we took our turn and out on the wing, all under the critical eye of Dudley who was watching as if it was just another exercise.

Every now and then the kite would give a lurch as if it was about to turn turtle. The Skipper went back down to make a last inspection as the kite gave a lurch. We called him to come back, but he just popped up, handing us a loaf of bread saying sternly: 'You missed some food,' then was gone again. Finally he came back and reluctantly abandoned his ship.

All this time the five remaining Ju88s had been circling and watching. It seemed just as if they had been waiting for Dudley to reappear, because as he got onto the wing, Mr Glass-Nose peeled off and bored in towards us. We all looked up at him and Dudley said: 'Sorry, I can't do any more for you boys; all I can say is if he shoots, jump.' I reckoned this was good advice so I stood at the leading edge of the wing between the fuselage and inner engine and watched the 88. As soon as I saw gun flashes I was going to jump, but there were no gun flashes. He just swooped low over us, waved his wings in salute and then they were all gone. I looked at my watch; it was 55 minutes from the start of the combat and I estimated the fight had lasted 40 to 45 minutes; it seemed like an eternity.

No sooner had we abandoned ship than we lost two dinghies and most of our gear. Pierre's wound dressings which had been kept dry till now became saturated; the salt water in his wounds must have been causing excruciating pain. Our recent elation at surviving went with the two dinghies and we wondered how long our remaining one would last. We organised ourselves as best as eleven men in a six-man dinghy could, with our legs and feet bunched up in the middle with Bamber's shattered leg on top. He sat stoically, occasionally coughing up blood, then he started complaining, not about his leg but about his watch! It had got salt water inside it and stopped. 'I paid a tenner for it, now look at it, it's not worth two bob!' He kept this up for some time until I finally said: 'Pierre, if you cut out your wingeing, I'll buy you a new watch when he get back to base.' He looked pleasantly surprised at this and I must admit he kept me to my promise. Anyway no further mention was made of his watch.

I looked across at the man opposite me and was surprised to see a strange face, also that he had a pale blue RAF battledress on. He noticed my perplexed look and solemnly held out his hand: 'John Eshelby,' he said. I took his hand: 'Peter Jensen.' I remembered then that our engineer, Lance Woodland, had gone to hospital for a minor operation and obviously John had been detailed to replace him. He had not come to briefing with us but had gone straight to the aircraft and had been sitting in the engineer's position all the trip. He had just joined the Squadron and this was his first Op – what an initiation! I then introduced him to the rest of the crew. I must admit that the incongruity of the situation did not dawn on any of us until some time later.

My watch was the only one still working and one of the crew kept asking me the time – as if it was of any consequence. After about the sixth or seventh time I began to get annoyed and said somewhat brusquely: 'It's about five minutes after the last time you asked me.' Dudley, who was sitting next to me, dug me in the ribs. I came to my senses and carried on in a changed tone: 'I can assure you the pubs will be closed by now.'

Dudley tried to keep our spirits up, and at one stage called on George to sing. I can still see George, sitting on the edge of the dinghy, a huge foam capped wave behind him, giving out a rollicking: 'Oh, a life on the ocean wave, a life on the rolling sea . . . .' in his magnificent baritone voice. Darkness came and George gave us a lecture on astro-navigation, but somehow none of us could concentrate too well. The moon came up and the wind dropped. Time became meaningless. We could only wait until daylight to try and fly the aerial kite, so we sat and waited, frightened to move unless the fabric of the dinghy was damaged and our last link with life would go. It was the longest night I have ever known.

Suddenly, it must have been about 3 am, we heard an aircraft. George fished out a 2-star red out of the bag and hung over the side and handed it to Dudley. Dudley pulled out the pin but nothing happened. Obviously the water had got into it. The engine noise faded away and our hopes with it. A few minutes later another, or the same aircraft came back. We had all switched on our Mae West lights and Dudley tried again with another 2-star red. What a sight – two beautiful red stars shot to the heavens and we cheered.

The aircraft turned and swooped towards us and we could make out the outline of a Catalina against the sky. It came down almost to wave-top height and switched on a searchlight. It was a Leigh Light Cat that hunted U boats at night. It stayed with us until dawn, circling, losing us, searching, finding us again. As dawn came up we saw that there was no cloud cover and our hearts sank. Tiger country is no place for a Catalina in broad daylight with no cloud cover; the 88s would have him for breakfast! We expected it to leave but to our eternal gratitude he stayed, still circling and obviously homing something – but what?

About 9 am he signalled us with his Aldis: 'Must go, short of fuel; help coming at 10.00', then he turned away and was soon lost to sight, so once again we were alone except for one small sea bird which had been with us since we ditched. Our spirits dropped to zero.

The sea was running in a huge oily swell and the dinghy was riding up and down like a cork. After a particularly high wave as we dropped into the trough, Bunny said in a quite matter-of-fact tone: 'Don't want to raise your hopes chaps, but I think I saw a ship.' No-one spoke but as the dinghy lifted again eleven pairs of eyes looked in the direction Bunny had indicated, and there they were! Five anti-submarine sloops under the command of Captain F J Walker CB DSO and three Bars.

How we cheered! But we weren't out of our difficulties yet. We held George in a standing position and he waved the bag that held the pyrotechnics but they couldn't see us. They reached a point about five miles from us and began searching. After a while the Catalina returned, obviously at the request of the ships, and he went to a point five miles the other side of us and began a search. We knew from experience that in a broken sea like this even a large ship is hard to see from the air, a dinghy almost impossible. Should we use our last flare?

Dudley made the decision and George pulled out the pin and dunked the flame float in the water and this did the trick. The Cat came over, waggled its wings and left for home again. The sloops then came over and lowered a launch and some matelots brought it over to take off our wounded. Pierre was carefully handed over to them then they insisted on taking Bob. Another launch towed us to the side of HMS *Starling* [U 66] which had a Jacob's ladder over the side and one by one we clambered up. When we were all aboard Captain Walker stepped forward and introduced himself and welcomed us aboard but when he discovered we were the crew of U/461 he could hardly contain his glee.

Much to our surprise, our Sunderland was still afloat and the ships went over to her. The tail was defiantly pointing to the sky, her tail and fin well clear of the water and its tail turret – 'my' tail turret, shattered by a 20 mm shell. Walker fired a D/C but it failed to sink her. It seemed a terrible indignity after all the old girl had gone through, so it was decided to leave it. As we sailed away we left our faithful, magnificent 'E' to find her own way to the bottom of the sea.

For Bob Webster, one incident remains firmly fixed in his memory:

At that particular time we used to carry a couple of pigeons in kerosene tins. Whether any ever made it back home I don't know, but when we ditched one was recovered from the aircraft. Unfortunately it had already drowned but I well remember Dudley giving strict instructions not to throw the bird away. He obviously thought we might need to pluck it if things became more serious!

The Catalina (FP237 'O') was a machine of 210 Squadron and its pilot was Flying Officer J A Cruickshank. At this stage he was unknown to the general public but John Cruickshank was to win the Victoria Cross on 17 July 1944 for his gallant attack upon U 347. Although badly wounded in the attack, one of his crew killed and others injured, he pressed on and his D/Cs sank the submarine. On reaching base he insisted on being helped back to the controls in order to land the Catalina safely. It was the same determination that on this September day he did not give up the search for Marrows and his crew until he knew them to be safe.

Cruickshank's crew on 17 September were:

FO J A Cruickshank	Pilot	Sgt S B Harbison	Engineer
FO J C Dickson	Navigator	FS J Smith	WOP/AG
FO J A Coulson	2nd pilot	Sgt D E Wallace	WOP/AG
Sgt G Cruickshank		Sgt C A Mitchell	
Sgt R D Stockden	Rigger	Sgt C J Webster	FME/AG

Only Dickson was still with him by the time of the VC action, and it was he who was killed in the attack.

Cruickshank had taken off from Hamworthy at 2119 hours on the 16th for a Percussion patrol. At 0305 they spotted a faint glow – the lights on the Mae Wests Peter Jensen refers to. They ran in and switched on the Leigh Light and illuminated the dinghy.

0305 Message to Base: 'Am over dinghy with live crew.'
0445 Message from Base: 'Remain with dinghy to PLE. Lib joins you at 0730.'
0816 Catalina set course for base at PLE.
0820 Sighted three sloops on course 180 degrees (4527/1110), also one Liberator searching. Identified with sloops and led them in direction of dinghy and gave distance over the R/T.

Cruickshank had already jettisoned his D/Cs to help fuel consumption and was staying far longer than was prudent. He had also been dropping Marine Markers to make sure he did not lose sight of the dinghy, but these were now almost used up. Because of the pressing need to leave due to his fuel state, Cruickshank radioed the sloops, in clear language, to make certain they could locate the dinghy. At 0825 they picked up the message from the Liberator: 'Dinghy sighted, Navy here.'

Liberator was 'A' of 53 Squadron, with its Commanding Officer, Wing Commander H R A Edwards AFC, at the controls, his navigator being Flight Sergeant Pledger. They had taken off at 0331 hours on the 17th, also on a Percussion patrol and had been diverted to look for the dinghy once Cruickshank's fuel state became critical. Their radio transmissions when they were in position 5104/0506 were:

0505 Message from Base: 'Proceed to position 4520/1108 and make square search for dinghy. Catalina in contact.'

0824 Message to Base: 'Over three sloops, Catalina just leaving area. Contacted Catalina on R/T asking for position of dinghy. Cat replied that dinghy was eight miles to the south – not marked as he had run out of markers.'

0855 Message to Base: 'Over dinghy in position 4535/1210, with 11 live bodies.'

0900 Message from Base: 'N5QN wants to speak to you. In contact with SNO.'

0907 Message to Base: 'Am over dinghy, Navy is here.'

0912 Message from Base: 'Are you in company with dinghy?'

0926 Message from Base: 'Resume patrol when rescue effected.'

1000 Message to Base: 'Three sloops arrived in area and one proceeded to rescue men from dinghy. A/53 asked to relay message to CinC Plymouth – "A whole crew of Sunderland E/461 – five officers and six NCOs, all Australian. One minor casualty. Sunderland E/461 was shot down by six Ju88s at 1600 on 16 Sept."'

At 1015 A/53 attempted to sink the Sunderland by dropping one D/C from 200 feet but it overshot slightly to starboard. Machine guns also used. The Navy also depth charged it and were still firing at the Sunderland when at 1022 the aircraft resumed patrol.

In October 1943, Dudley Marrows and George Done gave a broadcast on the BBC on their experiences on 16/17 September. It was one of those typical wartime broadcasts, script written by a journalist, but nevertheless, is accurate in its content:

WITH THE AUSTRALIANS IN BRITAIN
WE DITCHED IN THE BAY

GD: F/Lt Marrows had better start this story, for one thing he is a bit more used to this broadcasting than I am because he did a line shoot on pranging a submarine not long ago and for another, when the action started I was working at my charts in my cubby hole.

DM: Well, the first thing I heard was the tail gunner, Pete Jensen, on the intercom, saying: 'Aircraft on the starboard quarter.' At this time, we were flying through a very clear patch of sky with cloud cover about 30 miles away. Naturally we raced to the clouds and after a few minutes the tail gunner reported that he had identified the aircraft as six Ju88s. This is one of the finest cases of aircraft identification that I've heard of because at that time the aircraft were about 16 miles away, and he proved right as we found to our cost later on. The navigator went straight in the astrodome in order to control the fire of our boat and give a running commentary on the action so that I could take whatever evasive action that was necessary.

GD: That's right. I could see the Junkers coming in astern. When they got to within a couple of miles from us they formed up to attack, four on the starboard bow, and two on the port quarter, that is, four on our right and two on our left rear. They made simultaneous attacks and then formed up and started all over again.

DM: At this time we were flying about 4,000 feet and I started doing violent evasive action. It is extraordinary how you can throw a Sunderland flying boat about the sky!

GD: You're telling me! It's not so bad for you sitting down and strapped in, but I had to stand, hanging on as best I could to keep myself from turning somersaults.

DM: Oh stop binding, that's what you're paid for! Anyway, it seemed no matter which way we dived, turned or corkscrewed, there were always some Junkers ready for us.

After a few minutes, the tail turret was put out of action, and there was only one gun firing from the mid-upper turret. But we still managed to hold them off. After about 20 minutes, our two port engines were out of action and the hydraulics of the nose turret were shot away – this didn't make it any easier for me to carry out evasive action or for us to hit back as much as we would have liked to, but even so, we saw one Junkers break away and head for home with black smoke pouring from one of its engines; when we got back we claimed him as 'damaged'. With only two engines going, we were losing height rapidly and it was just about this time that the Hun spotted the fact that our rear turret was out of action.

GD: Yes, I couldn't make out how they didn't spot it sooner, but when they did, they changed tactics and the five remaining Junkers simply lined up behind us and let us have it, one after another – formed up and let us have it again. There were cannon and machine-gun shells simply tearing through our aircraft and it is a mystery to me how, with the exception of one member of the crew, we got through it as lightly as we did.

We carried on this action for 40 minutes which is a damned long time when your aircraft is in the state ours was by then – two engines shot up, rear turret out of action, front turret pretty well u/s, the mounting of the nose gun had collapsed and the air gunner, Sgt Bamber, was firing the gun, forcing it back onto the mounting; the port float holed, the wireless gear shot up, the masses of cannon and mg holes throughout the fuselage and hull. As far as the crew were concerned, by this time, the nose gunner had a bad leg wound, four others were very slightly wounded by shrapnel and one chap was scalded.

DM: Yes, he was the galley-gunner and was brewing up a pot of tea when the action started, and my violent evasive action knocked the kettle of boiling water over him. So we missed that cup of tea! When the Junkers put our starboard outer motor out of action we reckoned we'd had it and I ditched the aircraft.

GD: That was one of the best pieces of flying skill that I've ever seen. I can't make out to this day how you managed to land a Sunderland flying boat on one engine and one float in the Bay of Biscay.

DM: Well, as a matter of fact, I can't remember either, but anyway, we got down and proceeded to abandon ship. We had three dinghies and we nipped out into them. This was at 4.35 pm; I know the time because most of our watches stopped through being in the water and this was the time they showed. Well, we'd only been in the dinghies a few minutes when one of them started to sink – it must have been holed by some of the shrapnel.

GD: It was holed all right; I know, I was in it. Shook me a bit when it started to sink but I was soon in one of the other dinghies and took some of the gear with me. That one blew up after a quarter of an hour so we got into the last remaining dinghy with what gear we could which wasn't much because eleven blokes in a dinghy, that's meant to hold six, doesn't leave much room to spare.

DM: Room to spare! There never even seemed to be enough room for my feet! In case you're wondering what happened to the Junkers, they circled us for a bit and from the way they were flying we could see they were taking photographs, so perhaps one of these days we'll see a picture of ourselves in that dinghy, from the German papers. Then they flew off and we were left alone.

I gave out a tin of water for a man and gave orders that no rations were to be touched for 48 hours because naturally, although we'd sent a signal back to base saying that enemy aircraft were attacking us and giving our position, we didn't really know how long it would be before help came. We had seen some sloops on the way down and we estimated that they would be about 120 miles away from us, and spent quite a bit of time discussing amongst ourselves what the chances were of them finding us. When it started to get dark, I arranged watches to keep a look-out for aircraft or ships. We devised a shield that we held up over the side of the dinghy and this to some extent anyway kept a lot of the spray from coming in.

GD: Yes, that dinghy rode the swell pretty well, but every now and again, a big wave would break just over us and then we'd have to start baling, with a beaker and a shoe! However, we found that the best thing was to soak up the water in a towel and then wring it over the side. By the way, where did that towel come from? Do you know, Skipper?

DM: Yes, as we were climbing out of the aircraft into the dinghies I saw somebody's kit-bag hanging up with a towel sticking out of it and I reckoned the towel might come in handy, so I brought it along. I think it belonged to the wireless op. But to get back to the story, we were drifting back a bit, to the south, away from England. You can imagine this didn't please us very much. We watched the aircraft sinking, but it kept afloat for quite a long time because of the empty fuel tanks, and after a bit we could only see the tail sticking up.

It got pretty cold during the night and we had to take it in turns to stretch our legs. One bloke would say he was getting a bit cramped and we'd all have to jostle round a bit to give him enough room to get his legs out straight. Still, we saw the humour in it and kept pretty cheerful. We had a bit of extra company all night.

GD: Oh yes, the seagull. He spotted us just after we got into the dinghy and circled around us for the whole night. It was quite cheering to see him there. Then what else did we talk about in the dinghy?

DM: Well, it's hard to remember now, yet it's only a short while ago but there's one thing I shall never forget and that is the way we had to nurse that damned marine marker all night.

GD: Nor will I! And it's a darned heavy thing, believe me; about three feet long and six inches wide, made of metal. There was no room in the dinghy to lay it down so we had to sit it on our knees, and when we got tired of it, passed it on to the next bloke. Then the great thing happened at 3 am. We heard an aircraft which we identified as a Catalina flying boat. We directed it over us by means of our torches which were part of the dinghy equipment.

DM: We were all so intent on looking up that we forgot about our spray shield and got another soaking for our over-enthusiasm. I think it was about now that we started a sweepstake. They were really two sweepstakes, with an entrance fee for each of 2/–. One was to guess the exact time that we would be picked up and the other was for the first to sight our rescue ship. I'll tell you who won them when we get that far.

GD: The Catalina circled us all night and then at dawn went off to rustle up some help, and arrived back about 8.30 and flashed us a message saying that a ship would be with us pretty soon and that the Catalina's petrol was running low so they'd have to get back home. They hadn't been gone more than a few minutes when a Liberator arrived on the scene and took over the watch. It circled round us and at 9 am we sighted a sloop on the horizon heading towards us.

DM: And the sweepstakes were won by the same chap, F/Sgt Sidney, who incidentally comes from Sydney. He had the nearest guess as to the time we were picked up and was the first to sight the sloop. Not bad – he picked up four pounds for that effort! Well, pretty soon we were aboard the sloop. We found it was one of the ships commanded by Captain F J Walker CB DSO RN. Some of you may remember reading about him, he's the man who gave the order 'General Chase' recently when he was attacking three U boats in the Bay. He is a wizard chap. I was very proud to meet him even under these particular circumstances. Our clothes were dried and we were fed and and given accommodation on board his ship.

GD: And he certainly treated us royally, even ran us back to within a few miles of our base so we call him now, 'Walker's Air Sea Rescue Service' – pick you up in the drink and deliver you to your door!

DM: Well, there's the story and that's one of the action stories of a Sunderland flying boat. But remember that for our exciting moments there are hours and hours of unexciting ones. However, it's a good life and we get our spot of leave; we got some when we were rescued from the Bay . . . .

For his action over these two days, Dudley Marrows received the Distinguished Service Order, while Fred (Pierre) Bamber and Alan Neale Pearce were both awarded the Distinguished Flying Medal.

Thanks to the research by Chris Goss, fellow author and historian, as well as being a serving RAF officer, it was possible to identify the German Ju88 pilot credited with the destruction of E/461.

For some while a Gruppe of KG40 had been operating from the west coast of France, out over the Bay searching for Coastal Command aircraft. On 16 September 1943, six Ju88s from 14 Staffel of V Gruppe took off from Bordeaux at 1446 hours and after engaging a Liberator had found Marrows' Sunderland. While everyone had attacked it, final credit went to Leutnant Willi Gutermann, flying his 21st combat sortie in Ju88 coded F8+LY. After the war Gutermann became a lawyer and died in the early 1980s. He became a minor Luftwaffe ace with at least five victories: a Sunderland on 14 May 1943, a Blenheim on 20 May, Marrows on 16 September, a Wellington on 19 November, and a Beaufort in the Mediterranean on 8 March 1944.

When KG40 was disbanded in August 1944, following the invasion of France, its pilots and crews went to night-fighter squadrons or other units. Gutermann went to JG4's Sturmstaffel, so was lucky to survive the last months of the war.

And the photographs the Sunderland crew thought had been taken of them? Yes, they did appear in print, in the German Luftwaffe's *Adler* magazine, showing an almost plan view of the Sunderland and another oblique view, with the Sunderland, port wing low, tail high, and the Australians on the starboard wing shortly before launching their dinghies. Some weeks later British intelligence was in possession of a copy and soon the Australians had the unique experience of seeing themselves in the drink, the picture presumably taken by 'glass nose' as it flew over them.

CHAPTER SEVEN

ELEVEN DAYS IN A DINGHY

Whatever anxious moments Dudley Marrows and his crew lived through during their 18 hours in a dinghy, they were fewer than those experienced later that same month by another crew who had successfully attacked a German U boat in the Bay of Biscay but like so many others before and after them, the U boat gunners had inflicted crippling damage to their aircraft.

The U boat in question was U 221, a type VIIC submarine built at the Germania Werft (boat yard) at Kiel, and commissioned on 9 May 1942. Her commander was Kapitänleutnant Hans Trojer and both were to experience good and bad days during the Battle of the Atlantic.

Hans Trojer was born on 23 January 1916, a native of Birthähn-Sieburgen and had, prior to taking over his new command, been IIWO and IWO on U 34 and then in the first half of 1941, IWO on U 67. Before taking over U 221 he had commanded the training boat U 3. His nickname to the crew of U 212 was 'Count Dracula' and with them he would win the Knight's Cross.

Initially part of the 7th Flotilla, U 221 left Kiel on 1 September 1942 and after a stop at Kristiansand, joined Gruppe Pfeil on the 12th. Three days later she was in contact with convoy ON129 (GB to Halifax) but driven off. By the 22nd she had joined Gruppe Blitz and on the 24th, while attacking convoy SC100 (GB to USA), missed a target with two torpedoes.

On 3 October she was refuelled by U 116 and ten days later came success. Closing in with convoy SC104 she fired five torpedoes and was rewarded by the sinking of three ships. The first was the Norwegian freighter *Fagersten* of 2,342 BRT, followed by the British freighter *Ashworth* of 5,227 BRT and finally another Norwegian vessel, the freighter *Senta* of 3,785 BRT.

Staying in contact with this same convoy, Trojer attacked again the next day, this time his five torpedoes sinking two freighters. The

American *Susanna* of 5,929 BRT and the British *Southern Empress* of 12,398 BRT. Thus in two days U 221 could claim to have sunk a total of nearly 30,000 tons (29,681) of Allied shipping.[1]

With her successes behind her and her victory pennants waving, U 221 arrived at St Nazaire on 22 October. A month and a day later she left on her second war cruise, which was to prove vastly different from her first.

One day out of St Nazaire, in the dangerous Bay area, she was found by an aircraft at 1655 hours in position 4551/0425 (German Marine Quadrant BF5891), which her bridge watch officer described as a Liberator type. In fact it was a Halifax bomber of 405 Squadron RCAF. While 405 was a main force Bomber Command squadron, aircraft and crews of this unit had been loaned to Coastal to help with the long distance coverage of the Bay and Atlantic Approaches.

This Halifax II and its crew had become airborne from Beaulieu at 0814 but finding his compass u/s, the pilot had returned 45 minutes later and after the problem had been fixed, was off again at 1015. The crew was:

F/Sgt C C Stobel	Pilot	Sgt R Hart
Sgt J Bemister		Sgt R P Armstrong
Sgt W Koroby		Sgt A Whitteron
Sgt J Richardson		

Shortly before 5 pm that afternoon, and while on the homeward leg after a fruitless patrol, they were at 2,500 feet on a course of 316 degrees. In position 4529/0428, Stobel sighted what appeared to be a wake of a surface vessel about four miles ahead and just to starboard, on a course of 270. Stobel began to lose height in anticipation and at 300 yards, by which time he was down to 1,000 feet, he identified the object as a U boat.

Stobel immediately turned to starboard, made a 180-degree turn to port and lost more height. As the Halifax turned, the U boat could be seen diving, its conning tower and stern already awash. At 1658, the boat disappeared stern first as Stobel raced over the spot to drop

---

[1] Some historians seem to delight in stating that U boats or surface ships sank so many thousands of tons of shipping in a day, or a week, a month, or during a campaign, which to me seems rather pointless unless one knows how many ships this represents, and most laymen would not have any real idea. In the above sample, for instance, the freighters ranged from 2,342 to 12,398 tons, so it is difficult to try to make an average and then guess at the number of ships. However, all becomes a good deal clearer if the historian would say something like '. . . U 221 sank five freighters over the 13/14 October 1942, totalling nearly 30,000 tons.' After all if one takes the smaller ship, it could mean 12.8 ships, or the larger, 2.4 ships, neither of which would give any indication of the true number – five.

six depth charges from 200 feet. As they climbed away, the explosions were noted ahead of the swirl of the disappearing submarine, possibly 30-50 feet, but straddling the U boat's track.

Stobel circled, and continued to do so for five minutes but nothing else was seen and he had to leave, landing back at St Eval at 2023 hours. U 221 reported the attack to base, confirming no damage.

On 29 November, U 221 joined Gruppe Draufgänger. By the first week of December, U boats were closing in on convoy HX217 out of Halifax, Nova Scotia: a slower convoy, SC111 had sailed some days earlier. There were more than 20 U boats strung out across the Atlantic at this stage and 8 December was to see an amazing number of U boat sightings and aircraft attacks around this convoy.

The full story has been told elsewhere but 120 Squadron, operating out of Iceland, had the lion's share of the action. At 0928 and again at 1248, Squadron Leader T M Bulloch, one of the most successful anti-submarine hunters in Coastal Command, found and attacked three U boats. In the first attack (position 5725/3519) the U boat was claimed sunk, several bodies being seen in the water. At 1248 he attacked two boats, but one submerged. His last two D/Cs went down and subsequent attacks could only be made with machine-gun fire. Although for many years it has been difficult to assess which boat was sunk in the first attack, it seems now to have been U 611, which previously had been thought to have been lost on 10 December.

Terry Bulloch left the convoy at 1654, relieved by another 120 Squadron Liberator (FL932 'M') piloted by Squadron Leader D J Isted. Desmond 'Wizz' Isted had left Reykjavik at 1151 and located the convoy in position 5831/3241 at 1502 hours. After reporting to the SNO he was sent 30 miles astern of the convoy and at 1512 spotted two surfaced U boats. He immediately attacked one, releasing seven D/Cs, and as the boat crash-dived it appeared that two men were still on the conning tower.

By 1536 Isted was back with the convoy and heading out once more spotted another U boat at 1557 eight miles off, which he attacked with his one remaining depth charge. At 1616 he attacked another U boat with his .5 and .303 machine guns, something he and his crew repeated at 1652. At 1715, PLE was reached and he headed back to Iceland, landing at 2135. His crew had been:

SL D J Isted	Pilot	FS R T Bedford	1st WOP/AG
FO R A Crumpton	2nd pilot	Sgt R W Elder	2nd WOP/AG
FS D J Appleton	Navigator	Sgt A Allwood	3rd WOP/AG
Sgt A Richardson	Engineer		

U 221 reported being attacked by a Liberator at 1715 hours (German

time) in position 5815/3336 (German AK2577). Six depth-charge
explosions had been felt but again the boat suffered no damage.
However, due to the time it had to be Isted and crew who were above
them on this afternoon.

Disaster came at 2134 hours. The day's action over, the boats were
reforming in order to pursue the convoy during darkness but then
U 221 and U 254 collided under the grey seas of the North Atlantic.
U 254 sank and although several men escaped the sinking vessel,
U 221 were only able to rescue a handful from the icy sea. (The
number is given variously as four or six.) Her captain, Kapitänleutnant
Hans Gilardone was not one of them. In the past credit for the loss
of U 254 has been given to Terry Bulloch, but clearly, by the time
of the boat's loss, Bulloch was back at Reykjavik.

On the 15th, U 221 became part of Gruppe Raufbold but she was
then on her way home, arriving back at St Nazaire on 23 December
– in time for Christmas. However, this time there were no victory
pennants, and sadness for the loss of U 254 and most of her crew.

Some damage caused by the collision needed work, so it was not
until 27 February 1943 that U 221 again put to sea, joining Gruppe
Neuland on 3 March. Their luck returned on the 7th, sinking the
Norwegian freighter *Jamaica* of 3,015 BRT with two 'fish'. As
survivors took to the boats Trojer surfaced and took the ship's 4th
Engineer prisoner, but on 21 March this man, during an exercise
period, jumped overboard from the submarine and was presumed
drowned.

They caught up with convoy HX228 on 10 March and were again
successful. Hans Trojer fired off four torpedoes and hit three ships,
although one torpedo failed to explode. First to go was the British
freighter *Tucorinca* of 5,412 BRT, followed by the American *Andrea
F Luckenbach* of 6,565 BRT. The lucky freighter was the American
Lawton R Evans (7,197 BRT), whose crew felt the thud of a hit but
not the explosion.

On 13 March, U 221 joined Gruppe Dränger but four days later
she met up again with 120 Squadron from Iceland. Flying Officer
Sammy Esler, in Liberator FK244 'J', had been assigned to escort
convoy HX229. Taking off from Aldergrove (N Ireland) at 1102 he
headed out over the Atlantic. Their radar picked up the convoy at
1748, 30 miles ahead and seven minutes later the ships were in sight.
Instructions from the SNO directed Esler to a patrol area in 7/10ths
cloud at 3,500 feet, with cloud base at 3,000. Visibility was 30 miles
but at only 15 miles a U boat was seen in position 5121/3200 at 2005
hours. Approaching the target, another sub was seen in a more
favourable position on the port bow only ten miles off. As Esler
attacked they saw the first U boat go down. The Lib came in across

the boat's port beam, releasing five D/Cs from 100 feet a few seconds after this boat too crash-dived. After the explosions the boat reappeared at a steep angle, showing its conning tower and was on the surface for 35 seconds before going down again. Esler, being unable to raise the convoy's SNO for destroyer support, flew to the ships but still could not make contact.

Sammy Esler continued to patrol. At 2047 hours the crew saw three U boats on the surface, at ten, 12 and 15 miles, the approximate position noted as 6118/3231. Esler selected the middle boat and dropped his last D/Cs while his gunners opened fire, but the boat submerged, as did the others, and nothing more was seen. At least keeping them down reduced their forward speed, thereby letting the ships proceed to a safer distance. Esler's crew:

FO S E Esler	Pilot	Sgt F W Wallace	WOP/AG
FO D C L Weber	2nd pilot	Sgt J Kammelard	WOP/AG
FS T H Kempton	Navigator	Sgt A H Mealin	WOP/AG
Sgt G M Goodall	Engineer		

U 221 reported being attacked by a Liberator at 2010 hours in position 5127/3205 (German AK9846), although the crew only noted four explosions, but the boat had suffered some slight damage, and one man was slightly injured in a fall, but not badly enough to cause any problems.

Esler had indeed been busy this evening. At 2008, U608 reported being attacked, at 2010 he attacked U221 and at 2048, U 336. U 590 was one of the other boats seen by Esler to crash-dive, but was not attacked. U 441 also saw the attack on U 336 and was also attacked at 2059. He put his Liberator down at RAF Benbecula (Outer Hebrides) at 0507 hours on the 18th.

The next day Trojer closed with convoy HX229 and actually got ahead of it. His first attack was from his stern tube, then he turned and fired four more; he sank two ships. The first was the American *W O Gresham* of 7,191 BRT, the other the British *Canadian Star*, 8,293 BRT. Both ships had been carrying food and in all 57 men died when the ships went down. This time however, U 221 was subjected to a depth-charge attack by the convoy's escorts, but she avoided any damage. Heading home now, she entered St Nazaire on the 28th. It was now that Trojer received the Ritterkreuz (Knight's Cross of the Iron Cross).

Her fourth patrol began on 3 May. On the 12th, at 0940, she was located by a Liberator over the Bay but her gunners kept the aircraft at a distance and she was able to dive without being attacked. Trojer noted in the ship's war diary: 'Aircraft, Liberator. Flak. Aircraft circled around the boat. No approach. 0955 hrs Liberator disappeared in easterly direction.' That evening, at 2228 hours, she found a straggler from convoy HX237, the Norwegian tanker *Sandanger*, 9,432 BRT and sunk her.

Four days later she was supplied by Wolf Stiebler's U 461 and for the next ten days was part of Gruppe Oder, then Gruppe Mosel and finally Gruppe Trutz. With fuel running low she was supplied by U 488 on 12 June and returned to base on 21 July.

The fifth and last patrol began from St Nazaire on 20 September 1943. Seven days later she was found in position 4700/1800 by the Halifax of 58 Squadron and sunk, but not before she had damaged her antagonist and set it on fire. The full report of the action and subsequent ordeal is as follows:

Anti-Submarine Patrol in Halifax 'B' (HR982) 58 Squadron
27 September 1943

Crew:

FO E L Hartley	Pilot	FS K E Ladds	MU gunner
GC R C Mead	2nd pilot	Sgt R K Triggol	Rear gunner
FO T E Bach RCAF	Navigator	Sgt A S Fox	WOP
Sgt G R Robertson	Engineer	Sgt M Griffiths	Front gunner

Airborne Holmsley South 1138 hours. At extremity of patrol 47N, 18W, attacked U boat at 1712 hrs, believed broad beamer or 750 tonner. Approach at 50 feet and attacked 30 degrees to port bow, scoring hits with front and mid-upper guns.

Eight D/Cs dropped by Captain (pilot release) of which 2nd and 3rd straddled just aft of conning tower, D/C plumes observed, those straddling U boat being of black, oily nature. U boat having been fully surfaced at attack, was seen afterwards to be down at stern, bows rising to angle of 20 degrees out of water and from that position slid under.

'B' sustained at least one hit in the starboard wing, between the engines, in No.2 fuel tank, which burst into flame and spread quickly along the wing and breaking out in the fuselage at several points. Captain found aircraft difficult to manage, and suspected damage to rudder, the aircraft being kept straight by course use of engine. Order to transmit SOS was given and Captain then ordered crew to prepare for ditching.

The Ditching

Owing to difficulty of control, Captain was unable to jettison remaining D/C and unable to lower flaps, hence touch down was made at 110 knots, the urgency of the ditching, due to fires, being of primary importance.

The tail broke off, just forward of rear turret and water came in with a great rush through the nose, quenching the fires in the fuselage. The aircraft stood on its nose in the water, the trailing edges of the wings burning and aircraft visibly sinking slowly.

Seven of the crew left the aircraft; Captain through the pilot's escape hatch, FO Bach and Sgt Fox through mid-hatch and the remainder through rear hatch. GC Mead, Bach and FS Ladds took up ditching position in rest area, Sgts Robertson, Fox and Griffiths against rear spar. Sgt Triggol was in transit at touch down and was not seen again.

Owing to the attitude of the aircraft, the steam and flames and shock of impact, the crew got out as quickly as possible to find the dinghy inflated and at the end of the astrodome. It was right side uppermost.

Sgt Griffiths seemed completely dazed and could not support himself in the water, although FO Bach had attempted to inflate his Mae West and together with GC Mead to help him towards the dinghy. Due to the swell, Sgt Griffiths slipped from their grasp and was drowned; he was unconscious.

The remaining six boarded the dinghy, the 'painter' was severed as the aircraft sank. The scene of the ditching must have been about three miles from that of the attack, nothing more being seen of the U boat.

Owing to the speed of leaving the aircraft there was no dinghy equipment brought from the aircraft (ie: no dinghy radio, water, emergency rations pack, containing paddles and dinghy apron). An attempt was made to hand paddle the dinghy to the wreckage to pick up anything of value, but the wind and swell made progress impossible and the attempt was ceased.

The crew reviewed their position, set the sea anchor, dried out the dinghy, using a boot and socks. In view of the distance from base (7-800 miles) and the low altitude at which signals were transmitted, it was decided to assume that the spell in the dinghy would be a long one and therefore to eat and drink nothing for the first two days.

In the Dinghy
27 September: All crew wet and seasick during first hour, possibly through swallowing salt water. Spent the night in cold and wet condition.

28 September: Low cloud (500 ft) and slight drizzle with clear intervals. Took stock of our position and found we had –
> Four tins of emergency rations in pack (includes Horlicks tablets and a few barley sugar tablets).

Five emergency flying ration boxes (including Horlicks tablets, chewing gum, piece of chocolate, and a tube of condensed milk). Five pints of water (five tins).

At 1535 hours aircraft heard to pass overhead, above 10/10ths cloud on east-west course, therefore no chance of being sighted. Rigged up mast and prepared for the night. Slept on Mae Wests and had a fairly comfortable night.

29 September: Low cloud and drizzle at first, improving to excellent visibility, and broken cloud at approximately 1,500 ft. Dried clothes and made fishing gear out of wireless aerial and started daily diary. Condition of crew excellent in body and spirits.

A very little soggy chocolate was shared in the morning (about two ounces altogether). This was from pocket of Sgt Fox. Two Horlicks tablets to each at 6 pm.

30 September: Passed a very long and cold night. One on hourly watch throughout. One small piece of chewing gum issued to each in morning. Later used for bait without success. Now find we have 12 × 1″ Very cartridges instead of nine. The burnt hands of GC and Robbie, bound up by Field Dressing from Captain.

Wind light and variable. Visibility good. Cloud 6/10ths at 2,000 feet. Two Horlicks tablets each in evening. Continued practice of saying morning and evening prayers for those we love and for assistance. This practice from which we derived great spiritual strength was continued throughout.

1 October: Night was bad, with cold and wet and great discomfort. Horlicks tablets issued four times daily, one tablet per person. Started early to dry out dinghy and at about 3 pm things had gone quite well, until the sea increased quickly to an Atlantic swell. 35 foot waves and an unlucky cross wave broke on the dinghy and overturned it.

All got back safely but some kit was lost, and crew were badly shaken and exhausted. A wet bar of chocolate (two ounces) was divided out and eaten. Everyone thoroughly cold, wet and exhausted. The swell continued and night came without a great deal of improvement in our condition. Before dark the dinghy was continually swamped and constant baling was necessary with every available piece of material. Extra issue of tablet of barley sugar was made and this did everyone a power of good.

2 October: Passed very uncomfortable night, dozing fitfully in some three inches of water. All cold and cramped. No fish caught and no water used.

The day started with poor weather, low cloud and drizzle, which we caught on handkerchiefs and sucked dry. Weather improved and about midday, cloudless sky and calm sea. We took opportunity to dry clothes, and sunbathe. Drank first tin of water, 1/6th of a pint.

3 October: Prepared carefully for night, evening being quite warm. The night was clear and quite calm and cold. All were stiff and miserable. A false alarm was raised when Mars appeared low on the horizon giving impression of orange ship's light. No chances were taken and two Very cartridges were fired.

Now keeping constant day and night watch in turns. Our horizon very small, estimated at two miles. Dinghy behaving remarkably well, requiring little topping up. Ration still four Horlicks tablets per day. Everyone pleased at brightness of Very cartridges fired during the night. Morale still high, and fully confident of being rescued.

At dawn, all uncomfortable, but wonderful sunrise increased spirits with increased warmth. Another warm day, ideal for being spotted by aircraft flying at any height. Cloud only 1/10th. In afternoon bathed in turns from dinghy. Object to exercise limbs and dry clothes. Just at commencement two whales arrived to begin blowing on surface about 50 yards away, whilst 30 to 40 porpoises passed quite close, tearing along at about 20 knots. These later had close fighter escort of seagulls.

In afternoon constructed fishing net out of bellows handle and Ken's underpants, still without any result; fish too scared. All burns and slight wounds now better. After bathe we had discussion on next action to be taken, so far having relied upon wind and current to take us slowly eastwards towards more patrolled areas. We expected to be searched for but as the weather was bad, had an idea that aircraft might not have been able to operate, and had therefore stayed in area of ditching for six days hoping that our Wireless Transmission message had been received, and that the patrol on which we had been employed, had not been cancelled or superceded by others not so far west.

Now we felt that we should hoist some sort of sail and make better use of westerly winds, which prevail in this area, to carry us nearer the 'Bay Patrols' and convoy routes. Decided to make sail out of two shirts on the morrow and sea anchor modified to give less drag. All seem quite happy at having sunk U boat by direct method and now every effort to make more ground (or water) eastwards.

Later in evening we used net to catch jelly fish of which there were many. Still not possible to catch fish. We squeezed jelly fish in clean handkerchief in hope of extracting water, but result was so foul and salty, that after a despairing attempt to make it more palatable by the use of a water purifying tablet, we threw away this slimy, salty mess.

4 October: Night was rather better, sea quite calm, and wind still westerly. Only one tin of water used so far. Decided to reduce ration to three Horlicks tablets next day. Day started with low cloud and some drizzle. This had been expected and all had their silk maps ready, stretched between hands and mouth to gather moisture. However, the result was so foul tasting, that we cursed the man who did not foresee the possibility of silk maps being used for this purpose, and have some decent tasting waterproof on the 'handkerchiefs'.

The weather cleared before a warm sun, and we again attempted to catch fish, without success. This was getting exasperating, since we could get as near as touching them as we grabbed.

Made and mounted masts and sail, the latter consisting of two shirts sewed together by thin copper wire (from the wireless aerial) and tape (from the Mae Wests), the whole being rigged to the dinghy by six guy ropes from the W/T rigging. The masts were strapped on the emergency ration bag, on one side, and in the baling boot on the other. By this means it was hoped to save wear and tear on the dinghy.

The sail was a success and gave more speed than expected. In hoping to reach the patrolled areas we expect 1½ knots (or possibly two knots) in a more or less easterly direction. If the Gulf Stream flows in this vicinity there might possibly be this additional aid. Sea anchor was reshaped to give less drag and was close-hauled.

For days now we have been breathing though sea-wetted handkerchiefs and ducking our heads over the side and replacing helmet on heads still dripping in order to get moisture into the body by evaporation, or at least to conserve what moisture we already possess. It was hoped to have another bathe today but the weather was too cold.

After seven days in the dinghy hope is still very high. Nights are bad and everyone gets tired very easily, but the great thing is that everything gets done happily and in good spirit. In the evening cloud is 10/10ths and rain looks a possibility. At this time as on other occasions, the topic turns to food and strangely enough all join in and feel no irritation at the choice of such a subject.

5 October: Kept sail up during night although quite rough. Keeping up a good speed eastwards. During the morning the wind increased, also the dinghy speed, but much water being shipped and baling becoming necessary.

6 October: Night very bad. Sea very rough and torrential rain falling. Everyone had a good drink off face and hands by taking turns at sucking sail and handkerchiefs. All very tired, wet and cold, with no possibility of rest at all. Issue of chocolate and barley sugar during day. Weather improved during afternoon after passing through three large squally areas and wind swung round again to westerly. Constant manning of lookout for excessive waves and attempted to help dinghy to surmount bad ones had worn us all out and we were all thoroughly tired. Robbie began to show signs of becoming delirious and was no use for work or lookout.

7 October: Another difficult night with water occasionally splashing into dinghy. Last few days taken toll of our stamina and throughout night Robbie and Tom showed signs of becoming delirious on waking and required constant attention. Lookout therefore divided between the remaining four of us, who are finding it quite tiring to change position in dinghy. Still keeping up our hopes and morning and evening prayers. This night an additional prayer made for speedy deliverance, since we feel that although four of us could manage another three days or so, the position of the other three was becoming critical.

Weather cleared by mid-day but wind became northerly. One tin, (the second of the original five) of water shared out amongst us, and one piece of chocolate issued to each. My own estimate of position, having constructed route mercator projection and marked our approximate course is:

14 W, 46 N, some 220 miles off coast of Spain and bearing 140 T. Our present course being 160 T.

8 October: All now fairly well exhausted, owing to high seas and bad nights. Dinghy still behaving splendidly since we have found good distribution of weight. Still shipping water periodically and baling becomes quite a big effort. Wind westerly.

Dinghy dried out and topped up early, soon after dawn, but still ship water. Cloud 10/10ths. Now keeping hourly daily watch in turns, the remaining three resting and dozing.

At 14.30 hours, Ken Ladds on watch sighted mast of naval vessel. All became active, fired off three Very cartridges and found two destroyers slowly closing, the nearer one obviously manoeuvring to put us on their leeward beam. About twenty minutes later all picked up by HM Destroyer *Mahratta*, homeward bound from Gibraltar. Captain, Lieutenant Commander Drout [Lt Cdr E A F Drought, Ed]; doctor, Surgeon Lieutenant McRae. Doctor and ship's company took charge of us, giving us excellent and undivided attention.[1]

---

[1] In fact there were three destroyers: *Mahratta*, *Matchless* and *Valiant*.

10 October: Docked at Plymouth and shortly after lunch taken ashore in stretchers and admitted to Royal Naval Hospital, Plymouth.

Note: Ration boxes consist of following:
  (a) Emergency Pack – four:
       4 Barley Sugars, 40 Malted Milk Tablets.
       12 pieces of chewing gum.
       1 box matches and energy tablets.

  Emergency Flying Rations – five:
       1 bar chocolate.
       1 tube condensed milk.
       4 pieces chewing gum.
       33 Horlicks tablets.

This with five pints of water, Very pistol and 12 cartridges constituted our supplies.

E L Hartley

Eric Hartley and his crew had survived for 11 days. His 'second pilot' on this trip had been Holmesley South's Station Commander, Group Captain Roger Mead AFC. He decided to accompany the crew on what was their 27th operation, although Ken Ladds had flown more than 40 by this date. Hartley was an experienced operator having already flown with 502 and 612 Squadrons.

They were extremely lucky to have been spotted by the destroyer which was not searching for them, merely making its way to England from The Rock (Gibraltar). Hartley was later awarded the Distinguished Flying Cross, while Ken Ladds received the Distinguished Flying Medal, not only for his part in the attack, his guns engaging the U boat's gun crew, but for helping to keep spirits up during their time in the dinghy. The attack position was noted as 4700/1800, while the destroyer noted the rescue location as 4520/1533, timed at 1430 hours, which means Hartley's dinghy had drifted in a south-easterly direction for around 180 miles. Here was, of course, no happy ending for Hans Trojer and his crew, all 50 men going down with U 221 which slid backwards and down into 2,000 fathoms of dark water of the Atlantic.

Some years after this event, George Robertson wrote down his story from which he has allowed me to take extracts. He recorded:

> We had been allotted the Squadron's newest Mark VIII Halifax
> and learnt at briefing that, instead of making the usual trip into

the Bay, we were to proceed on a south-westerly course into the Atlantic.

Eric Hartley, a diminutive man but a first class pilot, could do almost anything with a Halifax and had earned our complete confidence. Tom Bach was our navigator, who came to join the RAF from the Argentine.

The most experienced NCO was Flight Sergeant Ken Ladds, now on his second tour. Sergeant Bob Fox, like Ken, was a Londoner and the only other married man in the crew. His wife, at the time, was expecting their first child. Sergeant Taffy Griffiths was our third WOP/AG, and our rear gunner that day was Sergeant Bob Triggol, who at age 19, had just joined us and this was to be his first operational trip. Apart from Bob, I was the least experienced crew member having joined Eric's team in April as a newly qualified flight engineer.

As anticipated our patrol was extremely uneventful. It was a gift of a trip really and I was secretly happy at the thought that there was no likelihood of our being jumped by Ju88s. Shortly after 1700 hours we made a fuel check and decided that we should commence our return, but as we were about to turn we got our sighting.

Eric saw it first, sitting on the surface about four miles away and as I handed him the binoculars he alerted us all, stating that we were going straight in to attack. We closed the gap with a corkscrewing motion in order to make it more difficult for the vessel's gunners and the final run in was dead straight and at low level. A good straddle was observed, with the second and third depth charges going in just aft of the conning tower.

I was unable to see the results but our gunners in the turrets suddenly became alive with cries of success and I later learned that the U boat was seen to be down by the stern, then the bows rose to about 20 degrees before she slid under. While this was taking place my visibility was confined to the wing areas and in the midst of this I was horror struck to observe the leading edge of the starboard wing erupt into flames.

I shouted a warning but in seconds the wing was a raging inferno with the fire spreading to the fuel tanks and breaking out in the fuselage. The skipper was calling '. . . ditching stations – we're going straight in!' I have only a hazy recollection of stumbling back to my ditching position, having witnessed the starboard wing breaking up and drifting away in blazing chunks. When in my position, I caught a momentary glimpse of Bob, making his way forward after evacuating his rear turret. He had nearly reached his ditching position when we made the first impact with the water.

The rear section of the aircraft disintegrated, Bob with it. There followed another crash and everything came to a halt.

I reached the escape hatch ladder having felt cold water hit me, and I seem to recall some pleasure from this as it gave some respite from the flames. I was half way through the hatch, not aware that the aircraft was standing on its nose, and looking for a wing which wasn't there. There was no time to ponder on this situation as I was the recipient of a good push and the next thing I knew I was in the water.

The fuselage was still pointing skywards, a blazing torch surrounded by floating debris. I swam to the semi-inflated dinghy, floating outside the ring of fire and grabbed at its flabby side wondering whether it had been holed by flak but it became firm under my grasp as it continued to inflate. I hauled myself in and then heard a voice calling for me to help him in. I was then conscious of the fact that others had reached the dinghy and we helped each other on board where we collapsed in an exhausted stupor. However, we had lost two of our number, Taffy and Bob. Bob must have been killed instantaneously when we hit. Taffy was seen by Tom and the Groupie floating in the water. Tom swam to him and tried to inflate his Mae West and guide him to the dinghy but he slipped from his grasp and was not seen again.

George's story now follows Eric Hartley's report, but we pick it up on 6 October. By this time the men were in a bad way and the weather had turned very nasty. George was also near the end of his strength:

After a bad night, a bad morning, as the seas show no sign of abating and the rain is still intense. There is no opportunity to rest at all. We now adopt different tactics to cope with the seas – two of us at a time kneeling to face the oncoming waves and pressing on the rim of the dinghy in order to ride out the foaming crests, the others reinforcing our weight when necessary. This is quite effective with the dinghy almost under water. After passing through three particularly nasty squalls the weather improved and the wind swung us round to the west. This pleases us as we now estimate that we should reach patrolled areas on or about the 8th.

That night was the worst yet. The seas were mountainous and we are surrounded by enormous waves continuously swamping us in great deluges of phosphorescent water. We have tied ourselves to the dinghy which is now almost fully submerged and riding below the water. It does not seem possible that we can survive these conditions being continuously pounded and swamped by colossal seas. It takes all our efforts just to breathe.

Somehow we still maintain our drill to surmount the crests and Ken and Tom are kneeling facing the onslaught, most of the time completely submerged. It seemed that we had been in this situation for an eternity when Tom sinks back exhausted and the Groupie tells me to take his place which I do. My last memory of that night is of wave after wave breaking relentlessly over me. Then oblivion. I must have passed out and from that moment I was never again in a fully conscious state.

With the coming of rescue, George became aware of the destroyer, looking up at the ship's side as it towered above him. He was hauled up onto the deck and the next thing he remembered was being in a cabin with plasma dripping into an arm. Slowly recovering, he and the others were put ashore and after some more treatment, were sent on a month's leave. George continues:

The Navy had taken aboard our dinghy, which then stood in the Group Captain's office as a memento. We understood it was badly worn and would not have lasted much longer even if we had. We wrote a thank-you letter to the manufacturers.

My leave was marred by one sad incident. Upon opening a newspaper one day I read with dismay that HMS *Mahratta* had been sunk whilst on Russian convoy duty and that there were only three survivors. It was hard to take in the fact that all those men, who had been so kind and caring towards us such a short time earlier, had now perished. For me that was one of the blackest days of the war.

CHAPTER EIGHT

US NAVY CATS AND LIBS

Most people in Britain thinking of aircraft engaged in the anti-U boat war would naturally think of RAF Coastal Command. However, there were several Royal Canadian Air Force squadrons engaged in anti-submarine work from bases on the east coast of Canada, and after Pearl Harbor, American army and navy aircraft (not to mention Blimps) operating too. As the war progressed some of the latter even flew under Coastal Command control, but most flew under their own airforce commands. This chapter is included in this book to bring to the reader an idea of how one American squadron flew in two unique theatres while engaged in anti-U boat patrols.

US Navy Squadron VP83 was activated in September 1941 at the Naval Air Station in Norfolk, Virginia, as part of the Fleet Air Detachment, Patrol Wing Atlantic. Its first CO was Lieutenant Commander Ralph Sperry Clarke USN, although they had no aircraft until November. The first six aircraft – PBY5As – were to be collected from San Diego, California, but immediately after the Japanese attack on Pearl, the Squadron began flying patrols off the Californian coast from San Diego into early 1942.

By the spring, however, VP83 was operating from Norfolk, out over the east coast, but with the spread of U boat operations, on 8 June 1942, a detachment of the Squadron was sent to Natal, Brazil, being the only American squadron in that country. Natal is on the most eastern extremity of Brazil, just south of Cape de S Rocque (just south of the fifth parallel). In September Lieutenant Commander Almon E Loomis took command.

Numerous patrols were flown out over the southern Atlantic and several U boats were spotted and attacked. In fact in December 1943, no fewer than 183 operational sorties were flown and seven submarines were sighted or attacked, two being thought to have inflicted some damage, but no kills were claimed. Success finally came on 6 January 1943. Flying Catalina No. P-2, Lt (jg) William R Ford, who would later take part in two more sinkings, was on his way back to base after participating in a three-day convoy escort. They were flying at 5,500 feet when AMM3c Billie Goodall, who had made two sightings previously, yelled to Ford that he could see a submarine.

Ford turned 90 degrees to port and tried to keep a small cloud between him and the U boat's position. Descending at 2,000 feet per minute he managed to approach the sub without being seen. The second pilot was in the bow and on the order to drop, toggled three bombs and a fourth a second later. The target did not appear to be crash-diving as expected and had allowed the Catalina to get down to 35 feet without any challenge from her guns.

Ford watched as he pulled up and to the left. Three explosions occurred close to the boat's starboard, abeam of the conning tower, and the boat appeared to rise out of the water and break into two pieces. Circling round, the American crew could see debris and some men in the water. Two life rafts were dropped while the stern of the boat rose vertically out of the water, bobbing up and down in the rough sea for about a minute before going down.

The U boat was U 164 commanded by Kapitänleutnant Otto Fechner, aged 37, previously the CO of a training boat, the position of the attack being 0158/3923. There were just two survivors rescued, a petty officer and a rating.

The Catalina crew were:

Lt W R Ford USNR Pilot	ARM2c Daniel W Dupree USNR
Lt Robert S Swan USNR	ARM2c Sidney B Hale USN
Ens Marian V Dawkins USNR	AMM1c Earl W Luck USN
AMM3c Billie Goodall USN	ACMM Robert B Stamps USNR

William Render Ford, from Crescent City, Florida, and known as 'Wild Bill' – at least, that was what was written below the cockpit window of his later Liberator – was awarded the DFC (four days after receiving the Air Medal), as was Billie Goodall, who came from Bessemer, Alabama. The rest of the crew were awarded Air Medals.

U 164 had had a short career. A type IXC, she had been built at the Deschimag, Seebeck Werft, Bremerhaven. Launched on 30 April and commissioned on 28 November 1941, her first cruise had been to the Caribbean, having left Kiel, via Kristiansand, in mid-July 1942. Her tower emblem was a shield with oak leaf and acorn. Having got through to the North Atlantic she had been attacked twice on 26 July by aircraft, at 0730 in the morning in position 6039/1800 (German AL3137) and again at 1215, in position 5933/1924 (AL2466), and slightly damaged both times.

Both attacks appear to be the work of 269 Squadron's Hudsons.

Aircraft 'B', piloted by Flight Sergeant T R Prescott, airborne from Iceland at 0333 hours, sighted a fully surfaced U boat at 0530 in position 6042/1802, describing it as very large (at first they thought it was a ship), brownish in colour with grey streaks. He attacked with four D/Cs but saw no results. Despite the time, the position is correct.

At 1013 hours, Flight Sergeant V D Croft, in Hudson 'E' sighted the wake of a boat from 6,000 feet, in position 6008/1853 and attacked it with four D/Cs just after the boat had crash-dived. Again the position is not far out despite the time difference. Some time later, Croft dropped two anti-submarine bombs on another boat in position 5950/1924 while his turret gunner strafed it.

On 29 July U 164 became part of Gruppe Pirat and early the next morning, made contact with convoy ON115. She missed with two torpedoes but followed the ships all day. In the late afternoon she was picked up by an escort vessel and depth-charged, but escaped injury.

Supplied by U 463 on 11 August she finally reached the Caribbean and attacked the dutch freighter *Stad Amsterdam* (3,780 BRT), on the 25th, with a four-torpedo spread. This brought aircaft out and on 31 August American aircraft twice attacked, but only suffered slight damage during the second one. On 6 September it only took one of her torpedoes to sink the Canadian freighter *John A Holloway* (1,745 BRT). Heading home via the North Atlantic, she was supplied by U 461 on 24 September and docked at Lorient on 7 October.

She left again on 29 November, this time for the Brazilian shipping lanes, sinking the Swedish freighter *Brageland* (2,608 BRT) on 1 January 1943, but once again the presence of a U boat brought aeroplanes to the area. At 1153 hours local time on the 6th, she went down for the last time, following the attentions of VP83, 65 miles from the north-east Brazilian coast.

Exactly one week later, on the 13th, Lieutenant (jg) Ludwig in P-10, attacked a submarine in position 0138/3952, not far from U 164's last resting place. His co-pilot, Lieutenant (jg) M G Taylor was the first to spot the wake. Ludwig attacked and dropped four bombs and a large oil slick was observed after the boat had submerged. They could only claim possible damage, but in fact their target was U 507, under the command of Korvettenkapitän Harro Schacht, which went straight to the bottom. Only much later was this credited to VP83 as sunk. Unfortunately his crew is not listed, although the navigator was Ensign Holt.

U 507 had been built in Hamburg, by the Deutsche Werft AG. Also a type IXC she was launched on 15 July 1941, commissioned on 8 October, and left on her first war cruise on 7 March 1942. The tower emblem was a carricature of the dog Bonzo. Harro Schacht was 33, a native of Cuxhaven, from a well-to-do-family, married with two young daughters; he had been in the Navy since 1926.

Heading out via Heligoland on the 12th, she was in contact with convoy ONS76 six days later but escort vessels slightly damaged her in a depth-charge assault. Next day she fired torpedoes at the convoy, but missed. She put into Lorient on 25 March.

She was out again on 4 April, this time headed for the Caribbean. She sank the American tanker *Federal* (2,881 BRT) on the 30th, but then had a run of no hits, firstly on 3 May, followed by three misses on the 3rd. After that her luck reversed. The American freighter *Norlindo* (2,686 BRT) went under from a single torpedo hit on the 4th, but surfacing, Harro Schacht gave food and water to the ship's survivors. The next day another single 'fish' sent the American tanker *Munger T Ball* (5,104 BRT) to the sea-bed, following this with two hits on a second US tanker, the *J M Cudahy* (6,950 BRT). On the 8th another single torpedo ended the life of the Bolivian freighter *Torny* (2,424 BRT).

Slight retribution came on the 9th and 11th with US aircraft attacks, both causing slight damage, but nothing the ship's crew could not fix. Having survived this, U 507 sank the US large tanker *Virginia* (10,731 BRT) on the 12th (having missed two ships over the previous 24 hours), and followed this up by sinking another American tanker, the *Gulf Prince* (6,561 BRT) with three torpedoes, on 13 May.

Some excitement followed over the next couple of days. At 0909 hours on the 14th, she fired a torpedo at the tanker *Eastern Sun*, but missed. However, the tanker had a gun aboard and U 507 had to make a hurried crash-dive. At 1138 hours she tried again with two torpedoes but neither struck home. Soon after midnight on the 16th, U 507 missed with a torpedo on the Honduras freighter *Amala* (4,148 BRT), and trying to do the job with her deck gun, still failed to score a telling hit. SOS calls brought forth an aircraft that bombed the sub 90 minutes later, but caused no damage. Schacht was obviously set on finishing this ship, for at 0400 hours he caught up again, and put a boarding party on her. They ordered the crew into their lifeboats, set scuttling charges and sank her.

The next day U 507 was subjected to depth-charge attacks by a sub-hunter, which caused some slight damage, but then she was on her way home. On 1 June, at 0802 hours, she was bombed by a twin-engined aircraft in the outer Bay area, which again caused some slight damage, but she made Lorient on the 4th.

This attack had been made by Hudson 'O' of 53 Squadron. The crew of Sergeants Henderson, Thomas, Stokes and Urquhart, located a fully surfaced boat at 0812 in position 4628/1159, dropping four

D/Cs from 50 feet, one being judged to have fallen right on it. The boat had dived leaving a brownish oil patch 50 × 100 yards, but nothing else.

War cruise number three began on 4 July, leaving port with U 130 for Brazil. Six days out a surface vessel found her and dropped D/Cs, slight damage being inflicted, but not enough to stop her. By the 28th she was way out into the South Atlantic and being supplied by U 116. On 16 August she was off Brazil and in two days sank five Brazilian freighters.

First to go was the *Baependy* (4,801 BRT) to a two-torpedo spread at 0012, then the *Araquara* (4,872 BRT) at 0203 hours. At 0913 the *Annibal Benevelo* (1,905 BRT) went down. In the afternoon of the 17th, at 1549, down went the *Itagiba* (2,169 BRT), followed by the *Arara* (1,075 BRT) at 1803, all four with one torpedo each. It was nearly six at 2237, but this torpedo missed its intended target.

The next day, 18 August, U 507 survived a bomb and machine-gun attack by an aircraft. Little did either side know of the other's identity, but in fact the aircraft was from VP83! Lieutenant (jg) Lacey, patrolling the shipping lanes in P-6, found the submarine in position 1352/3800, his four bombs making a perfect straddle across her bows. The American crew watched as the sub rolled over 90 degrees before sinking stern first, but it was not assessed as a kill.

On the 19th, U 507 found the 90-ton Brazilian sailing vessel *Jacyra*. Not worth a torpedo, the U boat surfaced and Schacht put aboard a party which sank her with a scuttling charge. Continuing her voyage of mayhem, she found the Swedish freighter *Hamaren* (3,220 BRT) on the 22nd but it took five torpedoes and gunfire to sink her. It is understood that following the sinking of the five Brazilian ships, Brazil declared war on Germany on 22 August, for they insisted they had been inside territorial waters. Germany insisted they had not.

U 507 next became involved in what became a famous incident in the South Atlantic. On 12 September U 156, commanded by Werner Hartenstein, sank the British former Cunard White Star liner *Laconia* (19,965 tons), now used as a troopship, crammed with British soldiers and their families, sailing from Suez. Also aboard were some civilian passengers, wounded servicemen, and 1,800 Italian prisoners of war, mostly captured in Libya, who had an escort of 103 Polish soldiers. In all there were some 2,732 souls on board.

Hit by two torpedoes, she went down with the loss of 1,619 men, women and children. Having discovered Italians amongst the survivors on and in the water, Hartenstein immediately called for help. Dönitz agreed a plan and ordered several U boats to the area, including U 507. When Schacht arrived at the scene on 15 September he took 161 survivors on board (129 Italians, one British officer, 15 women and 16 children) and towed four lifeboats with more people in them. By this time ships from neutral countries had been contacted and two days later U 507's 'guests' were put aboard the Vichy-French sloop *Annamite* but Schacht retained two English officers as prisoners.

Free of this rescue mission, U 507 headed for base, which she reached on 12 October, although she had had one of her crew die on the 7th of dysentery, which affected several crew members. She had been at sea for over three months, sailed more than 16,000 nautical miles and sunk seven ships, bringing her score to 16.

On 28 November she left for her final patrol, sinking the British freighter *Oak Bank* (5,154 BRT) on 27 December and the British freighter *Baron Dechmont* (3,675 BRT) on 3 January 1943, taking the captain prisoner. Five days later she sent the British freighter *Yorkwood* (5,401 BRT) to the bottom, taking her captain aboard too. Five days after that, on 13 January, she met her fate at the hands of VP83 with the loss of all her 55 crew. Schacht had earlier been awarded the Knight's Cross.

That same month of January 1943 came another change in command of VP83, Lieutenant Commander Bertram J Prueher USN, from Bloomer, Wisconsin, taking over.

On 15 March 1943, a Pan American Airways Clipper, en route from Africa to Natal, reported sighting a surfaced U boat and at 0850, Ensign T E Robertson took off in Catalina P-5. At 1035 he sighted the sub but she crash-dived before he was able to make an attack. For the rest of the day, a 'hold-down' was flown by aircraft of VP74 and VP94, and at 1600, Bertram Prueher, in P-4, took off to continue the 'hold' for the night.[1] The boat surfaced at 1900 and a run was made and four bombs dropped but athough a good straddle was made, no apparent damage could be seen.

Success came a month later, 15 April. Again Ensign Robertson was involved while on a barrier patrol in P-5. He was heading back to base at 7,300 feet. At 1500 hours, Ensign E C Morrison, the navigator, went forward to the bow window to take a drift sighting. While taking the sight, he was advised by Seaman E J Kloss that he could see a ship. Morrison immediately identified a submarine and scrambled back to inform Robertson. By this time they had flown past the spot, so Robertson began a turn to port, at which time the boat started firing. One bomb was dropped from height in an attempt to make the crew clear the decks of men. However, the boat was starting to go down.

---

[1] Hold down, the American term for trying to keep a submarine below in order for it to drain its batteries and use up its air supply so that when forced to the surface it cannot avoid aircraft by diving again.

Robertson nosed over from 7,000 feet in a 60-degree angle and reached an indicated airspeed of 245 knots. Down to 2,000 feet, the target was half submerged, but all four depth charges were dropped and directly after the explosions, the submarine surfaced and began to make erratic circles to port. These continued for some 20 minutes, seemingly out of control. All the while some heavy, greyish-black smoke came from the conning tower hatch and an area just aft of the tower. There was also a heavy trail of brown oil. Meantime, the boat's gunners maintained a spirited fire, keeping the Catalina at a distance.

Robertson sent a contact report back as well as making calls to other aircraft in the area. Lieutenant Bradford in P-12 picked this up and headed for the location. Making a run on the surfaced vessel, four bombs went down from 50 feet and then followed this up with four strafing attacks, requested by Machinist Jesse Bamber manning the bow gun. On the fourth run, Bamber turned to Bradford and said: 'Gee, Brad, they're shootin' at us!'

The submarine sank six minutes after the bombs went down and life rafts were dropped to around 30 men that could be seen in the water. It was in fact the *Archimede*, commanded by tenente di vascello Guido Saccardo. Laid down in December 1937 and launched on 5 March 1939, she was completed by 18 April. During her wartime patrols she sank at least three Allied ships. Sailing from La Verdun on 26 February 1943 her cruise area was to the Brazilian coast.

The survivors were seen on three rafts, just one of which was found 27 days later by Brazilian fishermen. It contained two bodies and one live survivor, although he was almost dead. His name was Guiseppe Lococco. He was taken ashore, treated and then handed over to the Americans to become a PoW. It was from him that the identity of the boat sank on 15 April was discovered.

It has not been possible to find the list of each Catalina crew but as each man was decorated with either a DFC or the Air Medal, I can identify the following personnel as members of both crews:

Aircraft captains and DFC winners:
    Ens Thurmond E Robertson USN, from Spatanburg,
       South Carolina
    Lt Gerald Bradford USNR, from Mobile, Alabama

Air Medal recipients:
    Lt Carrell I Pinnell USN – second pilot
    Ens Eugene C Morrison (Robertson's navigator)
    Ens George A Houchin USNR
    Ens Boyce S McCoy USNR

Ens Richard M Riggs USNR
AMM1C William T Hamilton USNR
AMM3c Carl N von Buskirk USN
ARM1c Thomas W Cowdery USNR
ARM2c Jesse Bamber USNR (Bradford's crew)
ARM2c Soloman Greenberg USNR
ARM2c Murray I Jorgensen USNR
ARM2c John W Pittman Jr USN
ARM2c Henry L Slusher USN
ARM3c Raymond M Scott USNR
ACRM Jack V Jenkins USNR
S2c Earl J Kloss USNR (Robertson's crew)
S2c Arnold P Burggraff USNR

On 15 May 1943, VP83 changed its designation to VP107, with
Bertram Prueher still as its CO, the Executive Officer being Lieuten-
ant Commander Renfro Turner Jr. The main squadron was still at
Norfolk, Virginia, but the Natal detachment continued. The old
Catalina flying boats were changed for Consolidated PB4Y-1
Liberators, fifteen being received, and on 20 June a six-plane detach-
ment took the new type down to Brazil.

Renfro Turner, at 0925 while on a training flight in B-7 on 22 July
1943, sighted and attacked a U boat in position 0423/3017. The six
bombs did no apparent damage and the boat submerged. Calling up
other aircraft, Lieutenant J T Burton arrived in B-8 at 1058 and made
a run on the sub which had come back to the surface, but due to an
error no bombs were dropped. One minute later, Turner dropped
his three remaining D/Cs and the boat went under once more. A
three-plane 'hold-down' was then maintained until the next morning,
by a succession of aircraft. At 0640 five aircraft took off to seek out
and sink the U boat. One of the aircraft was John Burton's crew,
taken by Will Ford but with Burton as co-pilot.

On station, Baldwin spotted the sub soon after sunrise, its wake
clearly defined, and at 0646 made an attack. Six D/Cs went down
but in the excitement, neither the pilot nor bombardier remembered
to arm the charges! Unlike the Catalina, pressing the bomb release
in a Lib didn't arm the charges. Nevertheless, two of the D/Cs did
explode, position 0405/3323, with the result that the U boat now
seemed unable to dive. One of the D/Cs had been seen to explode
by the boat's stern, possibly damaging the rudder or stern tube door.
In any event, the boat now seemed to be stern down. Baldwin stayed
out of range of considerable AA fire to await the other aircraft he
knew were on their way.

At 0705 another Liberator headed out to join the others having had a delay in take-off. The American warship, USS *Seneca* was also ordered to the area from Natal. By now, the first five Liberators had arrived in the area. Lib B-6, Lieutenant (jg) G E Waugh, made the first run. Lieutenant W R Ford, in B-8, was also getting ready to make a run when he saw Waugh heading in. Ford kept on, thereby making a co-ordinated approach which would divide the enemy's gunfire. Ford saw the other Lib's front gun send a line of machine-gun fire, the bullets cutting through the water towards, over and beyond the boat, then saw its D/Cs go down from an estimated 60 feet. As the Liberator cleared the stern of the sub it seemed to pause for an instant, then continued on course, but into the sea.

Lieutenant C A Baldwin, in B-12, still circling the combat area, saw the attack by his two squadron aircraft, and witnessed Goree Waugh's machine fly over the sub, whereupon the tail of the Liberator seemed to lift up and a second later the machine plunged into the sea. It seems as though it had been hit by the U boat's gunners although there was a question of whether the machine had in fact been caught by the blast of an exploding D/C. Neither Baldwin nor Ford, however, make mention of this, so the assumption must be that the boat's gunners downed the Liberator. However, it is possible the two surviving U boat crewmen reported that the D/C was responsible, but one has to wonder if they said that rather than court trouble by admitting their boat had shot down an attacker. Waugh's crew were:

Lt G E Waugh USNR	ARM2c Daniel J Ford USN
Lt R S Swan USNR	S2c Donald W McLatchie USNR
Ens William G Maierhofer USNR	ARM2c Anthony J Petaccio USN
Ens Donald R Besmehn USNR	ARM3c Walter G Seidel USNR
ACRM Edward L Chapman USN	ARM2c Stirling F Seymour USN
ARM2c John D Edwards USN	ARM3c George J Zukiewicz USN

Lieutenant Goree Edward Waugh A-V(N) USNR and his crew had arrived in Natal from Norfolk just three days earlier. Robert Swan, of course, had been the second pilot to Lieutenant Ford in the attack on U 164 on 6 January. Both Waugh, from Bluefield, West Virginia, and Swan, were awarded posthumous DFCs and Purple Hearts.

Meanwhile, Ford's bow gunner, AMM1c R L Damiano, had observed a bright white flash just aft of the U boat's conning tower immediately after Waugh's Lib ploughed into the water. By this time they were well straightened out into their run and as the explosions from Waugh's D/Cs were just subsiding, they observed the conning tower well out of the water and the Lib's forward gunners began firing. Ford aimed directly for the conning tower and at 0829 released a stick of six D/Cs.

Heading across the boat through spray, Bill Ford pulled out into a left hand turn to clear and look back. The sub was nowhere in sight. Where the aircraft had crashed there was a boil of water and on closer inspection they could make out life rafts and oxygen bottles from the aircraft, oil and powder residue from the sub attack, some boat's life rafts and about a dozen men in the water. When they finally left the area, there were four life rafts, two with men in them, one empty and one deflated. As they headed back to Natal they overflew the USN tug *Seneca*, and when she later reached the area, she was able to pick up the two survivors from the submarine.

Bill Ford received a Gold Star in lieu of a second DFC. Charles Arba Baldwin, from Kearney, Nebraska, also received the DFC. Ford's crew and that of Charles Baldwin, were:

C A Baldwin USN	Pilot	ARM1c H A Schneider	Top turret
Ens R M Riggs USNR	2nd pilot	ACRM S Greenberg	Radio
Lt D Davis USNR	Navigator	AMM1c S S Shedaker	Flight deck
Ens R M Shannon	Bow gunner	AOM3c M Striano	Tail turret
AM2c S E Nix	St'd waist	AMM2c G Ernst	Port waist
S2c F W Stern	Relief waist		

Lt W R Ford USNR	Pilot	ARM2c D W Dupree	Radio
Lt J T Burton USNR	2nd pilot	S1c D W Carpenter	Port waist
Ens N F P Butler	Navigator	AMM1c R L Damiano	Bow gunner
S1c R L Bohon	Flight deck	ARM1c P G Richter	Top turret
ARM3c G E Meyer	Radar	S2c F J Rackley	Tail turret

The stricken submarine was U 598, commanded by Kapitänleutnant Gottfried Holtorf, aged 30. A type VIIC boat, she had been built at the Blohm und Voss works in Hamburg. Launched on 2 October 1941, commissioned 27 November, the conning tower emblem was the coat of arms of Freiburg. Her first cruise had been to the Caribbean commencing 7 July 1942, from Kiel via Kristiansand. During a reprovisioning rendezvous with U 463 on 5 August, one of her crewmen had been swept overboard and although rescued, died soon afterwards. They took a replacement from U 463.

On 13 August she had been attacked by an (American?) aircraft in position 2051/7421 (German DN73, West Indies) but had suffered no damage. The next day, attacking convoy TAW12 with five torpedoes, she hit three British tankers, the *Michael Jebsen*, 2,333 BRT – sunk, the *Standella*, 6,197 BRT – damaged, and the *Empire Corporal*, 6,972 BRT – sunk. On 16 and again on 21 August she had been attacked by flying boat aircraft, again both American planes, been refuelled by U 509 on 3 September, and sailed into St Nazaire on the 13th.

Her second cruise to the North Atlantic beginning 26 December 1942 as part of Gruppe Sturmer proved uneventful, and she was back by 8 February. Cruise number three started on 6 March, again with Gruppe Sturmer. On 17 March she was depth-charged by a corvette while trying to attack convoy HX229 but escaped damage. The next day, she was located by an aircraft and attacked at 0847 in position 5503/2115 (German AL55). It would appear this was the attack made by Sunderland 'Z' of 201 Squadron, timed at 0850 hours in position 5438/1921, but as they dropped six D/Cs and the boat only noted machine-gun fire, there is a doubt.

U 598 then became part of Gruppe Seeteufel and was depth-charged again by escorts of convoy HX230 on 28 March. Resupplied by U 462 on 11 April she tried in vain to attack convoy HX234 on 23 and 24 April and being resupplied once again, this time by U 461 on 5 May, she returned home on the 13th.

Her fourth and final patrol, to the Brazilian coast, began on 26 June, being refuelled by U 487 in the central Atlantic on 10 July. Twelve days later, near Rocas Reef, VB 107 discovered her, and she was found again and finished off the next day. 44 of the crew died, only two being rescued, an Oberleutnant and a rating.

Lieutenant Commander Prueher attacked a U boat on 11 August[1] but was shot down in the action. It was assessed a definite kill and Prueher was awarded the Distinguished Service Medal but there did not appear to have been any submarine losses this date. However, once the facts became known, everything was clear.

Prueher had taken off from Natal at 0900 hours that morning to search for two reported submarines. At least one of these had been attacked on 3 August, by aircraft of VB129 and the destroyer *Moffat*. This had been U 604, launched from the Blohm & Voss works at Hamburg in November 1941 and commissioned on 8 January 1942. A type VIIC, she was commanded by Kapitänleutnant Horst Höltring, aged 29, who had previously commanded a type IID training boat from November 1940.

Höltring was nicknamed 'The Gangster' by his crew because he always carried a side-arm wherever he went, ashore or afloat. U 604 carried on her conning tower a shield containing a crested wave with a dolphin. She made six cruises and sank six merchant ships totalling almost 40,000 BRT.

She was detected by an American Navy aircraft of VB129, captained by Lieutenant Commander T D Thomas USN, off San Salvador, who

---

[1] The Liberator was due back at Natal on 12 August which is why some accounts of this action show this date rather than the 11th.

attacked her completely by surprise. In the engagement the first lieutenant and one lookout were mortally wounded, and Höltring wounded. Damage to the boat consisted of the port engine being wrenched out of line, the starboard switchboard and a diesel gravity feed tank torn off the bulkhead and one compressor wrecked. Both periscopes were useless and water began entering the hull at various places. She was later attacked by the USS *Moffat* and damaged further.

The location of the crippled boat was at extreme range so Prueher had gone off in Liberator PB4Y (32064) B.1 with the unprecedented fuel load of 3,400 gallons, intending to stay out for 15 hours.

Aircraft from VP107 searched for the missing men until hope of finding them ended on 1 September. The crew had been:

Lt Cdr Bertram J Prueher USN	ARM2c Donald W Gardner USNR
Lt (jg) Grover C Hannever USNR	AOM1c Gordon G Merrick USNR
Ens Robert Tehan USNR	S2c Joseph Milhalsky USN
Ens Eugene L Coupe USNR	ACMM Clyde A Smith
ACRM(A) Howard C Brandon USN	AMM1c John R Van Horn USNR

Prueher's flight plan was for them to set a course due east for 800 miles, and then north-west for 200 miles, intending to cover the area in which the U boat(s) had been tracked by DFs. At about 1130 he reported changing radio frequency and was not heard from again.

What Prueher found were three U boats, in position 0415/2120 – some 750 miles from land – at around 2004 hours on the 11th, U 185 (Maus), U 172 (Emmermann) and a damaged U 604 (Höltring). U 185 and U 172 had been ordered to rendezvous with the damaged U 604, take off her crew and also any remaining oil and provisions before scuttling her. At 1820 this day the UN Navy got a good DF fix on the target submarine, placing her within 100 miles of 04 degrees south and 23 degrees west.

Spotting the gaggle of boats Prueher went into the attack and was met by gunfire from the U boats, and the Lib was claimed by U 185 after it plunged into the sea. Prueher had dropped his bombs and his gunners had strafed the boat as they went over, and although none of the boats sustained more than slight damage as a result, some batteries had been cracked on U 604; however, one rating was killed and another seriously wounded, aboard U 172. Completing their transfer of men and supplies, U 604 was scuttled.

Taking the crew of U 604 home between them, U 185 (with 23 of U 604's crew) was found and sunk by aircraft from the USS *Core* on 24 August, survivors from this episode confirming what had happened

to U 604 earlier in the month. Höltring went down with U 185.
Prueher's place as Commanding Officer was taken by Renfro Turner Jr.

The Squadron now began to operate a detachment from Ascension
Island, way out in the South Atlantic, virtually mid-way between
South America and Africa. This was a strategic location to seek out
submarines heading north or south off the coast of either continent.
The first success came on 5 November 1943. Lieutenant C A
Baldwin was flying B-12 on an anti-submarine sweep south of the
Island, whence they had taken off at 0623 hours. They had been out
five hours when they began to make for base and Baldwin was transferring fuel from the outboard wing tanks, which required the radio
and radar to be turned off. At 1110, they were at 3,500 feet in position
1009/1800. Suddenly the bow gunner reported a ship through breaks
in the cloud, at which time both pilots saw it about five miles off the
port bow, confirming it was a U boat. Everyone went to battle
stations, the fuel transfer stopped and the radio was turned back on.
At 1½ miles Baldwin began a diving turn to port and came across
the sub on her port beam at 75 feet, letting go six D/Cs. Pulling up
and round, a second run was commenced, but the boat was turning
and Baldwin was unable to complete his run, so turned to line up
again for a third run.
This time his positioning was better and he was down to about 25
feet as he released his last three D/Cs but they exploded short.
Looking back they saw that the boat was still turning and trailing oil.
There was also some flak fire, belated and desultory because the Lib's
gunners had been keeping the German crew's heads down. Climbing,
Baldwin contacted B-4, Lieutenant Bill Ford, who was nearby, and
began homing him in. Meantime, the sub was still losing oil and
appeared to be down by the stern and steering an erratic course.
Ford too had been returning following a 600-mile sweep and intercepted the call from Baldwin at 1110 hours. He turned his Liberator,
with *Macahyba Maiden* emblazoned on its nose, and headed for the
action. They arrived on the spot at 1145 and closing to 1½ miles
began to receive flak fire from the boat. The flak exploded to their
port and below, so Ford, thinking they would quickly get the aircraft's
range, turned to port and lost height. Their next fire exploded to
starboard, where the Liberator had been. Ford now straightened up
and headed in, his top and bow gunners opening fire, scoring hits on
the conning tower, whereupon the return fire stopped. At 150 feet
Ford dropped six D/Cs and crossed over the boat at 25-30 feet, the
tail turret gunner then opening fire as they swept over.
Knowing he had dropped short, Bill Ford made a second run, guns
firing, this time dropping the D/Cs from 100 feet. It seemed better

but at least one D/C was 30 feet short. Climbing away, and now short of fuel, Ford headed for home at 1155. They landed at 1335, regassed, rearmed and then the Lib was taken over by Lieutenant S K Taylor, flying it off at 1513 to return to the scene, with almost the same crew, except for Ford and with a new third pilot.

By this time, B-8, with Lieutenant W E Hill at the controls, had taken off from Ascension and coming to the area, now made a run on the boat but met intense flak which smashed into the Lib's No.2 engine. The five D/Cs were dropped short, and streaming smoke from the damaged motor, Hill was immediately heading back to Ascension.

Now Lieutenant Taylor and B-4 arrived (having been in touch with Hill as he headed back), to find B-12 still in contact. Sam Taylor had also picked up radio messages that two B.25s had made horizontal bomb attacks on the submarine, from 1,400 feet. They had been close, but not quite close enough. The Mitchells were from the First Composite Squadron (Force 8012, USAAF), and in fact three were in the air, piloted by Captain Main, Major Akins and Lieutenant Carpenter.

Taylor spotted the oil slick, then the U boat, and manoeuvred for a good run, the boat turning with him and firing its guns. Taylor ran in, dropped down to 70 feet and released five D/Cs at an angle across the boat, while his top turret and bow guns had fired at the conning tower. A circling B.25's tail gunner reported that the drop looked good, but already Taylor was turning for a second run, this time dropping his four remaining D/Cs from 50 feet.

The boat seemed to be slowing and listing to starboard, and as he roared overhead and climbed, she appeared to be settling. Suddenly the front of the U boat reared up forward of the tower and then there was a terrific cone-shaped explosion. As this subsided, everything seemed to be swallowed by the sea. In the middle of all this some 25-30 men could be seen, with three life rafts and something that looked like a huge part of the submarine, which then disappeared. Some of them were on the rafts, some hanging on, but one of the rafts failed to open and sank. Taylor flew across and dropped another, and some men were seen to scramble into it.

An Army PBY (Major Orr of the First Composite Squadron) arrived on the scene and three more life rafts were dropped and after a short while, it flew off to search for HMS *Fort Cumberland*. Taylor's attack was timed at 1700, in position 1010/1812. Their radar located the surface ship some 35 miles distant. Taylor flew to her and by Aldis gave her the survivors' location. A last look at the survivors and then Taylor and the PBY headed for home. The battle had lasted for 5½ hours.

The submarine had been U 848, commanded by Korvettenkapitän Wilhelm Rollmann, from Wilhelmshaven, aged 36. Rollmann was an experienced U boat commander, having been in submarines since before the war. He had won the Knight's Cross in July 1940, commanding U 34, which he took over in October 1938, and already had an impressive record of 21 ships sunk, two captured and sent to Germany, plus another sunk by a mine laid by his boat. He had been in a shore job prior to taking over U 484.

A type IXD2, U848 had been built by Deschimag, Bremen and launched on 6 October 1942, commissioned on 20 February 1943. She had sailed from Kiel on 18 September on her one and only cruise. Via Kristiansand, she had headed out south of Iceland and been depth-charged on 5 October but was undamaged.

Reaching the South Atlantic she sank the British freighter *Baron Semple* (4,573 BRT) but three days later, VB107 ensured she would sink no further ships. All 63 of her crew perished, including the only survivor found drifting in a dinghy by the USS *Marblehead*, who died a few days later.

Bill Ford received a Gold Star in lieu of a third DFC, Charles Baldwin, the DFC too, and Samuel Kyle Taylor, from Whitesburg, Tennessee, also received the DFC. These crews were:

Lt C A Baldwin USNR	Pilot	AMM2c G Ernst	Bow gunner
Ens J Leonard USNR	2nd pilot	ARM1c H A Schneider	Top turrret
Ens L Arnold USNR	3rd pilot	ARM3c L G Ratka	Radio
Ens J C Kiefler USNR	Navigator	AOM2c M Striano	Tail turret
AMM1c S S Shedaker	Camera	AOM3c F W Stern	Port waist
AMM3c L N Tettlinen	St'b waist		

Lt W R Ford USNR	Pilot	ARM2c G E Meyer	Top turret
Ens H C Clark USNR	2nd pilot	AMM2c J F Bennett	Camera
Ens N Feckoury USNR	Navigator	AOM3c E J Fisher	Tail turret
ARM2c D W Dupree	Radio	AMM1c R L Damiano	Bow gunner

Lt W E Hill USNR	Pilot	ARM3c W E Ellis	Radio
Lt W Bofenkamp USNR	2nd pilot	AMM3c J E Schoolfield	Bow gunner
Ens W Scholar	3rd pilot	ACRM L M Bergstrom	Top turret
Ens W Dugan	Navigator	AMM3c R Geer	St'b waist
AMM1c W J Dickinson	Engineer	AMM2c T S Hammer	Camera
AOM2c J A Blair	Tail turret	ARM3c R A Wilson	Bomb bay

Lt S K Taylor USNR	Pilot	ARM2c D W Dupree	Radioman
Ens H C Clark USNR	2nd pilot	AMM1c R L Damiano	Bow gunner
Ens E G Whyte USNR	3rd pilot	ARM2c G E Meyer	Top turret
Ens N Feckoury USNR	Navigator	AMM2c J F Bennett	Camera

As far as is known, this is one of the only instances where crew members in the same aircraft attacked the same U boat, on the same day, in the same action – twice.

Before the month of November was out, VP107 gained another success, this time on the 25th. Liberator B-6 took off from Ascension Island at 0645 on an anti-submarine sweep with Lieutenant (jg) M V Dawkins in command. At 1040, while at 5,200 feet in broken cloud, the co-pilot, Ensign M E Eide, sighted a U boat 30 degrees off to starboard, range about ten miles. Chow was being served in the aircraft which initially caused some confusion but battle stations were quickly taken. Sending out the customary contact signal of 'SSS', Dawkins began a rapid descent through clouds and broke through at 2,000 feet, one mile astern of the target. Dropping down to 25 feet Dawkins brought his Lib in across the U boat and released six D/Cs which appeared to envelope the boat in one large detonation, one D/C actually hitting the decking. As they went over, the tail gunner opened up on a few personnel seen on the conning tower.

The attack had taken the U boat completely by surprise and no AA fire had been directed at the aircraft. However, Dawkins was struggling with his controls, for as he cleared the boat the aircraft's nose dropped while a loss of control was felt, and he almost hit the wavetops. Hauling back on the control yoke, the machine climbed slowly to 800 feet from where they became aware of some belated AA fire, but this was short and well below. Looking down they could see a trail of oil and it looked as if the boat had been blown 45 degrees to port.

The Lib radioman was having difficulty raising a nearby aircraft but base was contacted and the position given. Dawkins felt he had a problem with his machine and uncertain of the extent or nature, and seeing that the U boat appeared severely crippled, he felt it inadvisable to make a second attack. So while waiting for the other aircraft to arrive once contacted by base, Dawkins circled some way off but kept a keen eye on what the U boat might do.

However, his assessment that the U boat had been crippled proved correct for the next thing they saw was the crew abandoning the craft. Dawkins edged in to take pictures but then the boat exploded, an eruption blasting 200 feet into the air. The boat disappeared leaving survivors in the water. Her position was 0630/0540.

The target had been U 849. She was a type IXD2, built at the Deschimag works at Bremen and launched on 31 October 1942. Commissioned on 11 March 1943, she became part of the 12th Flotilla under the command of Kapitänleutnant Heinz-Otto Schultze. Holder of the Knight's Cross he was from Kiel, aged 28. He had previously commanded U 512 and U 432, and sunk 20 ships with another damaged.

U 489 sailed to the South Atlantic from Kiel via Kristiansand and Farsund on 2 October, assigned for a patrol in the Indian Ocean. On 17 November she had been spotted by an observation aircraft from the cruiser USS *Memphis*. Ascension Island had been warned which led to her being found on the 25th. There were no survivors from the 63 men aboard her.

Lieutenant (jg) Marian Vance Dawkins A-V(N) USNR, from Sumter, South Carolina, was awarded the DFC. His crew consisted of:

Lt M V Dawkins USNR	Pilot	ARM1c V C Roberg	Radio
Ens M E Eide USNR	2nd pilot	ARM3c J Simpson	Radar
Ens W A Grimm USNR	3rd pilot	AMM2c F S Renda	Port waist
Ens G H Valentine Jr	Navigator	AMM3c E J Kloss	Camera
AMM1c G Brownlee Jr	Top turret	AOM3c R D Gilpin	Tail turret

U 177 was another type IXD2, in fact the first of the type, built at the same Bremen works as U 849 but she had been commissioned earlier, on 14 March 1942. The IXD2s were called 'Uberseekuh' – overseas cows, due to their remarkable bunker capacity of 422 tons which made them suitable for long distance cruises; they carried 24 torpedoes for their six tubes. Her first commander was Korvetten-kapitän Robert Gysae, an experienced sailor who already had a distinguished career with U 98. He was with this boat for a year commencing March 1941 and had sunk a number of Allied ships and received the Knight's Cross in December 1941.

After her initial trials, U 177 was back in Bremen, but the docks became part of the target for Bomber Command's third thousand bomber raid and in the attack the U boat officer's quarters ashore was hit. U 177's doctor was killed and Gysae badly injured, suffering two broken legs and a badly injured hand. However, he was deter-mined to take his command to sea when it was ready, and on 17 September 1942 when it did so, Gysae, with crutches, was in control. His delighted crew fastened one of the crutches to the conning tower as a talisman and it was adopted as the boat's emblem, a 'U' with a crutch across the top of it.

They left Kiel and via Kristiansand headed out for the South Atlantic and eventually the Indian Ocean. Bad luck struck six days later, a coxswain being washed overboard and drowned during a watch change while proceeding through the Rosengarten in rough weather at 0605 hours. Then at 1330 came an air attack (position 6309/0935, German AE91) which she survived.

On 10 October she sighted an American battleship with destroyer escort, following them for five hours but finding no position for an attack and finally having to break off pursuit. Reaching the South

Top left: Wing Commander Jeaff Greswell DSO DFC, 172 and CO 179 Squadron who helped develop the Leigh Light and attacked the *Torelli* on 4 June 1942.

Top right: The *Luigi Torelli* bearing the scars of battle and of the rocks off the Spanish coast.

Above: Tenente di vasello Augusto Migliorini, commander of the *Torelli* and recipient of the Medaglia de Bronso al Valor Militare.

Left: Wing Commander H deV Leigh (right), with Wing Commander Peter Cundy DSO DFC, of 224 Squadron. The Lib is KG864 – note the Leigh Light beneath the wing.

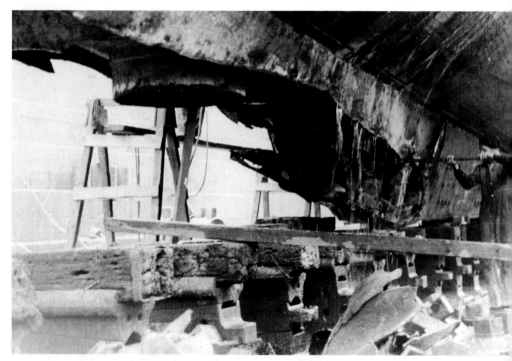

Top: The *Torelli*'s damaged (missing) keel section.

Above: Bullet holes in the *Torelli*'s periscope mounting.

Above right: U 373's first commander, KptLtn Paul Karl Loeser.

Right: Fred Giels, U 373.

left: U 373's conning tower with
...er's lion and von Lehsten's two storks
... babies.

right: S/Ldr A W Southall DSO DFC,
...Squadron, attacked U 373 on 6 July 1942
...was another who helped pioneer the
...n Light.

...ve: WC J B Russell and crew, 612
...dron, attacked U 373 on 1 January 1944.
...: Brignall, Underhill, Bedford, Russell,
...me and May.

...t: Ltn Johannes Glaser (left),
...Lehsten and Ltn Franke, U 373.

Top left: FO K O Moore, sank U 373 and U 629, 8 June 1944.

Top right: Sgt A A Turner, sole survivor of Q/172 Squadron which crashed onto U 459, 24 July 1943.

Above: Fred Giels (left) and Johannes Glaser, on holiday in Austria.

Right: Kayo Moore DSO and FO A P Gibb, his navigator, 224 Squadron.

Top left: Wolf Stiebler, commander of U 461.

Top right: Günther Paas, former crew member on U 461, did not sail on her fateful last cruise.

Above: U 461 supplying oil to another submarine, mid-Atlantic, with another standing-by.

Left: Erich Topp (in white shirt) of U 552, comes aboard U 461 during the refuelling of his boat. Stiebler in hat.

Top left: Clutterbuck and crew, 58 Squadron, August 1943.

Top right: Helmut Rochinski, last man off U 461.

Above left: Helmut Rochinski today.

Above right: Dudley Marrows and crew that sank U 461, 30 July 1943. Rear from left: Taplin, Tainer, Rolland, Marrows, Leigh, Sidney, Jensen; front: Webster, Watson, Pearce, Morgan (with dog), Bamber.

Right: Friends: Dudley Marrows, Wolf Stiebler and Peter Jensen with Sydney Harbour bridge in the background.

Top left: Don Conacher RAAF, survivor from B/10 RAAF, 1 August 1943.

Top right: Some of the other survivors: Sgt Jack Haslam, extreme left; FO John Portus, 2nd from left; FS Phil Cook, 3rd from right; Sgt Pete Petterson, far right. Centre is FL John Jewell DFC who was aboard HMS *Wren* when they were picked up.

Above left: Five survivors of B/10 Squadron cling to the remains of a wing.

Above right: FS E L J Brame (left) and Sgt E Beaudry, 269 Squadron; damaged U 489 on 3 August 1943.

Left: FO Al Bishop DFC, 423 Squadron RCAF.

Top: Sunderland ML783 on Lough Erne, 423 Squadron RCAF.

Middle left: Al Bishop's crew shortly before their last flight. From left, standing: Sgt 'Huck' Finn, Sgt 'Red' McDonnell; rear: FS 'Ginger' Horsburgh, FS 'Kel' Kelly, FO 'Bish' Bishop; middle: Sgt 'Ginger' Hadcroft, PO Harry Parliament, FO Murray Wettlaufer; front: Sgt 'Gos' Gossip and FO 'Art' Mountford.

Above: Huck Finn, Murray Wettlaufer, Al Bishop and Art Mountford at a postwar reunion.

Right: Art Mountford (left) and Murray Wettlaufer.

Top left: George Done, Marrows' navigator on 19 September 1943.

Top right: The downed Sunderland, photo taken by the Germans who shot it down. Note dinghies and crew on the starboard wing.

Above: Ju88C of V/KG40.

Left: The pilot who was credited with the victory, Willi Gutermann, of 14/KG40. (*Goss/Rauchbach*)

Top left: Sgt Stanley Beaton, killed in action 5 February 1944.

Top right: U 763 back at La Pallice. Note two white aircraft silhouettes now adorn its conning tow for her two victories on 4 & 5 February 1944.

Bottom left: Damage to the starboard dive tank caused to U 763 by Liberator A/224 Squadron.

Bottom right: Rudi Wieser today.

Top: Catalina J/259 Squadron on convoy patrol over the Gulf of Aden.

Bottom left: Catalina C/259 (FP126) on bombing practice, the aircraft which helped sink U 197, August 1943.

Bottom right: Len Eccles (left) and Oscar Barnett, 259 Squadron.

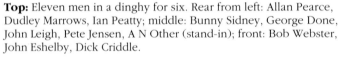

Top: Eleven men in a dinghy for six. Rear from left: Allan Pearce, Dudley Marrows, Ian Peatty; middle: Bunny Sidney, George Done, John Leigh, Pete Jensen, A N Other (stand-in); front: Bob Webster, John Eshelby, Dick Criddle.

Above: Eric Hartley and crew. From left, standing: Sgt A S Fox, -?- , FS K E Ladds, FO T E Bach, Sgt R K Triggol; front: Sgt M Griffiths, FO Hartley and Sgt G R Robertson.

Above right: Paddy Watson, ex-Marrows crew, who could only watch from another Sunderland as the Ju88s attacked.

Right: Paddy Watson.

Top left: Rescue at hand: the Group Captain is on the right with the fore-and-aft hat.

Top right: USN PBY Catalina, the type used by VP83.

Above: Lt William R Ford and crew, by Liberator B-4 named 'Macahyba Maiden', VB107 US Navy, November 1943. Ford wears the shoulder holster.

Left: Survivors of Hartley's crew being brought aboard HMS *Mahattra*, 11 days after being shot down.

Top: Lt Charles A Baldwin (second from left, front) and crew, with Liberator B-12 'Urabu', Novemb[er] 1943. Far right back row is AMM2c George Ernst; third from right is AOM2c Martin Striano.

Bottom left: KptLtn Ernst Cordes, commander of U 763, December 1943.

Bottom right: U 763 at Königsberg, July 1943.

Top: Lookout watch U 763, December 1943. Left, Ltn S Braun, Ob Mt Thorn, Rudi Wieser (in foreground) and Matr Ob Gfr Schwed.

Above: Smoke on sky line following the shooting down of the Liberator on 4 February 1944.

Far left: U 763's quadruple gun.

Left: Sgt Jimmy Fahey, killed in action 5 February 1944.

Top: U 197 – in trouble.

Above: The Barnett crew when led by FO Bill Tennant. Rear from left: Sgt W M Peters, Sgt Charlie Rouse, Sgt R Martin, Sgt J Ball, Sgt Collins; front: Sgt Brewster, Sgt R Anderson, Bill Tennant, FO Len Eccles, Sgt Ken Caligari.

Right: Ken Caligari DFM, 259 Squadron.

Far right: Norman Pearce, 259 Squadron.

Top: Hutton's crew, 36 Squadron. Front from left: R N Holton, J T Hutton, F S Foxon; rear: P C Kiln, I G Ricketts and Tom Layson.

Above left: Damage to Hutton's HF221 tail and rear turret.

Above right: Bamford's crew. Standing: Dick Bamford (left), 'Col' Colquohoun; squatting, Bill Medcalf (left) and Doug Cull, Blida 1943.

Left: Jack Layzell (standing), Ian Colquohoun (leaning), Tom Masters (left), Dick Bamford and Bill Medcalf, Atlas Mountains, 1943.

Top: 202 Squadron Catalina, Gibraltar.

Above: The Finch crew, 202 Squadron. Front, from left: FS Sheridan, Bell, J Finch, FO Goodhew and Sgt Wass; rear: Sgt Sugden, Sgt Radcliffe, FS Barber, Sgt Newman.

Above right: Commander of U 415, Kurt Neide.

Right: Mechanikers Obergefreiter (T) Günter Rautenberg, U 415

Top left: U 415 under attack by 612 Squadron Whitley, 1 May 1943.

Top right: Depth Charge going down from E/612 Squadron Whitley, 1 May 1943.

Above: Sladen and crew. Front from left: Sgt R W Wilson, WO J E Abbey, FL A I Sladen, FO A J Starr; rear: Sgt R B Lawrence, Lt R A Tunnell, FS J J Scott.

Left: U 415 coming into Brest, 6 January 1944.

Top left: Former enemies, now friends. From left: Hilly Hilliard, Jim Hoyle, Des Curtis, Kurt Müller, Raimond Tiesler, Gerhard Gneuss.

Top right: U 155 under assault.

Above: Les Doughty (left) and Ron Grimes, 248 Squadron.

Above right: Kpt Ltn Adolf Piening, U 155's first commander.

Right: Oberleutnant zur See Johannes Rudolf, Commander U 155.

Top: Mosquito VI, MM399 WR-S, 248 Squadron June 1944.

Middle left: Johannes Rudolf, sailing in Holland.

Above: Maurice Webb DFM, 248 Squadron.

Left: Harold Corbin CGM, 248 Squadron.

Top left: U 960 returning from her first patrol, with Günther Heinrich in front and Ltn Wolfgang Dalme, IWO, 1 September 1943. The emblem – 'Union of the Friends of the German Fleet' – is from the town of Potsdam.

Top right: U 976 under attack, 25 March 1944.

Above: A 57mm Molins gun.

Above right: FO Doug Turner (left) and FO Des Curtis, 248 Squadron Special Detachment, 1944.

Right: The damaged gun panel from Hilly's Mosquito.

Top left: Des Curtis (left) and Raimond Tiesler, skipper of U 976, 30 June 1996.

Top right: Hilly Hilliard and Jim Hoyle, 1944.

Above left: Hilly and Jim, 30 June 1996.

Above right: Günther Heinrich, commander U 960.

Left: Alan Peters (left) and WO L A Compton, 248 Squadron.

Top left: Corbin and Webb's crash-landing, 28 December 1944.

Top right: John Davenport (left) and his twin brother Peter, 502 Squadron 1944.

Above: Kramis' crew: L to r: FS W Stetsko, FS J H O'Kane, FL C Desmore, 1/Lt C D Kramis, FO J K Davenport, FS R Overden, Sgt J Robinson, Sgt J A Leavy, 502 Squadron.

Right: Karl Wahnig and John Davenport meet after 52 years.

Atlantic U 177 attacked a freighter on 2 November, but missed but that evening attacked again and sank the Greek ship *C Aegus* of 4,538 BRT. Gysae fired two torpedoes while surfaced and as the ship exploded she showered U 177 with debris. One week later she found the British freighter *Cerion* of 2,588 BRT but missed with four attacks and five torpedoes in heavy weather east of the Cape. Frustrated, Gysae surfaced to engage with gunfire, 3.7 and 2 cm guns being used but while they damaged the ship, she did not sink. Fearful that aircraft might soon be around following the interception of a distress call from the ship, Gysae abandoned the attempt.

Continuing on to the Indian Ocean, she attacked and sank the British tanker *Scottish Chief* (7,006 BRT) on 19 November, and the American *Pierre Butler* (7,191 BRT) the next day. Unfortunately for this ship, Gysae had intercepted her radio message that a ship was ablaze astern of her, thus enabling Gysae to search the area and locate the second ship. Then he made a mistake. At dawn on the 28th a ship was sighted which Gysae took to be an Armed Merchant Cruiser. Three torpedoes sent her to the bottom very quickly although the ship's gunners fired at the periscope until they were waist deep in water. Coming to the surface to inspect lifeboats, he found he had sunk the British transport *Nova Scotia* (6,796 BRT). On the latter ship were around 765 Italian prisoners of war, plus some interned Italian citizens, 134 South African troops as escort and a British crew of around 200. In all 750 men died, although two Italians were rescued and taken aboard U 177. Gysae quickly signalled base to get the Portuguese authorities to send help for the survivors. The frigate *Alfonso Albuquerque* was sent from Lourenco Marques (Mozambique) twelve hours later and managed to rescue 315 survivors, but bodies from the ship drifted ashore for days afterwards.

U 177's rampage continued two days later, sinking the British liner *Llandaff Castle* (10,799 BRT). Her first two torpedoes stopped her and Gysae then allowed 15 minutes for those aboard to abandon the vessel. Most of the 300 persons got away in the boats (being picked up two days later), and then a third torpedo sent her below the waves. The ship only suffered three crewmen lost. On 7 December the Greek *Saranikos* (3,548 BRT) went down, although Gysae surfaced and handed out medical supplies to survivors; on the 12th it was the turn of the British *Empire Gull* (6,408 BRT), which he hit but finished off with gunfire in order to save his last torpedo. Setting course for home he used his last 'fish' on the Dutch ship *Sawahloento* (3,085 BRT) on the 14th. U 177 arrived in Bordeaux on 22 January 1943 after 133 days at sea, having sunk eight ships and damaged another.

Following a long leave and with the boat fully serviced, she left for the South Atlantic and Indian Ocean again, on 1 April 1943. By the end of May she was off the Cape of Good Hope. Gysae found the Capetown-Durban convoy, CD20, soon after it had left harbour and attacked just before midnight of the 28th, but missed. Following the ships, he sank the American *Agwimonte* (6,679 BRT) at 0046 hours and the Norwegian tanker *Storaas* (7,886 BRT) at 0153. Gysae in fact claimed three ships, but he had attacked the *Agwimonte* twice, the second time while the ship's crew watched from the comparative safety of their lifeboats.

Following the convoy he missed a target on 3 June, and on the 6th, found a convoy but was spotted and the escort ships forced him deep and he had to break off the action. Later that morning a flying boat surprised her (3121/1640, German GR25) but she escaped without damage.

Two days later U 177 made rendezvous with U 195 (KK Heinz Buchholz) and transferred a sick crewman to her, as she was returning home. U 177 then headed into the Indian Ocean being resupplied by the German tanker *Charlotte Schliemann* in the third week of June. (This ship had previously been secretly refuelling U boats in the harbour at Las Palmas.) In all there were six U boats about the tanker, and as they could only work in daylight, it took almost three days to complete the task.

Returning to the area south of Madagascar, Gysae sank two more ships. In the evening of 5 July he found and attacked the Canadian freighter *Jasper Park* (7,129 BRT) but missed with two torpedoes. Gysae followed and in the late morning of the 6th sunk her with four torpedoes. Four days later, the 10th, he found the American *Alice F Palmer* (7,176 BRT), heading for Durban, damaged her with two torpedoes and finished her off with gunfire.

There was now a lull in sinkings but on the 29th, Gysae attacked the convoy DN53, sinking the 5,000-ton British steamer *Cornish City*. A week later she sank the Greek 4,195-ton *Efthalia Mari* with torpedoes and gunfire. On 17 August the British 6,921-ton *Empire Stanley*, a collier, was sunk. The explosion blew off the ship's hatches and rained coal down upon U 177's bridge.

With only one torpedo left, and that with a damaged tail, and having been out 4½ months, Gysae decided to go home. He arrived in the South Atlantic and fired his last, defective, torpedo at a freighter on 4 September, but missed. U 177 came into Bordeaux on 1 October, having been at sea for exactly six months!

While he had been at sea Robert Gysae had been awarded the Eichenlaub (oak leaves) to his Knight's Cross (31 May). He had now sunk a total of 12 ships and been at sea for over ten months in all.

The third cruise began on 2 January 1944. This time U 177 had a new captain, Korvettenkapitän Heinz Buchholz. Buchholz had been in command of U 15 when the war began and just three days after the outbreak he laid mines off the east coast of England, which in later weeks sank two coasters off Flamborough Head. He later commanded U 195 and sank three vessels between April and May 1943. Apart from the new CO, all the officers were new and some of the crewmen had left on promotion so it was a very different boat's company that left harbour.

Five weeks out, while about 540 miles west-south-west of Ascension Island, on 6 February, the lookouts allowed a VB107 Liberator to get within a mile of the boat before being sighted and even then there was a brief delay before the alarm was sounded.

The Liberator, B-3, piloted by Lieutenant C I Pinnell, who had been one of the co-pilots in the sinking of the Italian sub in April the previous year, and was now first pilot. They had taken off at 0700 hours following a report that a submarine was in the area of 1000/2400. As visibility was good, despite some cloud, radar was not used in case it should be picked up by the U boat. At 1025, at 2,600 feet, the bow lookout sighted an object at 12 miles and Liberator B-10 nearby was alerted. Pinnell turned towards the object which showed a heavy wake and then became recognisable as a U boat.

Despite what survivors said, Pinnell reported being met by light flak fire at two miles, at which time he put his aircraft into a power glide then pulled up. At ¾ of a mile and at 1,000 feet he began his attack run, the bow gun opening up on the conning tower and the flak ceasing. At 1029 six D/Cs went down from 100 feet as the Liberator roared over the boat, gun flashes now being seen from the conning tower again, returned by the rear gunner as they went over. They climbed to port in a sharp bank to 800 feet and circled.

The U boat had disappeared but as the water cleared the conning tower could be seen just under the water, so Pinnell came in again to drop his last three D/Cs. The boat appeared to have turned to starboard by some 75 degrees and the D/Cs fell ahead of the conning tower. Pinnell levelled off and climbed, making a slow turn to the left. As he flew back over the area the crew could see a number of men in the water and a life raft was dropped during a second pass over the spot. They then photographed the men in the raft, then circled until a relief aircraft arrived at which time Pinnell returned to base.

Survivors relate that the attack came so swiftly that Buchholz, who was about to go up to the bridge, had only just got out of the conning tower hatch when his command began to settle, water pouring down into the control room. In a few moments the U boat sank, taking down with her two-thirds of her crew. Two American vessels were contacted, the SS *Franka* and the USS *Omaha*, the latter arriving first to pick up fourteen men from the sea.

Lieutenant (jg) Carrell Ivan Pinnell USN, from Cammargo, Illinois, was awarded the Distinguished Flying Cross, to add to his Air Medal of April 1943. His crew was:

Lt C I Pinnell USN	Pilot
Ens J M Leonard USNR	2nd pilot
Ens J D Cook USNR	3rd pilot
Ens R S Swanson USNR	Navigator
AMM1c S S Shedaker	Camera
ARM1c W R Zudrell	Top turret
AMM3c H L Anderson	Bow gunner
AOM3c W H Phelps	Tail turret
ARM3c R L McKernan	Radio

Leonard and Shedaker, the latter the plane captain, had been with Lieutenant Baldwin in the sinking of U 848 the previous November.

On 10 April 1944, Lieutenant E A Krug Jr, in B-8, attacked a U boat in position 1537/1700 at 1141 hours. Six D/Cs were dropped and the sub circled for around 25 minutes before she slowly settled. She appeared to sink, but she was later discovered to have proceeded slowly into the Indian Ocean. This was U 843 on her way to the Far East.

A type IXC40, commanded by Kapitänleutnant Oskar Herwartz, this was another Deschimag, Bremen, boat, commissioned on 24 March 1943. On her first cruise beginning 7 October, she had sunk no ships and escaped an air attack. Now on her second cruise, to the Indian Ocean, beginning from Lorient on 19 February, she sank the British freighter *Nebraska* (8,261 BRT) on 8 April which had brought VB107 over her two days later. She gave her position as FT14 (1509/1645). Two months later she arrived at Batavia.

Coming home, commencing 10 December 1944 she was attacked by Mosquito aircraft from 235 Squadron in the Kattegat on 9 April 1945. Evading them she had wandered into a minefield, struck one and sank with the loss of 44 of her 56 crew.

VB107's last U boat sinking came on 29 September 1944, this time operating from Brazil. Three Liberators had departed Natal across what was thought to be a southbound U boat route. B-9, Lieutenant J T Burton, took off at 0005 hours, Lieutenant E A Krug Jr in B-7, at 0010, and Lieutenant Roewer in B-6, at 0040 following a mechanical delay.

At 0558, Burton made a visual contact with a submarine in position 1045/2530, still in a pre-dawn twilight.

Burton headed in at 0602 to drop five D/Cs from around 40 feet and following this, the boat appeared to settle stern down. Burton radioed Krug and Roewer, and indeed, Krug had already spotted anti-aircraft fire in the distance and was coming in, arriving at 0606. Just two minutes earlier, Burton made a second run, but his four D/Cs hung-up, although his gunner's fire seemed effective.

Heading out of the way, Burton saw Krug coming in but he was in a bad position due to the sub's evasive action, tight circles to port, and did not drop. Three minutes later both captains made co-ordinated runs, Burton's four D/Cs still not falling, but Krug let go six D/Cs but having over-estimated his speed, they fell short.

All the while the boat had been throwing up AA fire, and Krug turned to make another run, dropping his three remaining D/Cs and making a good straddle. Burton followed, having had his crew remove the arming wires by hand: he was able to salvo his D/Cs on the oil slick on the spot the U boat had disappeared.

After Krug's final attack, the U boat had been seen to blow up from about five feet forward of the conning tower to the bow, and survivors were seen struggling in the water. Thirty seconds later the rest of the submarine disappeared from the surface. Despite large quantities of AA fire, only Krug's B-7 had been slightly damaged, but not enough to interfere with its performance. Both planes now circled the survivors and dropped life rafts, and when Roewer finally arrived, he too dropped a third, and took pictures of the 15-20 survivors.

The U boat was U 863, commanded by Kapitänleutnant Dietrich von der Esche. He was aged 29 and had previously been watch officer aboard U 98, then CO of U 586. Built at the Deschimag works in Bremen, she too was a type IXD2 of the 12th Flotilla, and launched on 29 June 1943. Commissioned on 3 November she was ready for duty in July 1944, sailing from Bergen on the 20th for the South Atlantic and Indian Ocean, after leaving Kiel on the 18th. She was immediately found, attacked and damaged by a Mosquito aircraft from 333 Norwegian Squadron in position (German) AN34. Slightly damaged, but with three men severely wounded, she had to put back into Trondheim from whence she sailed on the 26th. Two months later she met VB107 to become a total loss. None of her 69 crew survived.

Lieutenant John Thomas Burton A-V(N) USNR, from Houston, Texas, was awarded the DFC, which he added to his Air Medals of 23 July 1943 and 2 January 1944. Lieutenant Edward Arthur Krug Jr USN, from Chicago, Illinois, who had received a Letter of Commendation for his actions on 10 April, now received the DFC. Their crews on 29 September were:

Lt J T Burton USN	Pilot
Lt R A Riley	2nd pilot
Ens P W Gallagher	Tech Obs
AMM1c W J Dickinson	Top turret
AMM2c E A Nicpon	Port waist
ARM3c A H Verity	Radio
AOM2c W H Mosher	Bow gunner
AMM3c F E Resner	Tail turret
ARM2c C W Hilgeman	Radio
Lt E A Krug Jr USN	Pilot
Lt M M Deutsch	2nd pilot
Ens G H Helfenbein	Navigator
AMM1c C W Richards	Top turret
AMM2c D M R Laux	Tail turret
ARM2c M I Jorgensen	Radio
ARM3c C A Pollard	Flight deck
AMM3c L A Palmer	Port waist
S1c G B Mangano	Camera
AOM3c C B Taylor	Bow gunner

On 1 October 1944 the unit's designation changed to Patrol Bombing Squadron 107. Its last operation was flown on 1 November and it then became engaged in an extensive training program. Although it did fly on a few other wartime patrols while so engaged, it did not see further action. Nevertheless, its eight sinkings made it amongst the most prominent of the US Navy's anti-submarine squadrons in WWII.

CHAPTER NINE

INTO THE TEETH OF FLAK

As the reader has already discovered, finding a U boat was one thing, making a successful attack was another. By the mid-war years an immediate crash-dive was a thing of the past, which only happened if the captain or senior watch officer thought they had time enough to get under the waves before depth charges came splashing down around them.

Once, however, it was fully realised that fighting back gave them a chance of survival, and later, in mid-1943, when Admiral Dönitz actually ordered his captains to remain surfaced and fight back, then aircraft crews started to discover just how vulnerable they could be.

Coming into a low level attack – it had to be low level in order for the depth charges to be placed accurately and to be effective – and provided the submarine's anti-aircraft gunners could keep a steady nerve in the sight of approaching death, the risk to the aircrew and aircraft was enormous. A huge four-engined Sunderland or Liberator, even a twin-engined Wellington, was a big target. Approaching aircraft didn't have any vast array of front armament to fire in order to keep the U boat's gunners' heads down or to affect their careful aim. A Sunderland, for instance, only had a lonely .303 Lewis gun at first, and other aircraft might only have two .303 Brownings. And the front gunner too was probably being shot at by the submarine.

Bob Yarston was a pilot with 269 Squadron and remembers a point very much in the minds of aircrew:

> In order for our depth charges to have their maximum effect, the aircraft would have to approach the submarine in level flight, (50 feet and at 160 knots in Wellingtons) so therefore we knew the German gunners would have a head-on 'no deflection shot'.
>
> I know that when operating at night we used to pray that if we ever located a U boat the gunners would be pointing away from us when we switched on the Leigh Light. If they had to

traverse their guns round it would give us a valuable few seconds before they opened fire.

We have already read about aircraft being shot down before or after dropping their depth charges, and there are numerous reports of aircraft signalling base that they were about to attack a submarine, and that was the last anyone heard of them. Untold (unknown) stories of great heroism might only be suggested by a simple note in a U-boat's log – 'attacked by aircraft, aircraft shot down.' Undoubtedly the U boat gunners were good, they needed to be and they needed to keep a cool head. None more so were those aboard U 763.

U 763 was built at the Kriegsmarinewerft, Wilhelmshaven as a type VIIC, and commissioned on 13 March 1943. Her commander was Kapitänleutnant Ernst Cordes, who was three months short of his 30th birthday, formerly WO on U 123 and then CO of U 560. U 763's tower emblem was a Unicorn rampant on a shield.

As part of the 3rd Flotilla, U 763 left Kiel on 14 December for the North Atlantic and on the 28th was part of Gruppe Rugen. From the beginning of the new year of 1944 she was sending weather reports back to U boat HQ. Seven days into the new year she was located by a flying boat using a Leigh Light, at 0040 hours, but it was kept at bay by her gunners.

Continuing with her weather reporting, by the beginning of February she was in the Biscay area, on the way to her new home at La Pallice, but on the 4th she was found again, this time by a Liberator of 53 Squadron, in position 4539/0745 (German grid BF4988), at 0829 hours. They had already been at action stations following nearby aircraft at around 0330. The boat's log noted (first person, the captain):

0435 Surfaced for recharging and ventilation.
0645 Searchlight illumination on bearing of 20 degrees; no contact. I decided to leave [the area] on the surface, and set anti-aircraft action stations and continued at full speed.
0650 At five minute intervals, five 'Aphrodite' activated.[1] Stood down AA action stations.
0759 Dawn twilight begins.

---

[1] Aphrodite was a German radar decoy carried by U boats. It comprised a hydrogen-filled balloon three feet in diameter. Once launched it would be anchored by a connecting 180 foot wire. On an aircraft's radar it would appear as a blip similar to that made by a U boat. It appeared to have achieved little, although it would seem that U 763 benefited from hers on this cruise.

0819 'Aircraft!' Immediately before diving an aircraft was reported on a bearing of 310 degrees, course 90 degrees, approximate distance 8,000 m, altitude 200 m, approaching in level flight.

0820 Naxos contact. Enemy turned and flew at low level over the boat to port from astern. I decided on account of the short distance available for defence to stay on the surface. At a range of 3,000 m opened fire with all guns and turned hard starboard at full speed. Enemy turned slightly to port and flew parallel to the boat at a distance of about 3,000 m.

0824 (signal to base) Being attacked by aircraft: marine quadrant BF 4888. (Immediately after submerging it was established that the radio-room had encoded the wrong quadrant, that should have been BF4988.)

0826 Enemy turned to port and went far back for its next approach.

0829 Enemy again flew over the boat from astern to the port side at low level (50 m). The boat again went at full speed and on opening fire turned hard to starboard. Enemy (type Liberator Consolidated 32) with American insignia [sic] returned fire with its aircraft guns and obtained hits on the conning tower on the port side. No personnel casualties. We ourselves scored hits on the wings and on the mid-fuselage. Darting flames and smoke trails were observed. After dropping a stick of bombs (6 to 8) which fell in the water diagonally to port at about 120 m distance (large wall of water), the machine turned on the inside curve and fired with its guns, affording thereby a good target. It flew off to about 5,000 m.

0840 The machine turned to starboard on to a new approach. 'Shot Down!' The machine pitched down on to its burning right wing and exploded on impact. Parachutes not observed. Because of the increased danger from the air and the favourable flying weather (middle height, broken cloud cover; bright daylight; good visibility) I decided to dive straightaway.

0845 'Alarm' – dive to 60 m.

Cordes also commented in the log:

'Those recommended to the boat by the Gunnery School at Schweinemunde proved themselves in the role of anti-aircraft fighters (uninterrupted supply of ammunition). The shooting by all weapons through all sea and weather conditions was very commendable.'

One of his gunners was Rudolf Wieser:

> I saw the Liberator as I was on duty on the port 2 cm twin flak gun. I immediately had the aircraft in the cross-hairs and received permission to open fire . . . . the aircraft swerved slightly to port. My line of fire remained good, even though the attacker succeeded in dropping his bombs. My flak attendant did excellent work on the ammunition supply. After turning for a new attack the machine cart-wheeled over on its wing.

From what is noted in the log, it seems obvious that the pilot knew his aircraft had been hit and set on fire but even so tried desperately to make a second run before he was prevented from doing so, but he then lost control and plummeted into the water.

The Liberator, far from being from an American outfit, was, as noted earlier, from 53 Squadron. Aircraft 'F' (BZ795) from St Eval had left to fly a Percussion R3 patrol at 2230 hours on 3 February. At 0811 it sent a Flash Report to base indicating it was about to attack a U boat. Like so many other signals during the war, this was the last. The crew were:

FL D A Bell	Sgt J W Churchman
Sgt T A Patey	FS E J Fowler RAAF
FS J O Lewis RAAF	Sgt R D Howard
FO N J Williams RAAF	Sgt C Lidgett
FS S G Hill RAAF	

Cordes took his boat away from the area, still heading for his French port. Night came again. Coastal Command, of course, were fully aware that there was a U boat in the area and further aircraft were looking for her. At 0133 on the morning of 5 February she was located. The captain's log continues:

0106　Surfaced for recharging and ventilation.

0133　'Aircraft'. Naxos contact. As the report came from the bridge, a searchlight lit up briefly on a bearing of 310 degrees. Aircraft approaching, altitude 100 m. Boat turned hard to starboard, both engines at full speed. Aircraft passed the boat obliquely on the port side at 100 m. Immediately opened fire. No hits observed. Enemy turned off to port and quickly disappeared from sight.

0138　Naxos contact. Enemy in sight in horizontal flight on starboard quarter, approximate course 150 degrees, height 100 m. Opened fire. Enemy released a stick of bombs and released a light marker. The U boat, steering hard to starboard, was not over flown; the bombs fell into the water 2-300 m to port. Hits [on aircraft] observed. No fire from aircraft guns. Aircraft (probably Lancaster type) pulled up immediately into the clouds. On this attack no searchlight was used.

The aircraft was another 53 Squadron Liberator (BZ815 'D'), out on an Air Sea Rescue search for the missing aircraft of Flight Lieutenant Bell and crew. It had taken off at 1755. At 0135 hours a radar contact was made at seven miles (position 4527/0654, German BF8135), which enabled U 763 to pick it up on her Naxos apparatus. Heading in, the pilot had sighted the U boat and attacked with five D/Cs (the sixth failed to release) – it only carried six as the crew were on an ASR sortie. They straddled the wake but intense AA fire shot some holes in the Lib's tailplane.

As the aircraft climbed and circled so the crew picked up what appeared to be a second and then a third U boat in the area. Homing procedure was undertaken until the aircraft reached its PLE when the pilot set course for base. The U boat(s) were still on the surface, and they also remarked that they had seen no sign of any dinghy. However, they had not been looking for the latter part of the patrol, being occupied with the U boats. In reality, they were probably seeing the Aphrodite decoys. The crew of D/53 were:

PO L L Esler RCAF	Sgt D M Holden
PO J L Knight	Sgt T W Ellison
WO W R Kinsman RAAF	WO R C Lauer RCAF
FS R J Crompton RAAF	FS F Clegg RNZAF
FS A W G Brown	

(Esler, as a Warrant Officer, and flying with Knight, Kinsman, Brown and Lauer, had attacked and damaged U 386 back on 3 July 1943, in an earlier Liberator 'D' – BZ731.)

U 763 continued on, but Coastal Command were far from finished with her yet. They had the scent in their nostrils.

0141   Naxos contact.
0159   Enemy [aircraft] in sight to starboard astern in level flight, height 5-600 m, range 12-1500 m, and order 'Hold fire'. I see a light-cluster fall quickly to the water; they are new floating light clusters. 6-8 bombs were dropped with short fuses. The enemy must have engaged Aphrodite. Continued running on an easterly course.

0203 Naxos contact; three Aphrodite activated. Enemy in sight
astern to starboard, at 400 m altitude, in level flight. No
searchlight. Aircraft intersected our course 100 m in our
wake, and was engaged with all guns. Jamming on both
twin guns. Light marker dropped. Hits observed, no bombs
dropped. No fire from aircraft's guns.

This was a Wellington from 172 Squadron out of Chivenor, aircraft
'M' (HF282), flown by FO C S Rowland and crew. They found a U
boat at 0206 in position 4539/0640, attacked, met AA fire and had
both wings and fuselage holed by cannon shells.

They had obtained a radar contact at six miles. As they turned
onto course they were distracted by some lights on the water and
decided to turn to investigate. As Rowland circled and was about to
illuminate the area, he spotted a wake half a mile away but too close
to be able to make a run in. He flew off to position the aircraft and
his radar operator picked up the target on screen. Coming in at 100
feet the Light was switched on and this illuminated a U boat on the
surface, and he attacked from 75 feet with six D/Cs.

No sooner had the Light gone on than the U boat opened fire, the
Wellington being hit in three places by cannon shells. The navigator
replied with the front guns. After the attack they climbed away to
the left, seeing the D/Cs explode astern. The aircraft became difficult
to fly due to the damage to the tail, so Rowland decided to head
back home.

FO C S Rowland	Pilot	WO J F Wilmer RCAF	WOP/AG
FO A Mason	2nd pilot	Sgt G B Schwinge	WOP/AG
FS D R Pledger	Navigator	Sgt E Oliver	WOP/AG

In their debrief report, this crew too believed there were three U
boats in the area.

0212 Naxos contact; searchlight beam. Enemy in low level flight,
astern to starboard . . . . , but no blinding effect, but a
glaring bluish light. Boat turned hard to starboard. Opened
fire but only a few rounds, since all guns on which jamming
had already been reported . . . jammed repeatedly. One
man (armourer) was slightly injured by a fragment (of
metal). Light marker released by the enemy.
0214 Enemy turned shortly before reaching our stern and
dropped a stick of five bombs which fell in the water 100-
150 m to port. Aircraft gunfire from rear and top turrets;
hits heard on boat.

0223 Alarm! Dived to 100 m, as all AA weapons unreliable. No bombs dropped. Hard starboard rudder applied. No further findings.

Another Leigh Light Wellington in the area was 'H' of 304 Polish Squadron (HF200), piloted by Flying Officer L Antoniewicz on a Percussion M2 patrol. It was on patrol from 2206 to 0837 hours. At 0325 it received a message from base telling it of the U boat which was being attacked on the surface. Antoniewicz headed for the area, which he reached at 0401, but could only report seeing flame floats and burning flares, but no contact with the submarine.

0416 Between the attacks the enemy was briefly seen repeatedly circling at a height of 6-800 m. But he always disappeared from sight quickly. Due to the long range (over 3,000 m) and so as not to betray our position and course, we did not open fire. The enemy bombing at 0208 had proved inaccurate. The aircraft did not hit the boat, and was doubtless deceived because of Aphrodite. On the boat's opening fire he had immediately launched a light-marker, and so marked the last position, flew off, orientated and turned on to a new attack. The attack was more skilful and more dangerous than the day before.

U 763 sailed out of immediate danger and later dived. During daylight of the 4th, she continued towards France and contacted base to set up the rendezvous with her escort into harbour. The log, continuing on the evening of the 5th recorded:

2016 Surfaced for recharging and ventilation. AA action stations manned immediately. Because of the favourable flying weather (bright moonlight) and the proximity of firing positions, I decided on the deception of the foe by the deployment of Aphrodite.
2033-
2038 Three Aphrodite activated.
2102-
2110 Three Aphrodite activated.
2205 Aircraft! No radio location signal identifiable, although Naxos apparatus was checked and found to be clear. Three light flares seen to port, estimated range 6-8,000 m. Immediately afterwards an aircraft was confirmed on the right and could not have had a radar contact as it did not make a direct approach to overfly the boat. Aircraft height

100-200 m, course 150 degrees. Boat turned hard astarboard and cruising speed maintained. At 1,500 m, all weapons opened fire; all weapons were well on target. Left side engine caught fire. Enemy turned slightly to port and opened fire from rear gun-turret. No bombs released and the boat was not overflown. Further hits were observed on the nose turret and the wing.

2209 Radio signal made: Attack by aircraft, marine quadrant BF8319. The aircraft (probably a Liberator, Consolidated 32) turned to port and flew about 400 m. The fire was getting rapidly larger as it flew off. We continued firing with the twin AA guns. It quickly lost height, and at 2211, crashed from a height of 50 m, and exploded on impact.

2211 'Victory'. Proceeded at full speed on course 150 degrees to crash location with all hands at action stations.

2220 Arrived at crash location. Large oil and petrol patch still burning in places. Switched to electric motors.[1] No survivors seen; only a no-longer-inflated life raft, a large landing wheel, and small pieces of wreckage. Returned to diesel engines and resumed course for base.

Rudi Wieser was again at his gun:

During the night of 5 February 1944 we were again located by aircraft, and deployed Aphrodite – metal foil balloons that misled aircraft. From between 0133 and 0223 hours the attacks were repeated; we submerged around 0223.

We proceeded submerged till 2016, surfaced and proceeded on the surface. At about 2205, another aircraft attacked, coming in low over us from astern. It had been attacking us from 2145 without success. At 2205 it had dropped a flare to see us better and at that point it offered us a clear target.

Immediate permission to open fire was given, so that all weapons were engaged in combat. Here too my line of fire was good, so that after only a few rounds the left-hand engines were on fire. My 2 cm twin flak gun had no stoppages. The other weapons were also in order. We assumed that we had shot down a Liberator, but today we know that it was a Halifax.

And indeed it was a Halifax, a machine from 502 Squadron. 'R' had taken off from St Davids, at 1721 hours to fly a Percussion patrol.

---

[1] Probably the reason for switching to electric motors was that being quieter than the diesel engines, it would give men on the bridge a better chance of hearing calls from any survivors in the water.

It was carrying four 600-lb anti-submarine bombs and 12 anti-submarine flares. The crew was as follows:

FO F T Culling-Mannix RNZAF   FO D J Williamson
FO L Woolcott RAAF   WO S Beaton
FO D E Celdart RCAF   FS I N Botsford RCAF
WO M J Fahey   Sgt C Ostler

It is easy to forget that each wartime incident brings forth untold grief to families of those involved. This story really began through the desire of Warrant Officer Jimmy (Paddy) Fahey's niece to know exactly what had happened to her uncle. She in turn contacted not only this author but also found Herr Rudi Wieser, and together we pieced together the story of U 763's encounter with aircraft of Coastal Command over these two days, which resulted in two aircraft being shot down, and two others slightly damaged by the U boat's gunners.

In February 1944, the Fahey family in Dublin had just started to grieve:

Officer Commanding
No.502 Squadron
RAF Station
St Davids
Nr. Haverfordwest
Pembrokeshire
8th February 1944

Dear Mrs Fahey,

I am writing on behalf of my Squadron to say how very deeply we regret that your son is missing from air operations. Matthew was Wireless Operator Air Gunner of an aircraft which took off on the afternoon of Saturday February 5th on an anti 'U' boat patrol. Unfortunately no message was received from the aircraft at any time during its patrol, however, the entire patrol area is being scoured. Our vigil will not relax and should our efforts be rewarded you may rest assured we will do all in our power to effect a rescue.

His Captain, Flying Officer F T Culling-Mannix, a New Zealander, was a most experienced pilot with many operational sorties to his credit.

Your son has been with us since May 1943. His courage and devotion were of the highest order and he always carried out his duties in a capable and cheerful manner no matter how arduous, or hazardous they were. The Squadron grieves the loss of a noble character and a gallant gentleman who was sincere in all he did.

Our sympathy which is both deep and sincere goes out to you
and all those who knew and respected Matthew as we did.

Yours sincerely,

(SGD) C A Maton S/Ldr

(for) Officer Commanding, No. 502 Squadron

(Fahey's first names were Matthew James, which is why Squadron
Leader Maton used Matthew in the letter, although the family always
knew him as Jimmy. On the Squadron, of course, it was Paddy.)

On the same day a letter also went to Jimmy's brother Colm, an
Aircraftman with 455 Squadron RAAF, based at RAF Leuchars, in
Scotland:

Dear Fahey,

I received your letter this morning and very much regret to say
that we have not heard any more news of your brother.

I am attaching a copy of the letter written to your mother which
gives all the details that are available. As nothing was heard of
the aircraft after it left its base we are unable to tell what has
happened.

The patrol has been covered by many aircraft since, but we
have not received any further information. During the period your
brother served with No.502 Squadron, he established a fine
reputation as a capable Wireless Operator Air Gunner and his
loss is a great blow to us all.

The Squadron extends its deepest sympathy to you in the sad
blow you have sustained.

Yours sincerely,

N M Bayliss, Wing Commander

U 763 arrived at La Pallice on 7 February, happy to have survived
the last few days crossing the notorious Bay of Biscay. On 19 March
she sailed on her second war cruise, heading out in company with
U 960. If they thought they might meet aircraft again, they were right.

On the 27th they reported that seven Mosquito aircraft (in fact
Beaufighters of 248 Squadron) attacked both boats in position 4609/
0135 (German BF6853) but sustained no damage. However, both
boats had to put back into La Pallice now that their presence was
known. They remained in harbour until 11 June. The Invasion of
Normandy had taken place and every boat was on the alert for
operations in the western Channel. Eight days later an aircraft came
over U 763 but it was kept from attacking by flak fire. Once more
she was back in harbour, this time Brest, in order to fix a problem
with her periscope. (See also Chapter 13.)

She sailed again, this time on 20 June, for operations in the Channel. Two days later she fired a torpedo at a destroyer, but missed, an operation she repeated the next day, although this time the boat was depth-charged by the hunting group of ships and she was lucky to escape undamaged.

She now headed for the Norwegian coast, and on 5 July, sank with three torpedoes the Norwegian freighter *Ringen* of 1,499 BRT, at 1803 hours. Four hours later she once more chanced a shot at a destroyer, missed again, and was once more subjected to a depth-charge assault which she survived. Not to be thwarted she attacked a hunting group on the 11th, but again missed the nimble targets.

On 15 July, U 763 was dicing with aircraft again, while trying to get back into Brest harbour. At 0206 hours, in position 4815/0455 (German BF5221), a Halifax of 58 Squadron located her. It picked the boat up on radar at eight miles while the second pilot was at the controls. On the captain's instructions the aircraft turned to port and headed in to drop flares and after identifying a U boat, turned and headed in again.

At 0208, at 1,400 feet, they saw three merchant vessels in a vic formation with a fully surfaced U 763 in the middle. The aircraft was too close to effect an attack so turned through 270 degrees to port as the escort vessels opened up with gunfire, then the flares burnt out. The captain took over the controls and climbed to 4,000 feet, dropping more flares and after seeing if they could bomb through some cloud, manoeuvred to come in again and despite the cloud and gunfire, dropped four 600-lb anti-submarine bombs.

They missed, and the Halifax had to fly off. An hour later it flew back seeing all the escort vessels still in evidence and the U boat still there, 1½ miles to the south. U 763 entered Brest on the same day, then went to La Pallice. The crew of Halifax 'Y' (HX178) of 58 Squadron was:

SL W D C Erskine-Crum	FO G H Hodson
FO R E Robinson	FS A R Keech
FL G L Conner	FS J L Mills
FS W D Dewar	Sgt S J Elliott
FO G B Loveday RCAF	

Cordes now handed over command to Leutnant zur See Kurt Braun and the boat was transferred to Norway. Braun, born in August 1923, had previously been IIWO aboard U 763. Converted to a schnorkel boat, she left La Pallice on 14 August, now that the Biscay ports were under threat from invading Allied forces, sailing the long way round England. She had almost reached Bergen but on 24 September was found once more by aircraft.

She was off Alden Island at 0415 hours, position 6100/0407 (German AN2415) and the pilot of the attacking aircraft was Squadron Leader John Downey, 224 Squadron. U 763's log records:

0500 Schnorkel run ends.
0506 Surfaced.
0524 Target indicated bearing 154 degrees, range 6,000 m, reducing to 5,000 and then 4,000 m.
0525 Aircraft! Brilliant searchlight ahead to starboard, range 600 m. Altered course hard to starboard. Stick of 4-6 bombs dropped, no fire from aircraft guns. All weapons quickly jammed. Overflown. Good bombing line. In flying away the aircraft launched small signal flares . . . Boat ready to submerge.
0528 Alarm! Crash-dive. Severe damage: starboard diving tank knocked out, both in couplings out of commission, both compressors misted, diesel air mast lost, both diesel blowers damaged, both bulkheads hit hard, 3 TV severely damaged, although it all seems to be temporary.

John Downey relates:

The U boat was fully surfaced and we, flying a box patrol over a calm sea, picked it up on ASV at some distance. Probably it had just surfaced. We homed straight in, but bent the course a bit to avoid attacking with the aurora borealis behind us, because it was particularly bright that night. I'm sure the U boat was taken completely by surprise, because it took no evasive action and didn't fire a shot. When we switched on the Leigh Light at about three quarters of a mile the deck crew were in the conning tower staring straight back up the beam. Our D/Cs fell across the stern and although our photo-flash failed to work, so that there was no attack photo, the rear gunner said that the stern was lifted out of the water. A photo taken on a run over the spot immediately afterwards showed a huge bubble.

Rudi Wieser, in the conning tower, explains why they did not fire:

After surfacing, we were, at 0525 (German time) attacked by a Liberator and bombed. Unfortunately we could not beat off the attack with our flak weapons this time. Our 3.7 cm gun had jammed, the starboard 2 cm gun had been lost in transit, and also my 2 cm port gun had jammed. All weapons were not yet free from water because we had only surfaced at 0506 hours.

A bomb fell on the starboard ballast tank, subsequently scarred the port side, slid down under the water and exploded a little behind the boat. Things at this moment were on a knife-edge. Later it was established that the diesel engine mounting had sustained hairline cracks.

So perhaps both had been lucky. U 763 was so nearly sunk but survived despite a successful straddle, and the Liberator because the U boat's guns had been ineffective. With their success on 4/5 February 1944, perhaps this was just as well for John Downey and his crew, in 'A' EW308:

SL J C T Downey	Pilot	Sgt R H Griffin	WOP/AG
FO M Kowalchuk	2nd pilot	Sgt R A Ranson	WOP/AG
FO H Sutton	Navigator	Sgt A R Wilson	WOP/AG
Sgt V Acourt	Engineer	FS A H Butler	WOP/AG
FO R W Lowe DFC			

The U boat reached Bergen the next day. Repairs from the attack kept her there for two weeks before she could sail, moving to Kristiansand to become a training boat. She was destroyed in a Russian air attack while in Königsberg, on 21 January 1945. Meantime, Oberleutnant Karl Heinz Schötter, CO of U 1195 had taken command of U 763, while Ernst Cordes, her previous CO, took command of U 1195, taking most of his crew with him, including Rudi Wieser. This boat was eventually sunk by HMS *Watchman* on 6 April 1945, but there were survivors.

John Downey DFC, a future Air Vice-Marshal, was to severely damage U 2365 on 5 May 1945, so badly in fact that she was scuttled by her captain, but was raised from the sea bed in 1956.

CHAPTER TEN

CATALINAS IN THE INDIAN OCEAN

One tends to forget that Coastal Command operated in a number of far-off places and not just around the British Isles or over Biscay and the Western Approaches. As we saw in chapter eight, long-range U boats went deep into the South Atlantic, off the South American coast, and also made their way round the Cape of Good Hope and into the Indian Ocean. While American units such as VB107 covered the South Atlantic, South America and the Caribbean, the RAF had units patrolling West Africa, South Africa and the east coast of that continent.

Len Eccles was a pilot with 259 Squadron, flying Catalina IB flying boats from South and East Africa, and gives us a very different view of life with that segment of Coastal Command. Len had been in a reserved occupation with GPO telephones when he volunteered for the RAF, and against all authority, they eventually agreed to release him provided that he returned should he fail the pilot's course.

He was inducted in September 1941 and with many others reported to Lord's Cricket Ground. Those men with maths were quickly posted to a streamlined ITW course at Torquay, and with one draft having been lost on the way to Canada, urgent replacements were wanted. So by October, Len was aboard the *Durban Castle* on his way to Canada. On arrival, despite all the rush, he and the others cooled their heels in a transit camp for two months, at Monkton, New Brunswick. Eventually they were sent for pilot training, Len going solo in late January 1942 from a base near Detroit, then progressed to Pensacola where he graduated in August.

Returning to England on the *Queen Elizabeth* in November, he was sent overseas in March 1943, around the Cape to Egypt. A month later he went to Mombasa, via Nairobi (in the grandeur of a BOAC flying boat and then a less luxurious Dragon Rapide). From Mombasa he was posted to 259 Squadron at Durban, and sent down with civilian passports by BOAC flying boat again, through neutral Portuguese territory. Len relates:

After a spell at Langebaan in the Cape we returned to Durban and operated for several months from Durban and St. Lucia. Night take-offs and landings at Durban were not permitted with a full load of fuel and D/Cs due to the congested channel, so we had to do our serious operations from St. Lucia lake in Zululand. It was here that several fatal crashes occurred, one just before I joined the Squadron at Durban. My first night there I was allocated a dead navigator's bed, with all his gear around. Not the best introduction to a squadron.

Mid-September we moved back to our own base at Dar-es-Salaam, via Tulear and Diego Suarez in Madagascar, and then in November we went on detachment to Aden, where we remained until mid-March, operating in the Gulf of Aden and around Socotra. Returning to Dar-es-Salaam, I completed my 'tour' in April, when I was going on leave to Kisumu. I flew as co-pilot with Bill Tennant in FP126, which he was taking to our maintenance base at Kisumu for a 'major'.

Coming in to land on a completely glassy surface of Lake Victoria at Kisumu, Bill either hit something – could have been a Hippo or a log – or he could have let the nose dig-in. Anyway, he performed a highly spectacular water-loop and we disappeared in a cloud of spray. Ken Grainger, a friend I'd trained with, who had heard I was on board and was watching us land, walked away, thinking that we'd had it. However, we surfaced again and when we came to rest Bill was lying across my lap (I was in the right-hand seat) in a dazed and shocked condition. As the starboard float was hanging on by a whisker I called to the crew to get out onto the port wing to keep the starboard wing out of the water. When Bill got ashore he was taken to hospital where he was detained for some time and that was the end of his flying career.

After my leave I returned to Dar and after checking out was flown up to Cairo where I was told that I had been seconded to BOAC and was to return to Durban to join them. I had wanted to fly a second tour on Liberators in the Atlantic, but could not get out of it.

Len recalls those less well known bases from where 259 Squadron operated:

DURBAN. For leisure activities there could not have been a more attractive place anywhere to be stationed than Durban. As the premier holiday resort of South Africa it had everything one could wish for. As an alighting area it left a lot to be desired. Aircraft were not allowed to operate at night nor were we allowed to operate with full loads as the one good run was a shipping lane alongside the wharf-side with not only a dog-leg in the middle but also the prevailing direction to take off took one over the city centre. Taking off from Durban we had to fly an hour up the coast to Lake St. Lucia in Zululand, fill up with fuel and from where we could make our mainly night take-offs. The alighting area here was not unlimited and as we were normally operating several thousand pounds over our maximum all-up weight it was an anxious time for the crew, sitting braced against bulkheads in the back during the long run at full power before we parted company with the water. I had to join them on a couple of occasions when we had three pilots on board and it was not a happy experience. I admired their stoicism during these interminable take-off runs before they could take up their operational crew positions.

From African bases we used to be supplied with canned foods to sustain us on our 20-hour plus flights. This usually took the form of canned soya sausages, canned guavas, and canned carrots and peas. We were also given a cash allowance of so much per crew-man for a few luxuries. The cans provided were invariably dumped into the bilges for emergency use and over the period between overhauls would mount up to a largish and progressively increasing contribution to our excess take-off weight. When over-hauls came along the bilges would be cleared out and the cans packed into cartons and passed to deserving causes. With the cash allowance (which came to a fair sum for a crew of 12 or 13), bacon, eggs, steak and potatoes would be bought and there was always some member of the crew who would supply well cooked and welcome meals. Canned peaches or apricots would round things off.

Inside the fuselage of the Catalina, below the central pylon where the engineer was stationed, we had a pair of 'A-frames' holding 45 gallon drums of fuel, which at some stage of the flight was pumped up into the wing tanks to extend our range. For cooking purposes we were fitted with an electric hot-plate, but of course, this was quite inadequate for the purpose so we fitted a couple of primus stoves which were also put into use towards meal times and these would be roaring merrily away within a yard or two of these drums of high octane! The fact that I am still here to recall this is evidence that we got away with this culpable disregard of all sensible safety practices.

ST. LUCIA base itself was a collection of huts on a hillock over-looking the lagoon. The surrounding shores were infested with crocodiles but they did not come anywhere near the camp. While we were at St. Lucia we were kept pretty busy and sleep was at a premium.

LANGEBAAN was a desolate strip of coast about half an hour

north-west of Cape Town where we had an advanced base to cover the approaches to the Cape. Accommodation was in the Panoramic Hotel, a run-down hotel owned by two brothers rejoicing in the names of Ossie and Ziggie. The alighting area was very extensive, but sadly during my stay there there was no call for our activities and the only time we used it was when we arrived, and taking off a month later to return to Durban. There was literally nothing to do but to wander up and down the beach, bored out of our minds. A night on duty as operations officer in the makeshift Ops Room was the only outstanding memory. Typically, there was nothing to report!

DAR-ES-SALAAM was our Squadron base. A former German colony it still had the appearance of its origins. The alighting area we used was up the river, which was obstructed in two places by ships sunk there during the Kaiser's war. When I was with BOAC we used to land and take off from the mouth of the river towards the open sea, but possibly the swell coming into the estuary would have been too much for a fully loaded Catalina in which we used to take off from as far back as we could go, towards the first of the half-sunken hulks. Many were the times when a quick decision to throttle back was necessary and another attempt made. This could happen several times in one take-off until enough fuel had been used up to lighten the load sufficiently. Frequent glassy surfaces didn't help.

From here we had an advanced base at Diego Suarez in Madagascar, and at Pamanzi, a paradise island in the Indian Ocean untouched by the 20th Century, and where we spent our spare time canoeing, in an outrigger canoe; fishing, gathering oysters off the rocks, and trading with the locals. One cigarette would get you a chicken or, not just a bunch of bananas but a whole branch full of bunches! Frangipani trees filled all the lanes in the town with perfume and covered the unmade roads with petals.

Our supplies arrived by a weekly steamer complete with weevil-infested bread. It is said that you could always tell an ex-desert rat by him tapping out his boots before he put them on, in case of scorpions. You could always tell someone who had come back from Pamanzi because he would tap his slice of bread on the plate to remove any weevils.

While we were there we gave a film show for the locals. All the dignitaries came. In the open air, the screen was the whitewashed wall of a building.

While we were there, we switched from Amatol to Torpex-filled depth charges and for a while had a good supply of fresh fish by combining the disposal of redundant D/Cs with simultaneous target practice and fishing. My job was dashing around after the explosion collecting the stunned fish into a canoe.

Operating in the tropics as we did caused clothing to be rather informal. Although nights could be cold, during the day, flying at comparitively low altitude, the standard dress was khaki shorts and sandals. Shirts were redundant as the metal components could become untouchable in the heat. All in all, though, it was a very pleasant way of spending a war.

ADEN was another of our detachments. We were quartered at the peace-time RAF base of Khormaksar. The buildings were superb although sparsely furnished. Also at the base was a peace-time RAF squadron who were occupied in fighting their own private war against recalcitrant Yemini tribesmen, for which purpose they were equipped with open cockpit single-seater biplanes.

Nearby was the USA staging post of Sheik Othman where transport aircraft on the run from America to China by way of 'over the hump' were refuelled. They had a superb open-air cinema to which we were invited and not only had they all the latest films but also visiting celebrities on the stage such as Bob Hope and Nelson Eddy amongst others we saw.

Aden was a very congested harbour and when we came to leave, on our way back to Dar, by way of Mombasa, we were the last of our detachment out, so had to take, in addition to our crew, 23 ground staff mechanics and their chests of tools, equipment and personal kit. The take-off was memorable because we barely scraped over the mess hall roof and it was about two hours before we could stagger up to 1,000 feet, by first burning off some fuel. While there, in addition to our normal operational duties we took part in converting Wellington crews to the type of work we did. It's good to see that they later had some anti-submarine success.

MOMBASA. Although a busy port during the war, the town itself was on the primitive side. The hutted camp was some distance out of the town, cut out of the bush. I did not spend much time there as it was not our base for operations but we did call in at times for various reasons.

When I first arrived in East Africa, I joined the group at Mombasa before posting. One of the airmen was bitten by a puff adder inside the camp one night while I was there and died in hospital. The surrounding vegetation was luxuriant and the night was filled with the throbbing of Native drums, probably dancing or some other kind of celebrations.

One very pleasant episode was when a Puss Moth, which had been on loan to our CO, had to be flown back to Nairobi from our base at Dar. I volunteered for the job and felt a bit like Jim Mollison as I flew it the 2½ hour trip up the wild east coast to Mombasa, where I reluctantly had to deliver it into other hands.

It was a most fantastic flight behind the single engine, in the cramped cabin, on my own, after the Catalina with its 12-man crew.

Ken Caligari was also a member of 259 Squadron, and, as we shall see, flew with Len Eccles later on. Ken was from Liverpool, although he spent most of his youth in Spalding, Lincolnshire. He became an aircraft apprentice in January 1939 and two years later was at RAF Waterbeach, in 3 Group Bomber Command. By May 1942, as a corporal he was able to transfer (volunteer) to aircrew. As a WOM/AG he became a sergeant.

Completing his training he was eventually posted overseas, flying out from Pembroke Dock in a Catalina with 259 Squadron's CO designate, Wing Commander W N Bisdee, on 23 January 1943. Via Gib, Cairo (where they spent four days sleeping in the Catalina, while messing in the BOAC boathouse), they then followed the Nile to Khartoum. From here they went to Lake Victoria, where the NCOs slept in glorified bashas, finding a plentiful supply of bed-bugs which fed on them hungrily. They ended up looking as though they had measles! The last leg, to Mombasa, was completed on 2 February.

This was the first of 259 Squadron's aircraft to arrive, and as far as Ken knows, was the only one to fly via the Mediterranean. All the others were routed via West Africa and the Congo, using RAF bases, and then the facilities of the civil airlines once inland. He remembers:

We spent the next few days settling in, did a compass swing, then no more flying till the 19th when we carried out our first operational anti-sub patrol in support of the Eastern Fleet. My first Skipper was PO Nigel Keeble but I only flew with him once more and then joined FP126 with Oscar Barnett as Skipper.

From 14 March, when we left Mombasa for Durban via Tulea (Madagascar), I was only in Mombasa for three days, during which time we carried out two A/S patrols, so my warm flying kit etc, didn't catch up with me until I had been back in the UK several months (around September 1944!).

The Squadron had several detached bases, spread from Langebaan on the west coast, 60 miles north of Cape Town, to Aden, Madagascar and for some crews, the Seychelles and other Indian Ocean islands. 259 Squadron's base moved from Mombasa, where it had shared the base with 209 Squadron, who had taken part in the Madagascan campaign.

I remember that Lake St Lucia was full of crocs and pelicans. Very illegally we used the crocs as targets on gunnery exercises. We all loathed St Lucia even though we were only there for five or six days at a time. All facilities were of the 'camp out' variety and in many ways it was a relief to fly. The food was eatable but I was always put off by the indigenous waiters sweating copiously from the hot kitchen stoves, dropping beads of sweat onto the plates.

At Tulea, Madagascar, we found a typical French colonial town with a good long stone jetty suitable for motor vessels. The snag with landing at Tulea was the high swell, especially if compounded by a stiff breeze in the right direction, that whipped the sea up. It fairly used to smack the bottom of the Cat with an alarming noise. I think Oscar used to do semi-stall landings there so that the boat dropped in the sea rather than plough through it.

Norman Pearce was an FMA/AG with 259 but not in the same crew, although he would be for a short period as we shall read. He too recalls Durban (Congella):

The mooring basin at Congella was enclosed by a concrete wall rising to about seven or eight feet at high tide, entry being gained by a break in this wall which, of course, also allowed the tide in and out. On one occasion we entered through the break and then began to be pushed towards the wall by the tide. Despite the use of our sea drogues and full throttle on our port engine, we drifted closer and closer to the wall. It was a losing battle so the Skipper cut the engines. I clambered out onto the port wing and prepared to jump off at the appropriate moment. The wall sloped upwards and outwards and from my position the drop would have been about six or seven feet.

I well remember the Skipper shouting: 'Go on jump, you so-and-so!' or words to that effect, but being by this time an experienced chap, waited until I was able to jump 'and' keep my feet dry. In any case I was wearing the shoes I wanted to wear that afternoon visiting Durban. I jumped and did manage to keep my feet dry, and to my surprise, was able to hold the aircraft off quite easily so no damage occurred.

This sets something of the scene for the Coastal crews that operated in this area. Along with 259 Squadron, was 265, and 209 Squadrons, also with Catalina flying boats. 259 had been formed at Beaumaris in January 1943 and was then attached to 209 Squadron at Mombasa, that had come to this area the previous year. 265 was formed at Mombasa in March 1943.

Operations were not so intense as flown from England of course, but once submarines were known or suspected to be in the areas covered, sorties were made no less aggressively as anywhere else. The story of this chapter covers the events in August 1943, against a submarine that had made its way round the Cape and was entering the Indian Ocean.

U 197 was, of course, one of the long-range IXD2 types, built at the Deschimag AG works at Weser. Commissioned on 10 October 1942, she was commanded by Kapitänleutnant Robert Bartels. Born in April 1911, the 31-year-old Bartels had previously been the watch officer in U 21 and then commanded U 139 and later U 561. He had been awarded the Deutche Kreuz in Gold for his leadership.

He took her out on her first war cruise from Kiel on 3 April 1943, heading for the South Atlantic and then the Indian Ocean. By 20 May she was down in Marine Quadrant FM22 (0609/1309), off the west coast of Africa. Here she found the Dutch tanker *Benakat* of 4,763 BRT. Hit by two torpedoes and finished off with gunfire, the tanker went down, but U 197 was later attacked by aircraft, slightly damaged and had one crewman killed.

Continuing round the Cape she entered the Indian Ocean and on 21 June was supplied by the German tanker *Charlotte Schliemann*, together with other U boats, U 177, U 178, U 181, U 196 and U 198. On 12 July she was located again in area KP33 (2321/3648) but escaped damage from at least three depth charges dropped near her.

Twelve days later U 197 sank the Swedish tanker *Pegasus* (9,583 BRT) and on the 30th attacked and damaged the American freighter *William Ellery* (7,181 BRT). Finally on 17 August she sank the British freighter *Empire Stanley* (6,921 BRT). However, in reporting the sinking of this her last victim, her location was picked up by shore-based HF/DF after a good fix was obtained. Her days were now numbered. Len Eccles:

> With a report of U boat activity in the area, we took off from St Lucia at 0230 hours on Friday 20 August 1943, and set course for our position to commence an anti-U boat search by CLA (Creeping Line Ahead). At 0300 Oscar Barnett, our skipper, went back for a sleep while I took over; he relieved me at 0700. Then I went to the rear for breakfast and after relieving Oscar again while he had his, I slept until 1030 – about three hours – when Oscar called me forward. I then took over the watch in the left-hand seat while Oscar went back for his rest period. This followed our normal pattern of alternating three or four hours off. Sergeant Martin was then taking lookout in the second pilot's seat, but was relieved at noon by Peters.
>
> With a shallow layer of strato-cumulus not far above us I climbed into it believing that this gave us the best chance of seeing any U boat before it saw us, since in my experience, most lookouts search the horizon rather than higher in the sky. We also had

switched off our ASV to avoid detection. There was a strong breeze at the surface and the sea was covered with streaks of breaking whitecaps, but at about 1240 I saw an especially long and persistent streak on the surface, about six or seven miles away, about thirty degrees on our port bow.

When it persisted I got the binoculars onto it. At first, all I could see was white spray, but then I got a glimpse of a conning tower shining white in the sun. I pointed it out to Peters and sounded the alarm, took out the automatic pilot, and started losing height while turning towards it.

Sergeant Peters disappeared from the cockpit as Oscar came forward rubbing his eyes, having just had a rude awakening, while I switched over to the right-hand seat. As Oscar took over control, I armed and set the depth charges.

At first Oscar couldn't see the sub, but when I pointed it out to him he went into a steeper dive to get down to our attacking height of 50 feet, turning further to port in order to attack the U boat from astern. We went into auto-rich, fine pitch, while our bow gunner fired a testing burst. I saw multi-coloured tracer crawl towards us from the U boat, then it whipped past our starboard wing.

Norman Pearce, our (relief) mechanic, was on the bow gun firing the .303 machine gun. This was a most vulnerable position with cannon shells whistling around his ears, but he 'stuck to his guns' as we approached the U boat.

Norman Pearce had been detailed to fly with Oscar Barnett's crew two days earlier, as his crew was on stand-down and Barnett's FMA/AG had gone sick. Norman Pearce recalls:

After some hours on patrol the klaxon sounded 'action stations'. I was in the bunk area at the time and immediately proceeded to my station, which in my own crew was the front-gun position, so I automatically went to that position now. Having been off watch when I dashed forward, my flying helmet was not to hand, and as manning the gun was my immediate priority, didn't wait to find it. Once in the gun position the two pilots would obviously have seen I was without it, and at a recent re-union, Len Eccles suggested that I must have scared the U boat gunners with my hair blowing wildly in the slipstream and thus put them off their aim – they missed, anyway.

Reaching the front turret, a manually operated one, I removed the top door and mounted the gun, a .303 Browning. The removal of the door enabled the gunner to stand upright and with his head out in the slipstream, operated the turret with his shoulders.

I saw the U boat at about one mile ahead and when we were

within 1,000 yards tested my gun with a short burst. The bullets fell just short so my estimate of range appeared correct, 800 yards being considered the effective range. Our attack was from an angle of 30 to 40 degrees to the U boat's course and return fire from it I could see passing to the left and right of us. I recall that for a fraction of a second I thought this was my bullets ricocheting at the most peculiar angles – silly me, maybe just as well. There appeared to be three men in the conning tower operating their gun, and, when we passed over them, two had disappeared and the third was hanging over the tower rail and showing no sign of life.

Len Eccles continues the story:

As all this was going on about us I heard a couple of explosions as heavier shells burst under our hull, then we were racing over the suddenly rough sea at 50 feet. I got the impression of the deck of the U boat as it flashed past underneath us and the depth charges were away; then the port blister gunner began hammering away with his .5 Browning gun.

We turned steeply to port and looking back I could see the sub surrounded by falling spray, but no other result. According to the port blister gunner, we straddled it with four D/Cs along the starboard side, with two more over, forward of the conning tower, and the sub was totally obscured by spray. (The photograph which we saw later seemed to show that owing to a sharp turn to port by the U boat, all D/Cs fell close along its starboard side.)

'Four years,' cries Oscar, 'Four years I've been looking for one, and now when you find me one I miss the blasted thing. Did you see where the bursts were?' I told him about the cannon fire and of possible hits on our starboard wing, but in the heat of the attack Oscar hadn't even been aware that we were being fired on.

We continued circling, wishing we had a couple more depth charges; every time we came within range we were fired upon by the boat's heavier gun, causing shells to explode behind our tail. After about half an hour the U boat suddenly submerged as we were turning away from it. We immediately dropped a flame-float to mark the spot and resumed our circling. Oscar went back to prepare a full report to send to base while I took over and kept on replenishing flame-floats with smoke-floats as they burnt out. With the strong wind and high rate of drift it was easy to get blown out of position without them.

After about half an hour of this, Oscar came back and took over again, and shortly afterwards, Sergeant Peters reported an oil patch on our port side, almost underneath us. As we started to have a closer look at this, the U boat surfaced about a quarter of a mile away to port, quite stationary. Our gunners fired a couple of bursts at it to occupy its gunners while we got out of range again.

For some time the boat remained stationary, wallowing on the surface, then after about twenty minutes it set a course of 150 degrees, true, and increased speed gradually, to about ten knots. Meantime its gunners fired at us with the heavier gun every time we came in range. Behind the boat there was a widening trail of oil and we could see it had a pronounced list to starboard. It was also weaving somewhat as though the crew was finding it difficult to maintain a straight course. Shortly we received a signal that a Catalina of 265 Squadron was en route to join us.

Oscar Barnett, as Len relates, could not recall return fire from the U boat nor of seeing anyone in the conning tower; however, he remembers:

After landing and taxying to the mooring at Tulear we noticed a small jet of water coming through the hull of the Catalina and impinging on the centre of the Captain's seat! We could find no rivets missing from around the plate, so I think it must have been a small piece of shrapnel. There was also, we found later, quite a deep dent to the leading edge of the starboard wing, otherwise we had no damage.

Also in the Catalina was Flight Sergeant Ken Caligari, the wireless operator, mechanic, who recalls:

We took off from St Lucia in Catalina FP126 (call sign, Onward C-Charlie) at 0110 hours local time, with full petrol tanks for a CLA to PLE, some 400-500 miles south-west of Tulea, Madagascar, where we would land after the search. This was our fifth patrol since 1 August and the 11th time we had been airborne, so we had been kept quite busy.

The patrol had progressed as many had done before, the crew shifting from gun watch in the blisters and forward on the flight deck; the flight engineer being relieved by the flight mechanic who would then do a gun watch/lookout, or rest on a bunk; the two WOPs and WOM rotating each hour, radio, ASV, gun watch, or forward lookout or a blessed hour on the bunk; the navigator doing a lookout when he could or snatching bunk time. The flight rigger usually volunteered to feed and water us in addition to doing his stint on gun watch/lookout.

By 1300 hours we were twelve hours into our patrol and starting to feel rather jaded. I think I was on gun watch in the port blister and Mick Peters was on radio watch, Joe Ball was either resting or on gun watch, Len Eccles had the flight deck, and Oscar was having a rest. I seem to remember Len calling for Oscar over the intercom, saying he thought he'd seen something, and then the alarm was sounded. Joe Ball took his position as flight engineer, I went on radio, Mick Peters went to the port blister .5 gun. Andy Anderson, the navigator, prepared and handed me a Sighting Report and I contacted Durban on 6666 Kc/s. While I was transmitting, Oscar was throwing the Cat about and delivering the attack, which incidentally was a perfect straddle as was to be expected of such a highly competent skipper. At the same time Andy Anderson was hanging out of the blister and must have been dangling while taking pictures with the camera.

I remember craning my neck to look out of the starboard window by the radio but all I could see was tracer drifting up toward us. After the attack, seeing the boat still on the surface was a bit of an anti-climax. Meantime, I was sending an attack report to Durban 'SSS' indicating that the U boat was damaged but still not out of action. We were all dismayed when the U boat later submerged. I recall hearing Oscar say: 'There goes my gong!' in that dry way of his.

The 'SSS' signal was the code to the ground station that a submarine had been sighted/was being attacked and meant that this, and subsequent signals, were top priority. Using 'SSS' was a 'shorthand' and easily recognised way of sounding the alert to all who received it.

After we had been searching around for about half an hour the U boat surfaced and I heard it had a list and was leaking oil. This too I reported to Durban and was told that another Cat was being sent to rendezvous with us. I was advised that N-Nuts of 265 Squadron wanted to home on us so I was able to contact them on HF and from then on sent frequent homing signals.

Unfortunately the power packs were giving off strong smells of burning so I managed to keep swapping them over to give each a chance to cool down, doing this until 'N' joined us about 1700 hours. Regarding this homing, I changed to a pre-arranged frequency and sent out a signal to anyone who needed it – the signal was to the effect: 'This is C/259, please take bearings and home on to me'; followed by a long continuous dash to allow those receiving the signal to use their Direction Finding loops/radio compasses to set course for us and keep on course for us.

Apparently the wireless operator in N/265 had difficulty in receiving my signal which I suspect was due to the problem I was having with the radio power supply.

Len Eccles continues:

We maintained contact for the next 2½ hours, the boat's gun crews firing at us whenever we drifted within range, sometimes using his heavy gun but at times with his cannon, covering the sky behind us with a pepper-pot pattern of bursts.

I went back to the blister to take some photographs, then at about 1615 I saw the relief aircraft approaching us about eight miles to starboard. He homed in on our continual signal with his loop aerial. We flashed him with the Aldis Lamp and as he seemed intent on going straight in to the attack, we tried to divert him by firing red Very lights.

We then signalled that the U boat should be subjected to a combined attack before going in with D/Cs, and to clear the gunners off the deck, we both circled anti-clockwise, both firing with our .5 guns from the port blisters. After a short burst of return fire all resistance ended. We saw our tracers bounding off the deck and conning tower and soon we were in danger of being hit by our own side!

Both aircraft ceased fire and Oscar made a dummy attack from which we saw that the deck was clear and the hatches closed. We stood off two miles, having learnt the relief aircraft was not from our own squadron as previously assumed. However, we were both on the same side, and we watched as the pilot made two copy-book attacks, but each time the boat made last-minute sharp turns and each time the attack run was aborted.

Time, however, was on our side. We made another dummy run to confuse them, followed by N/265 that made a perfectly judged attack, lined up perfectly and this time we saw his D/Cs fall along and over the target, raising two huge fountains of water and I got the impression that the sub broke in two. Both middle sections rose out of the water, before disappearing under the surface.

I grabbed the binoculars and all I could see was a huge mass of bubbling and seething oil and water. We circled around watching as the oil spread out until it covered an area of about 800 by 200 yards.

Norman Pearce:

We shadowed, according to my log-book, for four hours and 35 minutes until 'N' of 265 Squadron homed-in on us. Still standing in the front turret I remember that our starboard wing seemed to be dropping rather low. Turning round to face the pilots – still without my helmet – I noted the Skipper was not in his seat and that the co-pilot was 'driving'. He was turning to starboard and looking over his shoulder at the U boat. To me the wing was much too low so I banged on the fuselage to draw his attention to this fact. I'm not sure what he thought but at least the wing came up to a more, to me, comfortable angle.

On seeing that N/265 had the situation in hand we again attacked with our guns. This time our Skipper did not keep a straight course for obvious reasons, and the G-force (yes, even in a Catalina) was such that I found it impossible to operate the turret so decided that the only way to score any hits was to concentrate on firing only when the weaving of the aircraft brought the sub into my sights. This proved effective as hits could be seen striking home. I was unable to see the effect the blister guns had, but presume they too recorded hits. When N/265 made its attack, after at least two dummy runs, no return fire could be seen coming from the sub. In all I fired 1,200 rounds in the action.

Ken Caligari:

I really lost all track of time worrying about keeping the approaching Catalina homing in on us. Finally it arrived. When it was ready to make the attack, gunners in both aircraft pasted the U boat and the boat's gunners could not man the guns. After an initial pass, N-Nuts laid six depth charges diagonally across the U boat and down it went.

Both flying boats remained in the search area for some time but nothing more was seen except a very significant oil patch. We set course for Tulear and landed there after being airborne for 20 hours, 35 minutes.

Shortly before his death, Ernie Robin, the Canadian pilot in N-Nuts sent me the following account of this action:

We were about 500 miles south of Madagascar when we heard the 'SSS'. We immediately altered course for their position but we were about three hours flying time away and we could not pick up their homing signals. At 1500 we began to pick them up but they were so weak we could not home in. Finally the operator stopped sending and we were able to break in and get an updated position report which we immediately set course for and arrived about 1630. Despite the signal I had to depend on our superb navigator, Bill Wilson.

When we arrived, C/259 was circling the area and the sub was on the surface, making about ten knots on a southerly course. My first reaction was to set the D/Cs and head right in, but my crew had a better thought, and although the sub was firing at us and had longer range and better guns, my crew thought we should try to silence them first, which we did by circling close and using our .5s. The boys in the blisters were anxious to get their licks in and they were really accurate. They sprayed the conning tower and it was not long until the crew on the sub decided to clear the bridge, so with that done we were free to make a run-in without fear of being shot down.

I made a run at the U boat and the German skipper did the same thing as he did to Barnett, he turned about 90 degrees just when I was ready to press the button. There was no use in dropping my D/Cs if he was not in range, so another pass and we were out-manoeuvred again. However, the third time, by which time I was getting a lot of 'flak' from my crew, the German made his mistake and turned straight along our path and I hit the button. I recall we were very low and had to lift up to avoid the conning tower and masts. Three of the D/Cs landed right alongside the U boat and one on the deck. I think the reason there was not much debris to speak of was because when he went down to 25 feet, the D/C in his deck would have exploded and completely smashed everything.

We knew we had sunk the boat and there was great jubilation on the intercom. After circling for a while it began to get dark so we headed for Tulear where we landed some time after 2100.

The two crews consisted of the following airmen:

FL L O Barnett	Pilot
FO L W Eccles	2nd pilot
FS R Anderson	Navigator
Sgt J Ball	Engineer
FS K V S Caligari	WOM/AG
Sgt R Martin RNZAF	WOP/AG
Sgt W M Peters RNZAF	WOP/AG
Sgt N Pearce	FMA/AG
Cpl Henderson	
PO Woodhouse*	

* squadron signals officer, flying on a familiarisation flight.

FO C E Robin RCAF	Pilot
Sgt G Lynn	2nd pilot
PO W Wilson RCAF	Navigator
Sgt D Baty	FE/AG
Sgt J F Martin	FE/AG
Sgt S Oxley	WOP/AG
Sgt E J Hall	WOP/AG
Sgt S Angelo	Mech/AG
Sgt J Carter	WOM/AG

Oscar Barnett and Ernie Robin were both awarded the DFC, and Ken Caligari the DFM.

CHAPTER ELEVEN

OPERATION SWAMP

It's funny how things happen sometimes. On 18 April 1943, Squadron Leader George Williams, with 608 Squadron operating from North Africa, was returning from an operational sortie with his AOC, Air Vice-Marshal Hugh Pughe Lloyd CB MC DFC (of recent Malta fame), to land at Maison Blanche. However, due to bad weather they had to divert to Blida, which had a single runway, and as George Williams found, almost gale force winds were blowing right across this runway.

He knew he had a problem and was actually coming in into wind, the right wing pointing up the runway as he crabbed towards it. At the final moment, George kicked the rudder and put the Hudson down on what he was later to recall was perhaps his best landing ever. No doubt the AOC had been more than interested in the approach and landing, for as they taxied in he mumbled to George: 'Bloody good landing, Williams; bloody good.'

A few months later, George became tour-expired and was immediately posted to Lloyd's HQ North African Coastal Air Forces in Algiers, so the landing must really have impressed the AOC. He certainly hadn't forgotten George Williams, who subsequently became a Wing Commander.

Because of this posting, Williams was able to bring his recent knowledge of anti-submarine operations to help plan future tactics. He had himself been the instigator of the loss of U 595 on 14 November 1942. He and another Hudson of 608 had attacked this U boat and severely damaged her. Being unable to submerge, she was then attacked by Hudsons of 500 Squadron. U 595 subsequently beached herself on the Algerian coast and later sank. After the war the U boat's first officer confirmed it had been 608 which had done the major damage.

Ever since Operation Torch, U boats from both the Mediterranean and others coming into the Med via the Straits of Gibraltar, had caused concern to Allied shipping off Algiers and Tunisia. One of George's tasks was to improve the success rate against submarines, and he came up with Operation Swamp. He took his idea to Lloyd who supported it and getting full co-operation with the Navy, something not always readily available to the RAF, put it in motion.

George's idea was to swamp the area with aircraft once a U boat had been located and bring in the Naval anti-submarine vessels in a combined operation. Rather than possibly lose it, they would anticipate its area of operation, and constantly keep aircraft over the immediate area, increasing their number as required as the area of possible submerged escape was enlarged. As the U boats needed to operate initially near the coast in order to attack coastal shipping, he knew that the usual radius of action was halved: ie: the boat, once spotted, could only travel in a half-circle area heading in a northern arc. So, by keeping aircraft in the air over the suspect area, he knew the boat would eventually have to surface to re-charge batteries and to ventilate. At that moment she was tremendously vulnerable, being unable to submerge.

Operation Swamp was to gain several successes off the North African coast in the first months of 1944, either by aircraft, ships and aircraft or ships after aircraft had located and kept the boat down. However, one of the first Swamp operations occurred off southern Spain in January 1944, and while it did not 'bag' a U boat, it resulted in a spectacular series of events with the target boat being subjected to numerous attacks from which she defended herself very well.

Jeaff Greswell, whom we met in chapter one covering the first Leigh Light sortie against two Italian submarines, had, by early 1944 become Commanding Officer of 179 Squadron. Not being a CO to sit behind a desk, he was operating in Leigh Light Wellington XIVs from Gibraltar and with detachments in places nearby. He and his Squadron were very much involved with Swamp. The story of one Swamp operation, against U 343, began on 7 January 1944.

U 343 was a type VIIC submarine, built at the Nordseewerke, Emden GmbH. Commissioned on 18 February 1943 she was commanded by Oberleutnant zur See Wolfgang Rahn, born 31 October 1920, and previously the watch officer of U 458. Her first war cruise began on 22 October 1943 but apart from being depth-charged by escort vessels from convoy MKS30/SL139 on 20 November, she sailed into La Pallice empty handed on the 26th.

Exactly one month later, 26 December, she was ordered to break into the Mediterranean to join the 29th Flotilla. This she managed to do on 5 January, no mean feat, but then her ordeal began.

At 0035 hours on the morning of the 7th, a Wellington of 36

Squadron had located a U boat 30 miles north-west of Oran; as a result the biggest Operation Swamp in the Med was begun. Ten aircraft of 36 were deployed from Blida to Tafaroui (Oran) to carry out the Swamp, while 179 Leigh Light Squadron at Gibraltar were brought to Readiness. Night and day sweeps covered the area but nothing was found.

That night however, at 2225 hours, U 343 was located and attacked by a Wellington from 36 Squadron ('H' MP807) in position 3642/0200, flown by Flying Officer P Thrower. It was a brilliant moonlit night so no Leigh Light needed to be used. The Wellington maintained contact on radar for 14 minutes after the attack but then the boat submerged, obviously without any damage. Flak came from the boat but the aircraft was not hit. Twenty minutes later aircraft 'P' of 179 Squadron made an attack in roughly the same area and again the boat dived. At 2340 G/36 obtained a disappearing ASV contact, U 343 going to periscope depth. She came back to the surface at 0319 on the 8th. However, she had been found, and Swamp had swung fully into action.

No sooner had U 343 surfaced than she spotted a darkened ship and crash-dived. This was probably the Polish destroyer *Slazak* on patrol in this area. At 0330 aircraft spotted a surfaced U boat in position 3819/0029, off Alicante, which dived. This was U 952 which had seen the aircraft. This was reported but was obviously nothing to do with the U boat seen further east. Oddly enough there is no reaction to this second submarine for Swamp, ie: no second Swamp was ordered, so one must assume it was thought that there was only one U boat about. A couple of hours later *Slazak* found a diving U boat in position 3628/0253. It had not seen the destroyer and was diving merely because her crew had picked up a GSR contact. This was U 380.

For the rest of the day aircraft combed the area, but U 343 kept well below, planning only to surface with darkness to re-charge and ventilate. The day was a long one for all concerned. With night, she resurfaced at 1934 hours. Surface vessels were spotted three minutes later and down she went again, coming back to the surface at 2055.

36 Squadron maintained a constant presence over the area which was rewarded at 2134. Aircraft 'Y' of 36 Squadron (HF245) located the U boat in position 3654/0156. Although captained by New Zealander Flying Officer R D Bamford, at the moment of contact he was not at the controls. The full crew was:

FO R D Bamford RNZAF	Pilot
FO T J Masters RCAF	2nd pilot
FO L A Colquohoun RNZAF	Navigator

FO D G Cull RNZAF   WOP/AG
FO W L Medcalf RNZAF   WOP/AG
FS S W Layzell RAF   WOP/AG

The Canadian second pilot, Tom Masters, remembers:

We had been in a 'creeping line ahead' search for more than two hours and hadn't seen a thing. The night was clear and the moon was so bright you could read by it, which is why I did not use the Leigh Light.

We had been detached to Oran to carry out our search. I had come from 62 Squadron (Hudsons) after a tour in India/Burma and joined Bamford's crew as co-pilot. We alternated take-offs and landings, and we also changed every hour when flying. We commenced our search pattern with me flying, Bamford took over and I would relieve him an hour later. We had spotted something in the water earlier and were in the process of firing off the colours of the day for recognition since the wireless operator had not reported any activity in the area. When we received no reply we fired off a second cartridge.

Meanwhile, Bamford and I were changing positions. When we did not get a response I dropped down to about 500 feet and swung up-moon to have a better look. It came as a surprise to see a fully surfaced sub making no attempt to dive – and in bright moonlight. I went into a shallow dive, levelling off at about 50 feet and ran broadside to the sub. Expecting the usual light fire from it, I was most surprised when 'all hell broke loose'.

Because we were so low most of it went above us, but when I pulled up a little to drop the depth charges the flak began to hit the 'plane. I don't think we cleared the sub by more than ten feet. I wanted to keep low to avoid any chance of missing with the depth charges; the tail gunner thought we had hit it.

When we passed over the sub I felt a thump and thought we may have hit the sub's aerial mast but shortly the left wing started to burn. Thinking it might be the engine on fire we pulled the extinguisher but when it continued to burn I decided to ditch. One thought was to get as far away from the sub as possible in case they came after us. It was like daylight and the next thing we were in the water. I thought there was more than one vessel from the amount of gun fire we experienced. Obviously the sub had had plenty of time to be ready for us and with their heavy armament were well prepared to give us a warm reception.

None of us knew how we landed but I guess we hit the water hard because of the burning wing. Our time in the water is another chapter in an eventful night. Under ideal conditions the Wimpy was a good aircraft to ditch. However, when you are shot up and don't know how much of the left wing was intact, I can only conclude that we broke up upon hitting the water. I remember opening the cockpit hood over my head as we prepared to ditch but that's all. Next thing I was floating around in the moonlight, the crew were hollering at each other and the rubber raft was floating in front of us. Cull, Medcalf and myself swam to it but it was only partly inflated. In the distance we heard Layzell calling he couldn't swim. Later he said I swam over and got him but I can't remember that.

Anyway, we gathered alongside the dinghy and took stock of what shape we were in. Cull didn't have as much as a scratch; he had been in the rear turret. Medcalf complained about his foot, which turned out to be broken. Layzell was the worst. After Medcalf got in the dinghy and inflated to where it was firm enough for us to get in, we hauled Layzell in. This move caused him to scream and he passed out. His leg was almost severed about the ankle. The wireless equipment had come down on top of him. I had a broken foot and deep cuts about the face, legs and knees. Thank God for the salt water, it helped stop the bleeding.

I guess I kept passing out because what seemed like a few minutes was actually eight to nine hours before we were picked up. I think the credit for this goes to Layzell because he told me that as soon as he saw the flames on the wing he triggered an SOS switch on the wireless, so I guess someone got a fix on us. During the night a hospital ship, all lit up, passed close by. We hollered and whistled but it kept on going. I think we were still too dazed to care very much anyway. Thank goodness it was a warm night.

About daybreak the *Slazak* came out of the mist and sped by us. We thought it was going to keep on going but it did an about turn and dropped a net over the side with four burly seamen hanging on. Still going at a good clip, they reached down and hauled us out of the dinghy. I guess they didn't want to stop and be a sitting target for a lurking sub.

We sat on deck for a while having a smoke and some rum. The captain explained that the doctor was sick and that they were almost out of medical supplies, but one of the seaman would do his best for us. After a few shots of rum nothing seemed to hurt and the seaman began sewing up the cuts.

Bill Medcalf:

We took off from Oran at around 8 pm. Dick Bamford, our

captain, slipped on getting into the truck taking us out to the aircraft so Tommy started off flying the first few hours. Jack Layzell was on the radio, Doug Cull in the rear turret, Colquohoun was the Nav.

Going up the Spanish coast on the way to the Balearic Islands, a very big blip came up on the radar and we went to have a look. The night was clear, calm and moonlit. Tom got us in the moon track and said he could see a U boat and he would go down on the deck and attack. I had a look and there were two subs lying almost side by side. They were probably transferring something and having a bit of a yarn without going on the radio.

As we went in they were firing at us with cannon which set our port wing on fire. Doug Cull, in the rear turret, said the flames went 60 feet behind us! I remember seeing Ian Colquohoun take out the astrodome and discard it. I sat on the floor with my feet against the main spar. Cull did everything right; turned the turret on the beam and got rid of the door and undid his belt. When we hit the sea we hit tail first and shot Doug out like a cork from a bottle. We skidded on and left him behind. His oxygen bottle on the life jacket didn't work; when he tried to inflate it, with the emergency hose he dropped the screw-in valve. As he couldn't swim things looked a bit serious until he managed to tie a knot in the hose.

Tom and I found ourselves in the water hanging on the dinghy. He was badly cut around his face where he had gone out through the windscreen. My ankle was badly broken and crushed. Jack Layzell came alongside and his leg was broken in six places.

Tom and I managed to get in the dinghy and tied Jack alongside. We were too stuffed to pull him in immediately. Doug Cull was calling out and we managed to paddle over and help him in. Strange to say he was not hurt at all.

We sat in the dinghy and watched a Spanish fishing lugger sail around us for about an hour but it was not their war and they left us alone. The night was so calm we could hear the Polish destroyer coming and they were speaking in Polish, but by then we would have welcomed the entire German navy.

They tossed us a rope and took off flat out. I reckon we were the first rubber dinghy to water-ski on the Med. We stayed on board for two days and then they took us to Oran and an American hospital.

Stanley 'Jack' Layzell:

At 2130 we picked up two blips on the radar screen and I understand two subs were seen visually and the pilot, Tom Masters, announced we were going to attack and commenced the run.

My next recollection was of the aircraft receiving a number of hits, it sounded like a number of doors slamming, then we were hit on the starboard side which smashed the entrance to the cockpit to matchwood. (This is where I would have expected FO Bamford to have been.) Then I became aware that there were flames along the port side, but the run was completed and the depth charges sent away. FO Masters said on the intercom that the extinguisher had not put out the fire which by now was severe and to transmit an SOS which I did pretty quick realizing we were going to have to ditch which is what happened quite quickly and before I had time to brace myself. Then everything went blank.

Suddenly I was standing on something that was submerged with a lot of bubbles coming up and trying to stem them with my hand, and having the feeling that I had lost a leg. Then I heard someone shouting that his Mae West was punctured and he could not swim. Then someone grabbed me and asked if my Mae West was inflated: it was not. It was Tom Masters and he operated the air bottle for me, then it seems I must have blanked out for I next remember Tommy trying to heave me into the dinghy.

Next time I opened my eyes I was lying on some kind of shelf or locker. Tommy was lying on the floor and was having his face stitched up by a sailor. We were on the *Slazak* and there was a bell ringing.

Wellington 'M' then arrived (HF221), captained by Flying Officer J T Hutton. His crew consisted of:

FO J T Hutton	Pilot	FS C T Layson	WOP/AG
FS R N Holton	2nd pilot	FS P C Kiln	WOP/AG
FS F S Foxon	Navigator	WO I G Ricketts	WOP/AG

Ron Holton recalls:

It was the night after my 21st birthday, which I had celebrated not wisely but too well. The following evening three crews were called to standby, including ours, and were briefed in the crew room. Apparently a German U boat had slipped through the narrows of Gib on its way to a base at Marseilles. Some distance to the east of the narrows it had come upon an American troop ship and had promptly sent it to the bottom with enormous loss of life. Our job was to find the U boat and kill it. This was to be achieved by setting up what was known as a Swamp operation.

It was an ingeniously thought out plan that spelt doom for the U boats in the Med. We knew where the U boat had been, ie: the site of the sinking and we also thought we knew its destination. We knew its maximum speed under water and therefore had a fairly good idea where it was now and where it would be in so many hours time. If we 'swamped' the area with aircraft, gradually extending the area and the number of aircraft, eventually we would find it when it was forced to surface.

Our three aircraft were to form the first wave. Each of us was allotted an area. We knew that somewhere within the totality of the three areas the U boat was bound to be. All we had to do was keep searching and to remain alert. The search area was just off the south-east corner of Spain. We had the central area.

It was a brilliant cloudless night, almost full moon, when we set course and took up station. Looking up-moon as the jargon had it, the sea glittered with a myriad diamonds; it was a truly beautiful and peaceful night, although our purpose was anything but peaceful.

After a couple of hours or so of uneventful patrol, we suddenly received a coded signal from No.1 aircraft to the west of us. It gave its callsign, followed by the number '424', meaning he was about to investigate a suspicious target, followed by the position. After no more than five minutes it should then have transmitted either a confirmation or a cancellation, but after five minutes – nothing.

I was flying the aircraft (Jimmy Hutton and I always shared the flying on a 50/50 basis) and called to Mike, our navigator, to give me a course to the position given. It was close to the western edge of our area and in a very short time we were approaching the site when Tommy, who was on the radar, said: 'I've got a target bearing 050, distance seven miles.' As I turned on to the bearing, I noticed a fire on the surface of the sea, obviously the remains of No.1 aircraft.

Tommy continued to give me closing ranges, having sent off our own '424' signal, five miles, four miles and so on while I gradually reduced height and increased speed. We did not want the sub to crash-dive until we had had a good crack at it. Stan had already gone aft to lower the Leigh Light, when I noticed the sub on the surface about one mile off the Spanish coast and making a tremendous wake as it proceeded at maximum speed. I immediately told Stan not to lower the Light as this would give us ten extra valuable knots and also make us a more difficult target.

Tommy reported: 'Two miles, dead ahead!' I opened the bomb

doors and flicked the switches to prime the depth charges. Almost at once the flak started. I was amazed at how much was being thrown at us: there were large balls of orange fire which I knew to be from a Bofors gun. These came at us so rapidly, making hose-pipe patterns that I thought that at least one was bound to get us. In addition there seemed to be a mass of tracer shells coming from a number of guns. I could not see how we could get through all the flak and survive. Somehow I 'knew' that this was my last life about to be extinguished and I was terrified. I had been in many tight spots before but never had I experienced such abject fear.

Suddenly I seemed to be above and slightly right of my body. I could see my other self manipulating the aircraft and lining it up in accordance with all the training we had received: a thirty degree angle to the boat, depth charges to be dropped just ahead of the sub so that they exploded two on either side. I felt as calm and free from all fear as if I was out on a country stroll. I began to give a running commentary to the rest of the crew and told George, the rear gunner, to be ready to strafe the whole length of the sub as we passed over it. I realised that the port engine had been hit, and that now we were almost on top of the sub, the gunners below must have had a perfect view of our vulnerable undersides. As the bow of the U boat disappeared below our nose, I pressed the release button and felt the lift as the stick of four D/Cs fell away. As I did so, George's guns started chattering as he swept the decks of the sub, and the acrid smell of burnt cordite filled the aircraft.

Instantly I seemed to be back in my body and found myself struggling to maintain control. We were heading straight for the Spanish coast and there was no way we could avoid it. The port engine was out of action and my first reaction was to feather the propeller and increase compensatory power to the starboard engine. We were now over the coast and I had no idea how close to the ground we were. I only knew that we were far too close. The bomb doors were still open and I couldn't close them until I had jettisoned the remaining four D/Cs and I couldn't do that while we were still over land. In the meantime it was impossible to climb and I had to make a very gentle turn into the dead engine – contrary to good airmanship – therefore I necessarily had to penetrate further inland than I would have liked.

As we crossed the coast I remember George shouting excitedly over the intercom: 'We've got him! We've got him!', as the D/Cs exploded and smothered the U boat in foam and cascading water. But all my attention was on the aircraft. At last I completed my gentle left-hand turn and recrossed the coast. As soon as we were a reasonable distance from the shore, I jettisoned the remaining D/Cs (unprimed of course) and closed the bomb doors. And now I managed to gain a little height. Now that we were out of immediate danger I had time to glance over my left shoulder and look at the sub. She had stopped and seemed to be lying at an angle of about 60 degrees to her original course; the dispersing foam of the explosions was still about her. As I climbed away I saw the last remaining Wellington make its run in. It had no opposition and dropped all eight of his D/Cs in two sticks on the dying sub. In view of our disabled state we decided to divert to Bone, the nearest Allied airfield, where we landed safely.

This third Wellington of 36 Squadron ('B' HF236), with Flight Sergeant J Williamson and crew, who had also picked up Masters' sighting report and set course for the location, obtained a contact and headed in. He too saw the fully surfaced U boat in the moonlight and attacked it with eight D/Cs but the boat appeared uneffected and remained on the surface while the now impotent Wellington circled for the next 45 minutes keeping her on radar. Although this attack is timed at 2202 hours, and that of Holton at 2206, Holton saw the third Wellington attack after they had done so, therefore the times are slightly in error.

From the Hutton/Holton crew, Tom Layson relates:

We had been ordered to Tafaroui on detachment and that first night we were ordered on the Swamp and I see from my diary we were: '. . . recalled after sighting – did not take off again.' The next day, the 8th, we were relocated at La Senia and that evening we were once again briefed for a Swamp and I recall that at the briefing we were addressed by the AOC, Sir Hugh Pughe Lloyd, who had achieved some note as OC at Malta. I recall his final words were: 'It's a piece of cake boys!'

While on patrol, with Percy on the radio and myself on the radar we had received a signal of a sighting and made for the area, then I got a sighting on the radar and was guiding Ron Holton onto the target when I detected a blip on the far side of the U boat and presumed it was an aircraft coming in from the opposite direction. I informed the pilots and we broke off to make an attack when the space was clear. On the second approach I was again guiding us in when I got the message: 'We can see it.'

It was a bright moonlit night and the searchlight did not have to be used. I left my seat and looked out of the astrodome and saw a concentrated hail of flak directed at us.

Having dropped the depth charges, we realised that we had sustained some damage and Ron Holton had a hard job to keep the aircraft flying and later told me that when he did have a chance to look out of the aircraft, he was flying over land – Spain!

In the meantime, the lights and intercom had been knocked out and then Ricky in the rear turret, was flashing the visual intercom system so I went back to see what he wanted. I went down to the tail and knocked on the turret and Ricky opened his doors and came out. His face was covered in oil or fluid. He had realised that we had been hit and had swung his turret to one side, opened his doors and put his head out, and had been liberally sprayed with oil where a cannon shell had gone through the propeller boss without stopping the engine from turning over, but at a reduced speed.

He told me that he had been hit in the leg and he came out of his turret and I cut the leg of his trousers and, despite the absence of light, I could discern blood from his knee to his ankle. I cleaned his wound and put some bandage where I thought it was needed and then returned to the rear turret for the flight home. On landing I was amazed to see a whole fleet of cars, fire tenders, ambulances, etc, chasing the aircraft down the runway. Ricky, we then discovered, had stopped some small pieces of cannon shell in his leg but was otherwise unhurt.

Later examination disclosed that the tailplane had been hit by cannon shells and a shell had gone through the top of the turret. Ricky was a great lover of cigarettes and always had a tin of 50 on the side of his turret. He was most annoyed to find shrapnel had pierced the tin and cut most of his cigarettes in half.

Despite suggestions that there were possibly two U boats, it is quite evident from German records (confirmed by Naval Historical Branch) that neither of two other U boats off the Spanish coast (U 952 and U 380) was at any time in the immediate vicinity of U 343 and there were no others anywhere in the area. Neither boats observed the attacks upon U 343 nor did they engage any aircraft. These 'second' U boats could only have been Spanish fishing vessels or a small merchant ship proceeding coastwise.

As previously mentioned, U 952 was 80-90 miles away from U 343 and she only encountered one aircraft, at 0329 hours, five miles south of Alicante, which flew past the boat at about 300 feet. The sub dived but was not attacked and her captain assumed she had not been seen. However, the aircraft was R/179 whose crew had in fact seen the boat but did not carry out an attack.

Meantime, U 380 was south of Almunecar, more than 50 miles

from U 343. The crew only saw a Hudson and the masts of an escort group, although they picked up several Naxos contacts.

If there was a second vessel anywhere near U 343 it must have been a Spanish fishing vessel or some such craft. There were a number of Spanish vessels in the general area, among them the destroyer *Churruca*, although it is highly unlikely she would have opened fire on any aircraft.

The whole time U 343 was moving slowly north-east but hugging the Spanish coast. There were periods when she was steering a northerly course, others when she was on an easterly course, but the general movement was north-east. At no time did she double back.

With Williamson still circling the submarine, Wing Commander Jeaff Greswell's 179 Squadron Wellington arrived. The area could not be totally covered by Middle East aircraft, so AHQ Gibraltar were asked to assume responsibility for the *Salzak* position which did not include U 343. Greswell's crew were:

WC J H Greswell	Pilot	Sgt M M O'Hara	WOP/AG
FO M A Clifton	2nd pilot	Sgt L T Cutbush	WOP/AG
FO A E Stone RCAF	Navigator	Sgt M McInnes	WOP/AG

At the time of attack, O'Hara was on radar, McInnes on radio and Cutbush in the rear turret.

Greswell made his run at 150 knots and released his depth charges from 100 feet. They were seen to explode on the far side of the U boat level with the conning tower, although individual explosions were not clear. Flak came from the boat through the spray but it remained on the surface, turning to port.

Greswell attacked at 2214 hours but already another of his pilots was heading in, Flying Officer W F Mc Davidson in R/179. He arrived and made his attack at 2237, the boat still fully surfaced. Davidson approached from its stern, from 80 feet at 145 knots. His crew comprised:

FO W F Mc Davidson	Pilot	Sgt A G Fuller	WOP/AG
FO L J Frost	2nd pilot	Sgt R S Eminsang	WOP/AG
Sgt C Parker	Navigator	Sgt J V Dadson	WOP/AG

Davidson met heavy flak fire as he approached but levelled out for his attack run. The aircraft was hit moments before the depth charges went down, when about ¾ to ½ a mile from the target. Struggling with the controls and his port wing on fire, Davidson was forced to port but released his D/Cs. The burning Wellington carried on for about two miles then crashed.

Davidson was thrown through the windscreen as they hit the sea, suffering facial injuries but he found himself alone; the rest of his crew had gone down with the aircraft. He spotted the aircraft's dinghy about 15 yards away, swam to it and hauled himself in. Moments later he saw the U boat approaching from the gloom, so feigned unconsciousness.

The boat actually bumped into the dinghy, but whether the German lookouts actually saw him is unknown. If they did, they might have seen a face covered in blood and assumed he was either dead or unconscious. They made no move to pick him up.

Oberleutnant Wolfgang Rahn had his own troubles. He recorded in the boat's log that following the attack at 2237 by an aircraft which they shot down, U 343 was severely damaged and rendered unfit to dive.

By this time there was yet another aircraft approaching, a Catalina ('J') from 202 Squadron. It made contact and headed in, having also seen the gunfire five to six miles away. It too met severe flak fire. The Catalina's gunners also opened up but the flying boat was hit in the port mainplane and fuselage, and the flight engineer wounded by shrapnel in the shoulder. Both fuel tanks were also holed. The flak ceased and the pilot released six D/Cs from 30-40 feet, but with his aircraft damaged, John Finch headed away towards base. His crew had been:

FL J Finch	Pilot	Sgt E Wass	FM/AG
FO R K Bell	2nd pilot	FS A D S Sugden	WOP/AG
FO B J Goodhew	Navigator	FS L Radcliffe	WOP/AG
FS V Sheridan	Engineer	FS A P Newman	Rigger
PO A F H Barber	WOP/WOM		

Despite the damage, U 343 was still able to move ahead and continued her way north-east. She had survived seven separate attacks and her gunners had shot down two aircraft and damaged two others. Her initial trial was now over and on 19 January she limped into Toulon harbour. Then on 4 February she was damaged by an air attack on Toulon, so her repairs had to be extended.

She finally left Toulon on 6 March but four days later she was found and sunk by the armed Isles class trawler HMS *Mull*, in position 3807/0941, north-west of Bizerta. There were no survivors from her 51 crew.

Flying Officer Davidson was rescued from the sea by HMS *Active* at 0910 on 9 January, and later received the DFC. Tom Masters also became a recipient of the DFC.

CHAPTER TWELVE

U 415

This chapter could not have been written without the help of a former member of submarine U 415, Günter Rautenberg. He was born in October 1923 and joined the U boat service when aged just 17¾. Trained as a Torpedomechaniker, he served aboard U 415 from September 1943 until July 1944, at which time he was wounded as a result of the submarine hitting a mine as she left Brest. Günter has written a Chronicle about U 415 and her crew and has allowed me to use extracts for this book.

U 415 was built at the Danziger Werft AG, in Danzig, commencing 12 July 1941. She was launched on 9 May the following year to become part of the 7th Building Training Company (7 BLK). She was commissioned on 5 August under the command of Oberleutnant zur See (later Kapitänleutnant) Kurt Neide, to become part of the 8th U boat Flotilla, commanded by Korvettenkapitän Eckermann.

The boat moved to Kiel and by the begining of 1943, she was nearing readiness for sea. On 27 February she left Kiel for Kristiansand, as part of the 1st U boat Flotilla, then headed out into the North Atlantic, becoming part of Gruppe Seeteufel, which was operating south of Iceland, on 18 March. Ten days later her crew made their first attack, on a freighter, but their two torpedoes failed to hit. During the first week of April she was supplied by U 462 and then became part of Gruppe Meise.

On 21 April 1943 she sighted the convoy ONS3, and the five torpedoes she fired at it scored hits and sank two British freighters, the *Ashastian* (4,917 BRT) and the *Wanstead* (5,836 BRT). The next day she was attacked by convoy escort vessels but escaped damage. On the 25th she was resupplied by U 487 and then she headed for her new home in Brest harbour. However, she was to have a rough passage before getting to her pen. Her ordeal came on 1 May, although she had been sighted by aircraft over the previous two days, so her presence was already known.

1 May: Today is a holiday – 'Labour Day'. One would think
. . . . However, in the true sense of the word it would
not be very hard in the Biscay to describe the day as
'*eisenhalting*'.[1] A succession of comings and goings on the
surface involve engagements with Allied aircraft, in their
'Derange' patrol area.

0717: Surfaced.

0810: Quadrant BF7498. Alarm! A four-engined Halifax took
us by surprise flying out of a cloud from a bearing of 160
degrees. The first attack was parried by our 2 cm flak guns
and then we submerged. Five bombs were dropped astern
and there were many casualties in the boat.

One bomb fell ten metres behind the quarter deck. After
its entry it was ascertained that the bomb hit diving (ballast)
tank number one. Tank one and forward of the quarter
deck are damaged.

The aircraft was painted white underneath and was
difficult to spot.

Although in my book *Conflict over the Bay* (Wm. Kimber & Co, 1986) I
noted the first attack upon U 415 (incorrectly) as a Wellington of 172
Squadron, and only mention in passing an attack on 'another' U boat by
Flying Officer Houston of 502 Squadron, I was in error. The time of
Houston's attack is more in keeping with U 415's log entry, and, of
course, 502 Squadron were flying four-engined Halifax machines. This
crew, who patrolled between 0420 and 1459 hours, consisted of:

FO R Houston	Pilot	Sgt L S Collins
PO L McDowell		Sgt J S Pope
Sgt A N Excell		Sgt J Kershaw
Sgt E B Bruton		

1046: Surfaced. Quadrant BE7424. Sunderland due north. We
received six bombs while at a depth of 60 metres. A few
casualties.

This time is was a Sunderland from 461 Squadron, RAAF ('M' DV968),
flown by Flight Lieutenant E C Smith, who had been airborne on a
Derange patrol at 0515 hours. In position 4455/1030 at 3,500 feet, the
Australian crew had sighted the U boat on their starboard bow at 5-6

---

[1] It is difficult to translate this word into English but to the U boat men it meant
a long day containing iron in the air, eg: white water explosions, bombs, mines,
torpedoes, depth charges etc.

miles and immediately attacked but the boat was seen to be submerging when half way down, leaving a swirl on the rough sea. Smith was not able to get his most favourable position but released four D/Cs from 50-75 feet. They straddled the projected track of the boat at right angles, 18 seconds after she had disappeared.

The German lookouts had seen the approaching danger and as the Sunderland was making a turn to head in, the U boat captain decided to crash-dive. As the boat went lower and lower so the crew heard the detonations of the D/Cs close by, their vessel sustaining further light damage, but they escaped. Smith's crew had been:

FL E C Smith RAAF	Captain
PO C J Dawson RAAF	1st pilot
PO D A Sinclair RAAF	2nd pilot
FL F B Gascoigne RAAF	Navigator
Sgt L W Cox RAAF	Engineer
Sgt R V Stewart RAF	Fitter
FS H Smedley RAF	WOM
FS J Gamble RAF	WOP/AG
Sgt J Barrow RAF	WOP/AG
Sgt R MacDonald RAF	Fitter
PO E R Critcher RAAF	AG

(Smith and his crew would sink U 465 the very next evening, not very far from this same location.)

1400: A smoke-float was sighted near the periscope. It smoked like a world champion. It was dropped by an aircraft over the area of our U boat submerging, and facilitated the search by following aircraft or destroyers.

1516: Surfaced.

1735: Quadrant BF7198. A four-engined Halifax on a bearing of 20 degrees came at us by surprise from high cloud cover. The first air attack was parried and hits were obtained. The aircraft dropped four bombs and returned fire from nose and tail turrets. Several minor casualties in the boat.

After the attack we crash-dived. Two bombs exploded when we were at a depth of 40 metres: several minor casualties in the boat.

Rather than a Halifax, the attacking machine was a Whitley of 612 Squadron ('E'), captained by Flight Sergeant Norman Earnshaw. As he came in he could see the boat was staying on the surface although making a tight turn, which made a good approach more difficult. AA fire came from the conning tower but there is no report of any hits on the aircraft. As this was happening, Earnshaw's radio operator was preparing to get off a sighting report.

Earnshaw came in low and dropped his depth charges, then circled to come in again, dropping sea markers. His crew were:

FS N Earnshaw	Pilot	Sgt L J McQuiston	WOP/AG
Sgt M G Millard	2nd pilot	Sgt L Shaw	WOP/AG
PO L R Green	Navigator	Sgt B Dennehey	WOP/AG

> 1725: Message to base. Position 4418/1023, sighted fully surfaced
>   U boat 180 degrees, five miles, course 190 degrees, 15 knots.
> 1727: MTB. Attacked U boat.
> 1729: MTB. Second attack and dropped sea markers.

Earnshaw then remained in the area for 40 minutes but nothing more was seen. U 415 sustained further damage from these attacks but nevertheless had had great good luck. As the U boat chronicler noted:

> On looking back these were three passably favourable attempts to send U 415 to the bottom, but in the end the crew repaired the damage and was able, on 5 May, to limp into Brest.
>
> The repeated dogged attacks by the RAF shows with what determination our U boats were pursued in their passage through Biscay. For us, however, it must be said that the basis of our tactical decisions were those of our old hands, and with some good luck we came through those perilous days.

Captain's comment in the boat's log:

> The area is under constant air observation so that re-charging by day is almost impossible unless the sky is completely cloudless. The aircraft fly high and because of their white paint are difficult to spot. They then come suddenly out of a cloud in a steep dive, so that the boat, inspite of the best lookout, is always caught by surprise.

U 415 remained in harbour for over a month, effecting repairs and getting her crew back on their feet. Most of the noted casualties had been due to cuts and bruises from hitting the many steel projections inside the boat during air attacks, the exploding depth charges making the boat shudder and leap about.

This was at the time that Admiral Dönitz was ordering his crews to stay on the surface and fight back, but tactics had also changed to ensure that sailings into the war zones of the North or South Atlantic, or off the American seaboard, would be undertaken in groups of boats for mutual protection whilst crossing the Bay. U 415 sailed on its second war cruise on 12 June, and her area of operations was to be the Caribbean. She left in company with four other boats, U 68, U 155, U 159 and U 634. Two days later they were spotted:

14 June 1943. Biscay.

> 0643: Resumed surface travel in formation. Wind north-west, force one. Sea calm, with cumulous cloud and good visibility.
> 0903: An aircraft bearing 260 degrees, swoops down suddenly out of cloud, broke away from our flak fire and disappeared.
> 0913: Quadrant BE7642. Four fighter aircraft bearing 310 degrees attack the formation at low level. Combined flak fire from all boats. After one attack the aircraft flew off. U 68 had received hits and there were casualties on the bridge and the flak position.

The four fighter aircraft were in fact Mosquitos. Three were from 307 Polish Squadron, the fourth from 410 Canadian Squadron. The twin-engined fighters came down in line-astern, led by Squadron Leader Stanislaw Szablowski, going for the second boat in line, which was U 68. The second Mosquito pilot found his guns would not fire but continued to make a mock run.

Standing orders in fact precluded these aircraft from attacking U boats as their fire was insufficient to inflict major damage, and they would be vulnerable to flak. They were looking for boats and Ju88s, but if they found the former, their task was to report their position so that larger aircraft could be sent in. Thus the No.3 and No.4 Mosquitos did not attack.

And Szablowski's machine (HJ648) had in fact sustained hits from the U boat's gunners and was heading away trailing smoke from his port engine, but he managed to get back to Predannack, where he made a successful crash landing.

> 1015: A Ju88 appeared over us and made signals to the U boats and flew a few circuits around us.
> 1030: Quadrant BF7641. An aircraft at high altitude on a southerly course but apparently we remained unobserved. Fifteen minutes afterwards a contact on the 165 cm waveband.
>
> Because of personnel casualties resulting from the aircraft attack, U 68 [Oblt z S Johannes Altmeier] had to retreat and was escorted [back to Brest] by U 155.
>
> Our Kommandant assumed command of the remainder of

the group. We proceeded on a course of 230 degrees and travelled a further 15 sea miles.

In the late afternoon, a twin-engined aircraft attempted, without approaching, to maintain contact with us.

1554: Group submerged in order to shake-off the watcher. Our boat went down to 100 metres. As we reached 60 metres, four depth charges exploded nearby and several others further off. We again sailed on the surface from 1900 to 2000 hours.

This latter aircraft was a Whitley from 10 OTU, captained by Sergeant Manson, his sighting report timed at 1558. He began circling two miles off, hoping to call up reinforcements, but when his crew saw the boats going down, Manson attacked but his D/Cs undershot, although the explosions were heard by the U boat crews.

Once clear of the Bay area, the boats split up and went their separate ways. On the 26th, U 415 was supplied with fuel from U 170 and U 535, and became part of Gruppe Trutz. By 20 July the crew were working their way along the coastal waters through the Caribbean and were attacked by an American patrol aircraft. Three bombs fell and she was machine gunned but no damage was sustained. Flak fire was directed at the attacker.

On the 24th she found a convoy but its escorts drove U 415 off and then the next day another American patrol plane bombed and strafed her, but again without damage. Both attacks came in the German EE Quadrant. There was now a dearth of any sightings and the boat then had to be resupplied with fuel from U 847 on 22 August.

Heading back across the Atlantic, U 415's crew had one last moment of excitement, being depth-charged by three U boat hunters, but again she escaped damage. On the 8th she entered Brest.

War cruise No.3 started on 27 October. Two days out of Brest, while still in the cauldron of Biscay, aircraft once more found her.

29 October 1943. Biscay.

0357: Surfaced. Wind strength three from the east. Sky only slightly overcast with good visibility. With both diesels at half speed the boat proceeded on a southerly course.

0433: Aircraft bearing 340 degrees. At 2,000 metres range machine approached the U boat at a height of about 30 metres above the water and caught us in its brilliant searchlight. At full speed and with the rudder hard to port, the Kommandant presented the enemy with the smallest dimensions of the boat. Both twin cm guns opened fire immediately. The aircraft simultaneously opened fire with all its guns. Five bombs fell about 150 metres astern across our wake. The four-barrelled gun did not open fire on the retreating aircraft. Our newly shipped, thick-shipped corporal (a U boat term for a surface vessel), was perhaps too slow and was not yet used to the tempo of life on a U boat.

In the boat there were only slight casualties to report. After the over-flight the boat crash-dived into the cellar to a depth of A+20. Before and after the attack, no Naxos whatsoever was observed. We do not yet know from this whether the enemy aircraft was equipped with centimetric radar that our radar warning equipment cannot pick up.

In those two minutes fortune was on our side. We knew, however, that it might not remain so.

The aircraft was a Wellington from 407 Canadian Squadron, flying a Percussion patrol. Its pilot was Flying Officer J D Schultze, and his navigator was Flying Officer Greenaway. They picked up a blip at seven miles, homed in and turned on the Leigh Light at 0435. They sighted the fully surfaced U boat and dropped six D/Cs, which they thought straddled the conning tower and stern. As the aircraft circled to port they could see the boat emerging from the plumes and then submerge. They had indeed experienced flak during the attack. They hung around till dawn but saw nothing else. U 415 was in position 4603/0635 which matches pretty well S/407's 4611/0625.

> 2002: Surfaced. The transit through Biscay continued. Wind southerly, force two; sea slight, half overcast. Misty, phosphorescent.
>
> 2230: Contact on 171 centimetres, continuous tone but fading away. Submerged. The chums overhead are also not asleep.

30 October 1943. Biscay.

> 0505: Surfaced. Wind easterly, force one. Sea calm; cloudy, misty, strong phosphorescence.
>
> On the bridge stands the Kommandant, Obersteuermann [CPO navigation – first mate] Brins, with Bootsmaat [petty officer] Schindler and a few seamen. Under them, Franzel Ehrlicher and Schöntaube.
>
> A light drizzle has set in. The boat runs on both engines to recharge the batteries.
>
> 0542: Quadrant BF8155. Aircraft bearing 150 degrees with search-light. We turned hard to starboard at full speed.
>
> The aircraft flew directly at the conning tower at 50 metres

and opened fire with its guns. The First Mate and our No.2, leap immediately to the Pom-Pom gun, one cranked the traverse, the other the elevation through the gunsight. The target was raked with two bursts of fire. The machine's engine was on fire. The mixture of armour piercing and tracer gave a good line of fire on the target. The machine flew over the boat and dived burning into the sea, 50 metres abeam. Four depth charges dropped very close. One lifted the boat astern to the closed hatch and the water column fell on the quarter deck. Many casualties in the boat. However, after five minutes the LI reported everything all clear again for diving.

0547: Submerged for underwater running. A terse entry in the war diary reads:

'The four depth charges dropped very close . . . . The setting of the Pom-Pom by First Mate Brins and PO Schindler gave excellent shooting.' The Kommandant had not only extolled the courage of his own crew but acknowledged the performance of the foe.

As the First Mate reached the control room after submerging, he saw Ali Krieger behind the periscope column repeatedly raising his arms and jumping, shouting: 'We've shot down an aircraft!'

In the War Diary the Kommandant wrote:

'Because no Naxos whatsoever was established, the possibility of a new location method must be examined. The directional receiver was not tuned in but perhaps the short wave receiver interfered.'

By examining the damage while we were submerged, it was established that there was a fracture of the cast iron mounting of the lever on the disengaging gear of the starboard main coupling situated on the ship's side.

In addition, the rear shaft must have been distorted, since it permitted hardly any movement at all when we try to use the manual turning gear. Repair is impossible with our ship-board resources. Finally, after a deep dive attempt, it appears that there are severe leaks by the stern tube stuffing box as well as a succession of other items of damage, therefore a return of the boat to base is necessary.

It seems as if the aircraft which inflicted this damage just as it was hit and shot down, was Wellington C of 612 Squadron (HF205). It had been airborne at 2332 hours on the night of the 29th but nothing further was heard from the crew and this was the only aircraft which failed to return. The crew had been:

PO R S Yeadon	Pilot	FO W Wilson	WOP/AG
Sgt S R Jones	2nd pilot	Sgt W F Sills	WOP/AG
PO A M Davey	Navigator	Sgt B H Hall	WOP/AG

U 415's log:

> With these observations, our return to base was set in motion around 1600 hours, in BF8179. In addition to the further, but smaller damage, the Ju-condenser had been lifted off its mounting and lay on one side. By careful lifting it was fitted back into its former position and temporarily wedged to fit.
>
> During the evening surface running after 32 minutes, at 2004 hours in BF8158, an aircraft, barely discernible, was sighted bearing 70 degrees. Shortly afterwards there was a possible Naxos contact; there was a short lasting deep humming tone heard. Since the boat had apparently not been detected, the Kommandant ordered us to submerge at 2007, on full power. Three hours later we were again on the surface for re-charging.

U 415 put about and sailed back into Brest on 2 November. She was out of action until the 21st, at which time she was finally able to sail again. This time she escaped attention while making her way out across the Bay and in December became part of Gruppe Coronel and Gruppe Borkum. At 0118 hours on Christmas Eve she came across an escort-carrier, USS *Card*. U 415 fired three torpedoes at her, but missed, and also missed with a single torpedo against the escort destroyer USS *Decatur*. As was to be expected she was then subjected to a depth-charge attack but escaped without damage.

That same evening, at 2015 hours, U 415 put a torpedo into the 1,340 ton British destroyer HMS *Hurricane*, escorting convoy OS62, which sank. Thus the crew were able to celebrate Christmas with a significant victory. However, little more was found and soon U 415 was heading back to Brest. The Biscay gauntlet lay before them once more.

4 January 1944. Biscay.

> The boat has reached inner Biscay.
> 0728: Surfaced. Naxos contact during surfacing. Immediately crash-dived. The reflections of the Kommandant on it are: 'After several boats had been sighted in the inner Biscay by hostile aircraft, one has the impression that the enemy had put into action in this area continuous surveillance which made surface travel much more difficult. During submerged running the First Mate's stern compartment steward

produced a white silhouette of 'our' sunken destroyer and sewed it on both sides of the red sinkings pennant.'

1832: Surfaced.

1907: Quadrant BF4692, Naxos contact; crash-dived. As the boat goes straight ahead under the water, three aircraft bombs fell astern and strong concussions run through the boat. Almost all the command installations fail. The boat, however, through prompt action, levels out at depth 'A' and comes under rudder control. The damage is repairable with our on-board equipment.

This time U 415's antagonist was Halifax 'Y' of 58 Squadron (HX178). Airborne at 1615 hours, it found the U boat in position 4654/0721 at 1907 hours, which ties up almost exactly with U 415's position, just a minor variation on the second reference of 0715 west. The Halifax dropped six D/Cs which were seen to explode close to the target's stern, while her decks were awash. The crew were:

FL A I Sladen	Pilot	FS J J Scott	WOP/AG
Lt R A Tunnell USAF	2nd pilot	Sgt R W Wilson	WOP/AG[1]
FO A J Starr	Navigator	WO J E Abbey RCAF	WOP/AG
Sgt R B Lawrence	Engineer	FS O H Turner RNZAF[2]	

Algernon 'Toby' Sladen, also known as 'Moonpath' as he tried to develop a method of attack on moonlit nights (without having to switch on the radar and thereby risk detection from the sub's Naxos equipment) by trying to place the target in the moon's reflective light, was to receive the DSO later, having flown over 100 sorties. Apparently he was often seen in the Mess with hands swooping in a light beam, planning future attacks. He had been a sergeant in the Cambridge University Air Squadron and even had his own aircraft – a Tiger Moth which he had actually won in a raffle. He had already flown a tour from Iceland (612 Squadron) and also carried out some early experiments with Leigh Light aircraft. By the time he joined 58 Squadron his total flying hours topped 1,200. His first sub patrol with 58 was as second pilot to Eric Hartley (see Chapter 7).

'Twinkle' Starr and Abbey received DFCs; Abbey had been on the radar during the attack on U 415. Sladen only died a few years ago, preceded one year earlier by Twinkle Starr. Sladen had taken him into his own home when his former navigator was suffering from cancer.

---

[1] Sergeant 'Blondie' Wilson was a ground wireless operator who, when the Squadron was short of WOP/AGs, volunteered to take a gunnery course and subsequently joined the Sladen crew.

[2] Not a regular member of the crew.

There he spent the last years of his life. The American pilot, Bob Tunnell, later flew Mosquitos with the American 8th Air Force. He was shot down escorting B17s to Schweinfurt but he survived as a prisoner.

5 January 1944. Biscay.

0357: Surfaced. Wind northerly, force two; half over-cast but good visibility.

0431: Quadrant BF5449. Naxos contact, becoming louder. After the experiences of the previous days, the Kommandant let the boat remain on the surface. A zig-zag course was steered at full power and 'Aphrodite' was deployed. Simultaneously the command: 'Machine guns out!' and transmission of short signal 0431/5/56: 'Coming under attack from aircraft in BF5449,' signed Neide.

A minute later and a further short signal: 'Am 36 hours from rendezvous with escort,' signed U 415.

As the contact again disappears and nothing more follows, we dived at 0450 hours. The boat goes to 100 metres.

0914: Received signal FT.0546/5/62: 'To U 415, U 625; escort for Neide and Benker await at position 344, 6/1, 0630,' signed 1. U-Flotilla.

1815: Surfaced. No cloud, good visibility. In plotting our position we had to make an alteration to 254 degrees and by 12 sea miles.

1848: Naxos contact, becoming louder. The boat remains surfaced. Aphrodite deployment but no attack comes.

1857: Crash-dive. Why repeatedly does no attack follow? What has Tommy cooked-up? That's what the crew ask themselves.

1900: Aphrodite deployed.

2202: Received signal FT.1736/5/77: 'Neide, Benker; five M-boats with sweeps out, outward bound on route Polar Bear.'

2243: BF5469, Surfaced. As the Kommandant opened the tower hatch, there on the port beam hung a bright flare above the water. Expecting an immediate attack by an aircraft with a searchlight, he ordered the machine guns out. Both engines at full power ahead.

The boat is very quickly at defence readiness. Then it became apparent that the flare was over the Aphrodite position, deployed at 1900 hours. Further flares fell at shorter range. Repeated Aphrodite engagement.

Naxos contact. The Kommandant ordered a zig-zag course to be steered. We are gradually acquiring proficiency in this game.

2300: Wind southerly, force three. Sea moderate; cloudless, bright moonlight.

Attacked by a four-engined bomber from the starboard beam, level flight. Previous release of five flares in sight, altitude 200 metres, 1,500 metres off. Turned hard to port. Flak defensive fire opened with both twin guns and Pom-Pom. Position of target hard to discern because of strong blinding flares. Aircraft released four bombs of heavy calibre which fell on the port beam, nearest about 100 metres. During attack the boat ran at full power straight ahead. 'Main' was connected up. Short wave receiver plus directional receiver.

2304: Short signal transmitted: 'Attack by aircraft, BF5469' – U 415.

2305: Further flares dropped. Naxos contact still to be heard. Then there followed an attack of the same kind but with aircraft's guns only. The boat also defended herself against this attack.

2306: Crash-dived. The boat goes to a depth of 100 metres – no casualties registered.

Thus this cat-and-mouse game continued with the iron crew on the Wekker.

It had been another 53 Squadron Halifax that had located U 415, aircraft 'R' (HR983), flying a Percussion M3 patrol. At 2148 hours the crew had set course for base, seeing mostly trawlers on their radar. They were investigating yet another possible trawler, located at 22 miles at 2257 hours. This time, however, they spotted the submarine. Six D/Cs were dropped and 500 rounds of machine-gun fire directed at the boat, the boat, as related, returning fire with red and white tracer. Then she went under.

The RAF crew reported the position as 4700/0538, and although they circled the area for some time, had eventually to head for home, PLE having been reached. They landed at Predannack at 0329 hours the next morning. The crew consisted of:

FL I J M Christie	Pilot	Sgt W Heron
FS J M McCubben RAAF	2nd pilot	FS W A Rabig RAAF
FS F Chadwick	Navigator	FS H Finley RAAF
FL A Swain		Sgt L Griffiths

U 415's log:

Because of the long enforced underwater travels since 4 January, electrical and air reserves have fallen severely. Because the Kommandant reckoned on further attacks being made he decided that the quickest escort rendezvous was imperative, and he decided to report in.

With the last radio signal in hand, the old man perched on his bunk, trying to plat his beard, as radio operator Niewerth observed, and thought over the situation once more. Concern for the boat and her crew, continuous Naxos contacts, only a few amps in the batteries, almost no more air left in the bottles, the diesels already damaged, and with very little sleep, this was all playing on his nerves.

Making rendezvous with her escort vessels, U 415 entered Brest the next day. She was in port for almost two months, but sailed again for the Atlantic on 2 March 1944. The following evening she was found by Wellington 'U' of 304 Squadron in position 4645/0555 (German BF5491). The Polish crew recorded their attack time as 2208 hours, position 4705/0540.

Squadron Leader J Werakso, who had been with the Squadron since the previous September, was flying under 4/10ths cloud at 3,000 feet, the aircraft at 700 feet, above a rough sea, although visibility was ten miles. The aircraft picked up radar contact at four miles dead ahead and with a bright moon there was no necessity to use the Leigh Light. Werakso headed in, spotted the sub and released six D/Cs, two being seen to explode in the wake of the sub, the others along its track. The crew reported no flak, so assumed they had taken the boat by surprise. Their attack was deemed good and should have been lethal, but with nothing else seen, no claim could be made or upheld. In the event, U 415 suffered no damage. Her luck was still holding. The Polish crew were:

SL J Werakso	Pilot	Sgt A Herman	WOP/AG
FS K Kurnik	2nd pilot	Sgt Z Lender	WOP/AG
Sgt K Pakula	Navigator	Sgt T Edelman	AG

On the 13th she joined Gruppe Preussen but four days later she was depth-charged by three escort ships of convoy CU17 which caused severe damage. Aborting her cruise, U 415 limped again into Brest, on the 31st.

Kurt Neide handed over command of his boat to Oberleutnant Herbert Werner, and under his command U 415 slipped out of Brest on the evening of D-Day, 6 June 1944. Along with other boats, she was tasked with attacking the vast Allied invasion fleet off Normandy.

As one might expect, at the western end of the English Channel, with so many Allied aircraft and ships trying to ensure that no submarines could get close enough to cause mayhem to the invasion fleet, actions and counter actions would be highly confused. It is known that on 7 June, there were at least a dozen U boats in the area and all were in some sort of action with aircraft of Coastal Command.

To say with any certainty which aircraft attacked which boat, or which aircraft was shot at by which boat, is simply impossible. What can be ascertained is that U 415's flak gunners fired at an aircraft that attacked them and shot it down. It seems fairly safe to say that this was Liberator 'B' of 224 Squadron (in all Coastal Command lost three Liberators and a Wellington this night). The Lib crew were:

FO R H Buchan-Hepburn RAAF	Pilot
FS G J Fairs	2nd pilot
FS P Hogan RAAF	Navigator
FS J D Whitby	2nd nav
FS L Barnes	WOM/AG
FS M Dickinson	WOP/AG
FS B Hands	WOP/AG
FS A Kennedy	WOP/AG
FS H Earl	WOP/IR
Sgt A Collins	AG

U 415 was initially attacked by a Sunderland at 0220 hours which dropped four depth charges near them, and then a Liberator was engaged, followed by the same or another Sunderland a few minutes later. B/224 had been airborne from St Eval at 0034 hours on the 7th and its only message to base at 0207 hours said: 'Am over enemy submarine in position 4833/0451.' Then silence.

Also believed to be in the action was a Wellington 'G' of 179 Squadron, piloted by Flight Lieutenant Hill and they watched a Liberator's last actions. They had taken off at 0121 hours and at nearly an hour later spotted the feather of a wake half a mile on the starboard bow. As they circled they saw a Liberator heading in for an attack, its front gunner firing and the U boat firing back. Hill continued to circle and watched as the Liberator made a second approach but the U boat dived. However, another U boat was seen ahead and the Lib continued towards her in the moonlight, but then gunfire from a third, hitherto unseen boat, began to lace the night sky.

Hill was now making his move, picking the third U boat for attention and estimated his six depth charges to have made a good straddle. However, at 0230 the Wellington crew observed a brilliant flash on the surface of the sea as well as sustained fire, which must have been the Liberator crashing into the water.

Having sustained damage, U 415 headed back to Brest, docking the next day. On 11 July she sailed for Biscay but had to return two days later but set off again on the 14th. In the outer lock she struck a mine and was sunk! All but two of her crew escaped.

CHAPTER THIRTEEN

MOSQUITO BITES

Not only the large Coastal Command aircraft were used against the U boat in WW2, but, as the war progressed, versatile Beaufighters and Mosquito twin-engined fighter and fighter-bombers became useful weapons in the fight. Both aircraft were used in many roles and in many parts of the world.

Although not always capable of sinking a U boat on their own, both were used to locate boats heading into ports or skirting the enemy-held coasts of both France and Norway. Having successfully negotiated the terrors of the Bay of Biscay, returning boats – or even those heading out – had then to negotiate the inshore coastal waters through minefields laid by RAF aircraft. They were helped and escorted by minesweepers, sperrbrechers and even destroyers. These ships would be more than sufficient to see off the larger Coastal aircraft, but the more nimble Beaus and Mossies, with their 20 mm cannon armament, could attack more readily.

For tired crews within sight of home base, or those expectantly heading out on a war patrol, the last thing they wanted was the attention of these RAF fighters, and Coastal Command knew they were the answer to their inshore problem.

One squadron which had been developed to carry a bigger punch than the normal Mosquito units, was 618, formed initially to train with and then launch a dambuster-style bouncing bomb in order to attack German capital ships, notably the *Tirpitz*. Trials with a spinning bomb known as the 'Highball' took many months but in the end, the suicidal nature of an attack on *Tirpitz*, together with the fact that she hadn't moved to an anchorage suitable to attack with the bouncing-bomb, meant that the attack was cancelled. Therefore other ways of using 618 Squadron had to be considered.

One idea was to use their special weapon against U boats, but this was virtually a non-starter, and was soon dropped. The Squadron was then assigned to the Far East, but a detachment was given a new task, to carry in their Mosquitos the 57 mm Molins Gun. This gun, apart from its obvious punch, was one which encompassed automatic loading for the six-pound warhead. The idea had been hatched as early as March 1943 and by the autumn of that year, the 618 detachment – designated 618 Squadron Special Detachment – was sent to join 248 Squadron (Beaufighters), then based at Predannack, Cornwall, with Coastal Command.

The Detachment was on a trial basis to see how effective the gun would be against U boats and whether Mosquito aircraft could use them satisfactorily. Someone came up with the idea that at least four attacks on U boats would be necessary to assess future use. It was a case of 'First, find your U boat!' Unknown to the Mosquito crews, of course, was that Enigma gave Coastal Command HQ a fairly good idea of where U boats were, and where some would be as they approached the Biscay coast.

The Mosquito variant was called the 'Tsetse' after the African insect, not unlike its cousin the disease-carrying mosquito. Both had bites ranging from annoying to deadly, so 618's Mosquito 'bites' were hopefully going to be at least the former if not the latter.

The Detachment was ready by October and the first U boat (U123) was found and damaged off the Bay coast. Eight shells were fired at it, causing some damage, but then the gun jammed. The Mosquito crews, Flying Officer A J L Bonnett RCAF and his navigator, Flying Officer A M McNicol, together with Flying Officers D J Turner/ D Curtis, A H Hilliard and Warrant Officer J B Hoyle began carrying out almost daily anti-U boat patrols, either in pairs or on lone sorties, although generally escorted by aircraft of 248 Squadron. Escort with anti-flak aircraft was especially needed following the Bonnett/McNicol attack, for the Germans were now even more anxious to escort their boats into and out of port. Other Mosquito crews flew for periods with the Detachment too, which now moved to Portreath. The Germans also put up more Ju88 patrols over the areas off the Brest peninsula.

There was no more major U boat excitement until 25 March 1944. A signal from Group HQ sent two Mosquito XVIIIs off at 0700 hours, crewed by Turner/Curtis and Hilliard/Hoyle, in MM425 'L' and HX903 'I', and escorted by four Mosquitos of 248 Squadron. Their target area was off St Nazaire, the formation heading to the west of the Ile de Yeu which would bring them to the mouth of the harbour. Des Curtis relates:

> On 25 March I was leading navigator of a small force of Mosquito aircraft charged with seeking out German U boats in the shallow waters off the Bay of Biscay coast. The formation comprised two

Tsetse aircraft of 618 Squadron Special Detachment with four Mark VI Mosquitos of 248 Squadron as escort.

The Bay coastline was heavily mined by Allied aircraft, and the German Navy maintained a minesweeping operation to keep open seven narrow channels from the 60-metre water line to the ports where the U boat pens had been built. Once in a channel, the U boat was unable to dive safely and therefore proceeded at full speed on the surface. However, time to transit the channel was quite short.

The briefing order from 16 Group was very simple: 'Two Tsetse with escorts to proceed to a line C, ETA . . .' The time given being soon after full light. The task was to arrive at a point out of sight of land at that precise time, then to turn onto a heading of 030 degrees true, along the channel to the port of St Nazaire.

Leaving RAF Portreath as the first rays of light appeared in the east, we headed initially for a point some 25 miles west of the lighthouse at Ushant. Navigation lights were turned off as soon as the formation had settled at 400 feet and radio silence was mandatory. My task was to keep a constant check on the surface wind speed and direction, by watching the spume flying from the tops of the waves, and looking for every small sign of a wind lane.

Minor corrections of course were essential. Before passing to our left the flashing light of Ushant, we came down to 150 feet to avoid the risk of RDF detection. Then a major change of course to the south-east, still checking wind and ground speed. The navigation chart on which I worked was some 22 inches square, and that covered the area from the south of England to the north Spanish coast, and no assistance was possible from electronic aids.

On our updated ETA we turned onto the designated 30 degrees, coming as close to the water as safety would allow. At that point, before stowing my navigation kit in its bag, I gave my pilot two courses – one to Ushant then another to Cornwall, in case I was put out of action, and he lost sight of the other Mossies. Then I grabbed by bulky hand-held camera, made sure it was switched on, and concentrated on the horizon ahead. The other navigators would watch for enemy fighters.

The weather was fine but hazy, with a slight sea, and about six-eighths medium cloud. At wave height, the horizon is about eight miles distant, and at a speed of 270 knots, we would be very quickly onto any possible target. Suddenly, there were some minute shapes ahead, with the outline of the coast behind them. My pilot, Doug Turner, opened the throttles and began a gentle climb. Immediately he broke silence with: 'Target ahead.' There

was our target, a U boat with four armed minesweepers pro-
tecting it.

On full throttle and with Hilliard and Hoyle in the other Tsetse
moving out to position themselves to our stern, we climbed eastwards almost over the Ile de Yeu, to make our attack out of the
sun. The convoy below had recognised us as hostile, the U boat
beginning a series of sharp S-turns, and it and the escorting minesweepers opened fire with all guns.

The time was 0918, and we were at 1,500 feet about to turn
hard to port to make our first attack. As soon as the U boat had
disappeared from sight under our nose, Doug put the aircraft into
a steep 30 degree dive, and took aim to fire the first shot from
the 57 mm gun. Meantime, I was trying to get some photos with
the bulky camera, through the windscreen – a not too easy task
as the windscreen was at full arms' length from where I was
strapped in. Therefore my view of the battle was through the
camera viewfinder, making it appear that it was all happening
quite some distance away.

With a blinding flash and a bang we fired the first round. Its
tracer tip sped towards the waterline of the U boat. That noise
was backed-up by the clang as the heavy brass shell case was
ejected from the breech, immediately behind my seat, and fell
into the steel box below. Then the next round was rammed into
the breech with a resounding thud, before the whole noisy process
began again. In the time it took to dive at over 300 mph from
1,500 feet to sea level, Doug had separately aimed and fired five
rounds.

I saw the tall plume as each shell hit the sea, every time very
close to the waterline below the conning tower. I knew some of
the shells, at least, had found their mark.

We levelled out and climbed away easterly again to position
for the next run, as Hilly began his attack. I stopped taking
pictures and looked back, and I recall being amazed at the turning
rate of the U boat, and it was changing direction visibly in the
seconds of our dive onto it. On our fourth run the firing from
the U boat had almost ceased, so we knew they were in trouble.

The minesweepers were still pumping away at our formation.
The coastal batteries from the nearby Ile de Yeu had joined in
the firing, with both anti-aircraft and heavy guns. Their gunners
had been trained to fire heavy shells into the sea just ahead of
us; the volume of spray from a shell was enough to bring an
aircraft down if one couldn't avoid flying into it.

Minutes after first sighting this small convoy, I could see brown
oil on the surface around the submarine, telling us that its fuel

tanks were ruptured, and it was almost at a standstill. The oil patch quickly spread to about 100 yards long by about 30 yards wide. We knew that the U boat was very severely damaged. The battle was over, even though our Mosquito escorts and the mine-sweepers were still exchanging fire. There was no point in hanging about in the danger area, as without doubt German fighters were already being scrambled. Doug called up to abandon the attack and we headed north west and got back down to sea level. Looking around I could see the other five aircraft safely easing into a loose formation. With the need for radio silence long since gone, there was a sense of exhilaration in the voices of the pilots – a 100% success, with the target pretty well destroyed and all of our aircraft safe.

There was no need to stay far to seaward of Ushant light, as the Germans knew all about us by then. So, at low level and high speed, we skimmed across the rocks at Ushant, then turned almost due north for Cornwall.

The next pleasure was to see the happiness on the faces of the ground crews as we taxied into our remote dispersal. Our gun had been fired, what was the story? It was difficult to appreciate that the actual attack had been completed in about nine minutes. Many years later, I learned that the U boat was U 976, and it had been sunk, with four of its crew mortally wounded.

Aubrey 'Hilly' Hilliard in the second Tsetse machine, recalls:

The weather was hazy and visibility not good, about one and a half miles. Once we found the convoy, Doug Turner made three or four attacks before I positioned myself for one and I fired a couple of shots at the submarine, then got mixed up with an enemy destroyer which fired at us. I returned fire on them before turning quickly away.

Hilly's navigator, Jim Hoyle:

We were flying in broken cloud and I remember spotting a destroyer, two minesweepers and the U boat, later identified as U 976. It is my recollection that we followed Doug in his first attack with Hilly firing the Tsetse gun but it all happened very quickly and I did not see any actual hits. I think now that I may have been wrong about this, particularly after hearing of the U boat Commander's account of the action. After our attack we did not linger in the area and made our way back to Portreath. Our flying time had been four hours five minutes.

The escorting Mosquito crews had been:

FL L S Dobson	LR413 G	F/Sgt L A Compton	LR352 M
FO C Hardy		Sgt A D Peters	
FO V R Scheer RCAF	LR378 C	F/Sgt L D Stoddart	LR363 X
FO R W Twallen		F/Sgt C Watson	

Alan Peters recalls:

> Warrant Officer Compton and I were briefed to fly in Mosquito
> LR352 on 25 March and to act as anti-flak aircraft, with two 57
> mm cannon bearing Mosquitos forming the main attack element.
> On sighting the U boat and escort, the whole formation climbed
> to about 1,500 feet and on the command: 'Attack, attack, attack!'
> we started a shallow dive towards the target. At about 600 feet,
> Compton opened up with both cannon and machine guns, scoring
> hits on the deck and conning tower of the U boat. I really did
> not observe much myself being engaged at the time, taking
> pictures with a hand-held camera which weighed about 20 lbs
> normally, but suddenly increased its weight by a factor of two or
> three as we pulled out of the dive at about ten feet above the
> attack periscope of the submarine.

Oberleutnant zur See Raimund Tiesler, commander of the boat, later
recorded in the log of U 976 how devastating the attack had been by
the two Tsetse Mosquito aircraft:

> 0920   Aircraft sighted to port.
> 0921   First attack from starboard by Mosquitos. Permission to gun
>   crews to open fire. Aircraft firing only heavy cannon. One
>   dead on the bridge, several wounded manning the 2 cm
>   gun. Port side twin-gun destroyed. More attacks out of the
>   sun by 4-engined aircraft (sic). After three attacks the
>   automatic loading of the 3.7 cm anti-aircraft gun was out
>   of action, so re-loading had to be done manually. Boat
>   became heavy to control. I assume we are hit in Tank 1,
>   and order Tank 2 to be emptied, then all tanks to be
>   emptied and valves closed.
> 0930   The LI reports water coming into the galley; a little later,
>   that the boat cannot be saved. I give the order: 'Abandon
>   ship.' The boat was cleared and the wounded were hoisted
>   to the bridge by Engineer Leutnant Gneuss and Zentral-
>   maat Masch. Mt. Reckordt. Meantime, further attacks,

usually in groups of two to four aircraft and they only fire heavy weapons.

After the fifth attack, the 3.7 cm gun completely out of action although the breech was loaded. Some of the crew who were trying to abandon ship take cover behind the conning tower. The starboard twin-gun, coolly operated by Mtr.Ob.Gefr Rosin, is now the only gun in action. Three further attack, two from the starboard, one from port. About 30 seamen not protected by the conning tower are swept overboard on the starboard side; the rest are on the bridge and the fo'c'sle.

Both engines are still running at half speed. To keep the boat manoeuvrable, the WOII, Ob.Fshnr. Borchert, re-enters the tower and carries out steering orders, staying until the last moment until I call him to the bridge.

Finally the submarine began to sink by the stern but the Mosquitos had departed before that event. The crew were picked up by the escort vessels. One petty officer had been killed on the bridge, with two more and one seamen mortally wounded; others had varying degrees of wounds. Tiesler later recorded that the intake of water into the galley area and the battery room, plus damage to both 1 and 2 tanks, possibly No.5 also, made it impossible for the boat to be saved.

U 976 was built at the Deschimag AG Works as a type VIIC, commissioned on 5 May 1943 with Tielser in command. As part of the 7th Flotilla she had left Kiel, via Kristiansand on 25 November for her first patrol and been part of Gruppen Coronel, Amrun and Rugen. She had been fired upon and depth-charged by three surface U-boat hunters on 9 January 1944 but arrived safely at St Nazaire on the 29th.

Cruise two began on 20 March but was recalled on Dönitz' orders on the 23rd, to become part of Gruppe Marder. On her way back, having been picked up by the escort vessels, the Tsetse aircraft had found her. Tiesler, who had celebrated his 25th birthday on 7 March, had formally been watch officer of U 578 and then commanded U 649.

Two days later Turner and Hilliard were again successful. Two U boats had been reported sailing from La Pallice and their presence had been monitored for several days. They were U 763 and U 960. Des Curtis, again flying with Turner as lead navigator, recollects:

Two days later we were again ordered to proceed to Point C and to search the channel to St Nazaire. The time was again just after 0900 and in almost the same position along the channel, we spotted ships on the horizon, and, with the adrenalin pumping, we climbed slightly. I couldn't believe our luck. There dead ahead, were two U boats in line astern, but this time surrounded by a very formidable convoy of warships. Admiral Dönitz had learned a hard lesson and had reacted swiftly, and protection was being provided by four M-class minesweepers and two sperrbrechers. A sperrbrecher was a floating flak-platform, with a formidable array of anti-aircraft guns, a much more lethal floating base than, say, a destroyer.

The enemy ships began firing as our formation of eight Mosquitos opened out. I had no time to watch what our colleagues from 248 Squadron were up to. Hilly Hilliard's radio had gone u/s soon after we set off from base, an added difficulty when so much would happen in seconds. Hilly turned in front of us to make the first attack, and as we started our dive, we could see the splashes near to the second of the U boats where some of his shells had landed. Then, camera pressed to my face, I saw through the viewfinder the small shape of the U boat and the curve of its wake, and of course, the spurt of smoke from its guns as they fired at us. Then the crash, bang, as Doug loosed off rounds from our own 57 mm gun. The camera was being dragged away from my face by the G-force as we turned steeply over the small convoy.

With my limited vision through the viewfinder, I was not able to follow every shell, but between the two Tsetse Mosquitos we had registered at least four hits on the second of the two submarines. As far as I could judge, some of our shells had not landed as close to the target as two days earlier. This may have been due to the distraction of the heavy curtain of anti-aircraft fire that was exploding around us.

We broke off the attack, and Hilly flew alongside to show us that his aircraft had been hit in the nose section, blowing open the machine-gun covers, but fortunately leaving the Mossie still flyable. In addition, five of the six escorting Mosquitos of 248 Squadron had also been hit in those ten minutes, one of which crash-landed back at Portreath.

Jim Hoyle, Hilly's navigator, remembers the attack only too well:

Doug Turner again led us on the 27th, but this time we were escorted by six aircraft from 248 Squadron. During our pre-flight checks, we quickly discovered that the VHF radio and the intercom was u/s, but we decided to continue with the trip although we knew that we would be incommunicado. Because of the noise from the engines, Hilly and I had to rely on signs to one another as we could barely make verbal communication, though I was shouting as hard as I could. It was just a case of keeping station with the rest of the formation, following the familiar route down the west Cornish coast, skirting the Isles of Scilly and then cross to the island of Ushant, round the Ile de Seine and then past the Ile de Groix, Belle Ile and Ile de Noirmoutier.

After rounding the Ile de Yeu, we were moving towards the Ile de Ré and closer to the French mainland when we came across two U boats escorted by four M-class minesweepers and half a dozen other ships. Some of them were sperrbrechers which had a rather fearsome reputation for being armed to the teeth with anti-aircraft weaponry. Flak from these ships as well as from distant coastal batteries became quite intense and we were surrounded by flak bursts. I can still remember the odd, lonely feeling of being incommunicado and seeing the other Mosquitos milling around the convoy without knowing precisely what was happening and being unable to hear what orders were being given.

Suddenly, Hilly peeled off and went into a headlong dive straight at one of the U boats, firing the Tsetse gun as we went in. Another Mosquito, which we later discovered was piloted by Flying Officer Jeffreys, had latched itself on to our port side from where Jeffreys attacked one of the adjacent escort ships, whilst other Mosquitos singled out the other ships in the convoy for their attacks.

This time I had picked up my hand-held camera – quite a heavy piece of equipment – and was busy taking photographs as we attacked. One of them later showed a direct hit on the conning tower.

We flew straight over the top of the U boat at roof-top height and sped out to sea. As I put the camera down on the floor in front of me, I was horrified to see that the inspection cover door over the machine guns had opened up and was flapping away in front of me. I can remember pointing this out to Hilly who nodded grimly to indicate that he was already aware of the fact that we had been hit by flak. As we made our way back along the French coast, I had visions of one or both of these doors breaking away in the slipstream and wondered whether they would land on my lap in the cockpit or crash into the aircraft's tailplane. Neither was a prospect that I viewed with any pleasurable anticipation!

In the event they did not break off but continued to judder in front of us all the way home, and after a trip lasting four hours 15 minutes, we were finally able to make a safe landing at our base at Portreath.

Hilly Hilliard:

No sooner had we seen the convoy than we climbed. As I reached 2,000 feet I spotted a U boat with a sperrbrecher astern, both being at the rear of the convoy.

I dipped my port wing and went down towards the U boat, my nearest escort Mosquito going for the sperrbrecher, leaving the rest of the aircraft at this time still climbing. I fired seven shots in my dive, with bags of flak coming up at us. Just before I skimmed over the U boat at zero feet, I saw the German gunners pull their 3.7 mm gun upright. There was a thud as we went over and the machine-gun doors in front of the cockpit blew open! At first Jim and I thought the nose would soon split open totally.

Coming out of the attack we continued on our northerly course, getting away from the ships as quickly as possible. The shore batteries had also joined in so we altered course to port for a while to get out of their range.

On the way home Jim and I were concerned about the machine-gun doors flapping up and down in case they snapped off and damaged some vital piece of the Mossie, but we got home and landed safely, without brakes and almost out of fuel. One gauge registered zero the other ten gallons. We'd been very lucky that day.

Jim Hoyle continues:

After Hilly had 'parked' our Mosquito, we clambered out with quite a sense of relief and soon spotted a large jagged shell hole under the centre nose cone of the fuselage with surrounding shrapnel damage from the exploding shell. We were fortunate that the Tsetse Mosquitos were among the few planes to carry heavy armour protection in the nose section and without doubt it was this armour that had saved Hilly and me from serious injury or worse.

The six escort crews were:

FL J H B Rollett	LR352 M	F/Sgt C R Tomalin	HJ828 R
FO R Blanchard		WO G Phimister	
FL E H Jeffreys DFC	LR378 C	F/Sgt L A Compton	LR363 X
FO A D Burden		Sgt A D Peters	
FO F R Passey AFM	MM430 Q	F/Sgt P T Wilkinson	MM399 S
FO D G Williams		F/Sgt S Bertram	

Alan Peters:

On the 27th Compton and I flew in Mosquito LR363 again on an anti-U boat strike. This time we attacked one of the escort ships with 20 mm cannon and machine guns. As we pulled away over the target ship I heard a noise rather like canvas ripping, at the same time Compton swore loudly and pulled away in a wide climbing arc. It was obvious that we had been hit and Compton soon discovered that the rudder controls were no longer fully effective. I set a course to pass about ten miles west of Ushant and we climbed away to the north-west. After passing Ushant without further troubles we then set course for the Lizard. We had a little discussion as to whether we should try and land at Predannack or to go on to Portreath. Portreath won and we made a more or less routine approach. However, just as we touched down a violent swing developed, the wheels came off and we found ourselves scooting across the grass sideways only to come to a halt just short of the taxi-way. We climbed out through the side door and apart from a good shaking neither of us was any the worse for our crash-landing.

Ralph Blanchard:

On the 27th we were leading the escort to 'I' and 'L' in an attack on two U boats in the vicinity of St Nazaire which had an escort of nine flak ships. We suffered some damage to the tail of our aircraft but I don't think it was serious.

At least half of operational sorties in which I was involved whilst I was with 248 Squadron I was the lead navigator. A bit wearing at times but usually worth it.

Charlie Tomalin:

With my navigator George Phimister, I attacked two armed trawlers. The flak was pretty fierce and our Mossie was hit and we sustained a large hole in the port wing which also damaged the underside of the engine nacelle, which in turn shattered the tyre.

We knew we would have a problem when we returned to base but we managed to avoid further damage on landing, for which I received a green endorsement in my flying log book. [In other words – a well done! Ed]

Günther Heinrich, the U boat commander, recalls:

Attacks by Tsetse fighters were especially effective against U boats coming in and out of the Bay of Biscay. The shells of the 5.7 cm gun caused remarkable damage to our boats. The gun, originally constructed for a British tank, was about 3.6 metres long and was installed under the Mosquito's nose angled down slightly. From a total of 24 shells a shot could be fired every second automatically or fired singly. It caused extreme recoil and created a flash of fire some metres long.

U 123, with Horst von Schötter, had been attacked in the Bay on 7 November 1943 on the way to St Nazaire harbour and damaged. The first important attack was by two Tsetse aircraft on 25 March 1944. Escorted by four Mosquitos the two Tsetses attacked U 976 – Raimund Tiesler – in convoy and about to enter St Nazaire. The effects of the hits had been so severe that after the flak of the boat was put out of action, the incoming water was so swift that the crew had to abandon it shortly before sinking.

Although we didn't know it, and even our highest U boat Command had no idea, the current code of our wireless telegraphs between U boat Command and the boats at sea were often decoded at Bletchley Park, in Buckinghamshire. Therefore, practically all movements of U boats could be tracked. With this knowledge the Allies were able to inflict heavy losses on our boats. In this situation, much luck was needed.

I had been submerged three times crossing the Bay without any enemy contact and we were running at high speed during daylight with good visibility, passive radio detection, a strong lookout – eight men – and with our flak armament manned and ready to fire.

When U 960 was attacked by the Tsetse we fired with all our guns and one was hit immediately just before it flew over. However, at almost the same moment, a 5.7 cm shell went through the starboard side of the conning tower, through the post of the periscope and exploded inside the attack periscope. The periscope and its post was smashed and split open, and flying metal pieces and shrapnel pieces wounded everyone of us on the bridge and at the flak guns. Fortunately, our accompanying boat, U 763, was not hit. [See also Chapter 9.]

After entering the harbour at La Pallice I was, together with eight of my crew, sent to the Navy Hospital at La Rochelle instead of the expected Boat-party. After a stay of three weeks in this hospital, my boat had been repaired and all but two of the more seriously injured who remained in hospital, were ready for action once more.

One of the wounded crew members was Kurt Müller, who was celebrating his 21st birthday on 27 March! Günther continues:

> The RAF pilot who attacked us, and the few remaining crew of U 960 who are still around, have met and gained respect for each other. As often happens after a war we became friends. We have known each other as opponents and now as former comrades in arms.

On 1 November 1996, Hilly Hilliard moved house. From his home in Hamburg, Günther arranged for a pot plant to be sent to their new home, the order routed via Berlin, but the plant duly arrived on 2 November, much to the surprise and delight of Hilly and his wife. The two men have met several times; the war, while not forgotten, is now the source of their friendship.

In May 1944, Günther Heinrich took his U 960 into the Mediterranean. It was no mean feat getting through the dangerous channel between Gibraltar and the northern coast of Morocco. On 19 May she became the victim of a Swamp operation following detection off Oran. Attacked by aircraft and American warships and then kept down for several hours, Heinrich had finally to surface. Gunfire from the destroyers sank the submarine which went down with several of her crew. Heinrich, still not fully recovered from his leg wound from Hilly Hilliard's attack, was wounded again, in the back, but was picked up from the sea and taken prisoner.

He retired from the German Navy in 1978 with the rank of Fregattenkapitän, having spent many years in Washington, DC as a staff officer with the German Military Delegation to America and Canada.

CHAPTER FOURTEEN

MOSQUITO MAYHEM

Submarine U 155 was a successful boat, surviving, but only just, nine patrols and sinking a total of 25 ships. She had been built as a type IXC at Deschimag AG Weser, Bremen and commissioned on 23 August 1941, Kapitänleutnant (later Korvettenkapitän) Adolf Cornelius Piening being given command. Piening was born in September 1910 and he joined the Navy in 1930; prior to commanding U 155 he had been ten months as second in command in U 48. He would win the Knight's Cross with his new command.

As part of the 10th Flotilla, U 155 sailed on her first war cruise from Kiel on 7 February 1942, heading for the east coast of America. Just fifteen days later, on the 22nd, she sighted Convoy ON67, helped by the first use of HF/DF. Attacking with three torpedoes she hit and sank the Norwegian tanker *Sama* of 1,799 BRT, and the British tanker *Adellen*, 7,984 BRT. Buoyed up with this instant success, she came down to earth on the 27th, missing a freighter with two torpedoes.

The pendulum swung back on 7 March, one torpedo being sufficient to sink the Brazilian freighter *Arabutan* (7,874 BRT). Three days later she lost one of her watch officers overboard, Oberleutnant zur See Rentrop.

The next day, the 11th, no fewer than six torpedoes were fired at a freighter, but all missed. However, with three kills on her first sortie she sailed triumphant into Lorient harbour on 27 March. Less than a month later, 20 April, she sailed for the Caribbean. On 14 May she sank the Belgian freighter *Brabant* of 2,483 BRT, following this up three days later by sending to the sea bed the British tanker *San Victorio* (8,136 BRT) and the American freighter *Challenger* (7,667 BRT).

Three days later she picked up a message from U 502 about a small convoy (OT1) she had spotted. Hurrying to the location a single torpedo put paid to the Panamanian tanker *Sylvan Arrow* (7,797 BRT)

off Trinidad but this time an escort ship depth-charged her, and
U 155 received some slight damage, but survived.

A miss on a freighter on the 22nd was followed by success on the
23rd, sinking another Panamanian ship, the *Watsonville* (2,220 BRT),
and before the month was out, down went the Netherlands ship
Poseidon (1,928 BRT), on the 28th, and the Norwegian *Baghdad*
(2,121 BRT) on the 30th, although these had taken four and five
torpedoes respectively. She returned to Lorient on 14 June 1942,
having increased her tally of kills to ten.

U 155 set off for the Caribbean again on 9 July. On the 28th four
torpedoes were needed to sink the Brazilian ship *Barbacena* (4,772
BRT) but only one, followed by surface gunfire, to sink another
Brazilian vessel, the *Piave* of 2,445 BRT. Next day saw the Norwegian
Bill (2,445 BRT) sink below the waves, although they took the captain
prisoner. On the 30th one 'fish' finished the American *Cranford* (6,096
BRT), followed on 1 August by the Dutch *Kentar* (5,878 BRT) and
the British *Clan Macnaughton* (6,088 BRT).

A miss on the 3rd was rectified by a hit with two torpedoes on the
British ship *Empire Arnold* (7,045 BRT) on the 4th, the captain again
being taken aboard as a prisoner. The next day she surfaced to fire
at a freighter but return gunfire proved too hot and the engagement
was broken off. However, the Dutch *Draco* (389 BRT) later sunk.
On the 9th two torpedoes finished the British *San Emiliano* (8,071
BRT) and the next day U 155's deck gun sank the small Dutch ship
Strabo (383 BRT).

Retribution was now at hand. Off the Brazilian coast, in area
EP4184 (0703/5157) at 1318 hours on 19 August, she was attacked
by a twin-engined seaplane, but its three bombs failed to cause
any damage. However, at 2029 hours, a flying boat attacked and this
time severe damage was caused, and a crewman was lost overboard (EP4113 – 0745/5203). Unable to dive, U 155 called for
assistance.

It took the crew almost a month to get their damaged boat back
to Lorient, ably assisted by U 510 and later by U 460 who had brought
out spares for her. Still unable to dive she was escorted back by
U 704, and finally made Lorient on 15 September, her battle penant
showing a further ten scalps, in all twenty ships sunk.

Repairs took some weeks so it was not until 7 November 1942 that
U 155 was able to put to sea once more. She became part of Gruppe
Westwall and with the Allied 'Torch' landings in Morocco, she was
employed to Gibraltar. On the 15th she attacked convoy MK1 west
of Gibraltar with four torpedoes and sank the British escort carrier
HMS *Avenger* of 13,785 BRT, damaged the American freighter and
troopship *Almaark* which had to be towed back to Gibraltar, and

sank the British troopship *Ettrick* (11,279 BRT). Three days later an attack on another convoy failed.

On 21 November medical assistance had to be sought from U 118, Adolf Piening having been taken ill. However, it seems he had recovered sufficiently by early December for on the 6th, U 155 sank the Dutch ship *Serooskerk* of 8,546 BRT from the convoy ON149. U 155 was back in Lorient on the 30th, in time for New Year celebrations.

It was back to the Caribbean starting 8 February 1943. On 2 April four torpedoes were fired at the Norwegian *Lysefjord* (1,091 BRT) which sank, and the next day the American tanker *Gulfstate* (6,882 BRT) went under. Making her way back to France, she was located by a Leigh Light Wellington of 172 Squadron at 0411 hours on 27 April.

Wellington 'X' was flying in the Derange area, having taken off at 0043 hours. At 1,500 feet radar picked up a contact eight miles to port. Despite 10/10ths cloud, visibility below was good but the night was very black, the sea rough. The radar operator homed in his pilot and at one mile the two pilots spotted the tell-tale wake. Having come down to 400 feet, the Leigh Light was switched on at ¾ of a mile, which illuminated U 155 still on the surface, position 4430/1100 (German BF7424).

At 0411 six depth charges went down over the boat's port quarter to its starboard bow, from 100 feet, seen to explode close to its stern. As the Wellington swept over, the rear gunner hammered off 120 rounds of .303 into the conning tower area. The pilot put his aircraft into a 180 degree turn and came back over the flame-float, but the sea was empty. U 155 had made a rapid crash-dive and survived without sustaining any damage. The Wellington crew were:

FO M N Davies	Pilot	Sgt J A Muldowney	WOP/AG
Sgt M T Sennett	2nd pilot	Sgt A L Peterman	WOP/AG
Sgt I M Shuck	Navigator	FS D A Barden	WOP/AG

The following night, the hunt still on, U 155 was located once again by a Leigh Light Wellington, this time aircraft 'C' of 407 Squadron RCAF. U 155 put into Lorient on the 30th.

War cruise number six began on 12 June 1943, this time heading for the Central Atlantic. This was the period of group sailings for protection, so she headed out across the Bay in company with U 68, U 159, U 415, and U 634. As we read in Chapter 12, the boats were attacked in a strafing run by a Mosquito of 307 (Polish) Squadron, which damaged and caused casualties to U 68 and U 155. U 155 suffered five crewmen wounded, and both boats had to return to base.

Having survived this experience, U 155 came out again on 30 June heading for the Caribbean, but this time she was diverted for use as a tanker boat, supplying fuel to U 183, U 188 and U 168 over the three days 21-23 July, then returned to Lorient on 11 August.

Cruise seven began on 18 September, back to Brazil, although she popped into Brest for a couple of days. Down in the South Atlantic she was refuelled by U 488 on 4 October. Continuing on, she found and sank the Norwegian freighter *Siranger* (5,393 BRT) her 25th and last sinking. They took the ship's 3rd officer prisoner, who was wounded, and who was operated on by U 155's doctor. For those interested in tonnage sunk, her 24 freighters and tankers amounted to 125,752 BRT, plus HMS *Avenger*, 13,785, bringing the total to 139,537. (It was not known during the war that U 155 had sunk *Avenger*, only after post-war research.)

On the 29th two U-boat hunter ships found and depth-charged her, but she escaped their clutches without damage, but on 21 November a twin-engined aircraft caused severe damage in an air attack at 1652 hours in position 0127/4139 (German FB4638). U 155 headed back home and arrived in Lorient on New Year's Day, 1944.

There was now a change of command as Piening took a position with the 7th Flotilla HQ at St Nazaire. The new skipper was Oberleutnant zur See Johannes Rudolph, born in April 1916, who had joined the Navy in 1937 and had formerly been IIWO aboard U 155. He took U 155 out for its ninth patrol on 11 March 1944 but by 12 April, ten men had become ill with food poisoning including two officers, so they were forced to head for home. By the 23rd they were off Lorient, picking up their escort vessels, when the RAF found them again.

Undoubtedly the radio intercepts had picked up the fact that she was returning with sick aboard, and Coastal Command were informed. The Mosquitos of 248 Squadron was one unit alerted for inshore searches and six crews were briefed:

A/C	Pilot	Navigator
NT225 'O'	SL R A Atkinson DSO DFC	FO V C Upton
HX904 'E'	FO A H Hilliard	WO J Hoyle
HJ828 'K'	FL L T Cobbledick	FO W R M Belcher
HP907 'R'	FO K Norrie	FS B J Bland
HR158 'W'	FL L S Dobson	FO C Hardy
HP908 'P'	FS L C Doughty	FS R Grime

The first two aircraft were Mark XVIIs, the latter four Mark VIs.

They took off at 0408 hours and the pilot of one of the aircraft takes up the story. Les Doughty:

No. 19 Group, so we were told at our briefing on the morning of 23 June 1944, had received news by radio via the French Underground movement, of a U boat believed to be damaged, and making its way back to its base in Lorient, due to arrive in the early morning. My observer, Ron Grimes, (who sadly died in May 1991) and myself were one of a flight of six Mosquito aircraft, each armed with two depth charges and the usual four cannon and four machine guns, ordered to fly a controlled search for this reported submarine.

The briefing was as follows: We were to make a pre-dawn take-off on our navigation lights and formate on our leader at about 250 feet. When in formation the leader and the rest of us would switch off the navigation lights then switch over to our formation lights. These were small pin-prick lights set into the wings of our aircraft near the tip, which allow one to safely maintain a formation but are themselves not visible from the ground.

We were then to proceed to Lorient harbour, by which time day-break would be underway. Should the sub not be found at Lorient we were to turn to seaward and sweep into Biscay to continue the search.

However, in pitch black conditions, with no moon, we successfully formated and all switched off our nav lights. To our horror the leader failed to switch his formation lights on so no one could see where he was. Flight Lieutenant Dobson, the No.2 in command, then repeatedly called the leader asking him to flash his nav lights and switch on his formation lights, but with no success.

In view of the utter confusion and not wanting to risk a collision with one of our own aircraft, I pulled well away to one side and asked Ron to prepare a course for Lorient in case we never met up again. While he was doing this Dobson was constantly calling the flight leader but to no avail. After about ten minutes the R/T went completely quiet and we had no further contact with the rest of the formation, so I set off under Ron's guidance for Lorient in the hope of meeting up with the rest of the aircraft there.

Ron and I were now flying at about 50 feet above the waves and about a mile or so from the French coast on our way to the area off Lorient. Surface details very gradually began taking shape and more discernible as dawn slowly broke. I asked Ron for an update on our position and he pointed to a headland in the distance and said when we fly round that we shall be on the approaches to our target area. True enough, as we rounded the headland there was the Ile de Groix to our right and Lorient on our left – and approaching fast. Our next surprise was flying straight over a U boat, presumably the very boat we were seeking.

I immediately climbed to about 1,200 feet, all the time trying to contact the rest of the Flight on the R/T but all to no avail; we were on our own. We decided to attack, seeing it was only about 400-500 yards from the harbour mouth. I opened the bomb doors, armed the two depth charges as I went into a long shallow dive, and opened up with both cannon and machine guns. At about 50 yards from the sub and about 30 to 40 feet up, I released the depth charges.

We were now subjected to intense flak, both from the harbour and its surrounds, as well as from batteries on the Ile de Groix, and from which we sustained slight damage to three exhaust stub outlets on one of the engines. However, we were soon out of range at about 325 knots, took violent evasive action, and lost no time in heading away and setting course back to base.

The U boat received severe damage, while two men were killed and seven others wounded. She limped the last few hundred yards into harbour, repairs taking so long that although fit for sea by early September, she had then to leave her French base or risk capture. She was transferred to Norway, sailing on the 9th under the command of Oberleutnant Ludwig von Friedeberg, aged 20, former IIWO and IWO of U 548. He took with him a shipment of mercury and arrived in Kristiansand on 17 October. On 4 May 1945 the boat was surrendered in Fredericia, Denmark. At that time her Commander was Oberleutnant zur See Fritz Altmeier, aged 24, who had previously served on U 80, U 508 and commanded U 1227.

Johannes Rudolph, the submarine commander, recalls:

At the beginning of the war I started in destroyers, the *Dieter von Roader* and the *Z.27*, and I took part in the attack on Narvik. After this I went into U boats.

I was the first officer under Commander Piening on several trips before I took over as commander of U 155. The ninth cruise was to the Gulf of Guinea. Outside Freetown we were attacked by three British destroyers, but we managed to evade them. We then operated near Duala, but did not find any merchant vessels. After 14 days cruising we started the return trip. We had no schnorkel, and therefore had to sail on the surface by night to recharge the batteries. The trip was without any difficulties and we sailed past the Spanish coast into the Bay of Biscay.

We then met the pilot-boat outside Lorient, which took us to
the harbour entrance. As we sailed into the harbour a low-flying
plane came towards us from the land. I told my first officer, who
was standing next to me, that it cannot be a German plane, as
they were forbidden to fly towards a U boat. All our guns were
manned, and I gave the order to clear for action.

When the plane was at a distance of 300 metres, I gave the
order to fire at will, and to the 'Zentrale': both engines full speed.
At the same time the plane fired from all guns at our conning
tower, and dropped its bombs in our wake. We suffered two dead
in the conning tower and three badly wounded at the 2 cm guns.
Now, 50 years later, I learn that we also damaged the plane.

At the entrance of our submarine pen we were greeted by
music. I ordered an ambulance and asked for the music to be
stopped. After docking I handed over the boat to our Flotilla
Commander, Korvettenkapitän Kuhnke in front of the crew lined
up on our deck.

For his determined attack, Les Doughty received the Distinguished
Flying Medal and was made a Warrant Officer. The recommendation
of his award stated:

Squadron Commander's Remarks

F/Sgt Doughty has done excellent work throughout his present
tour of operations. On 23/6/44 he was Captain of an aircraft
detailed to carry out an A/S sweep before first light. While proceeding to patrol he became separated from the formation in the
darkness and continued to the anticipated position of the U boat
alone, flying along the French coast to Lorient.

He reached the entrance to Lorient harbour at first light and
encountered intense flak from the shore batteries. At the same
time he observed a fully surfaced U boat escorted by four surface
vessels. Having attempted to contact the other aircraft by R/T
without success he decided to attack alone and approached the
enemy force for the second time as it was passing through the
harbour booms.

Very intense flak was encountered from the ships and the shore
positions but F/Sgt Doughty pressed home his attack with
complete disregard for his own safety, scoring numerous cannon
strikes on the U boat and releasing two depth charges. Unfortunately, owing to the poor light and the heavy opposition, results
could not be observed.

In making this attack F/Sgt Doughty displayed the highest

standard of gallantry and devotion to duty. The immediate award
to this airman of the Distinguished Flying Medal is most strongly
recommended.

Station Commander's Remarks

Recommended.

Air Officer Commanding's Remarks

The fighting spirit of F/Sgt Doughty is typical of the whole of 248
Squadron. To pursue the enemy to the very gates of his own
harbour with a single aircraft is a most courageous act. Recommended for an immediate award of the DFM.

The award was duly approved and promulgated, the actual citation
recording:

This airman has proved himself to be a skilful, courageous and
determined pilot, qualities which were amply demonstrated on
the occasion of an attack on a U boat at the entrance of Lorient
harbour. In spite of intense fire from various ships and from guns
sited on the shore, Flight Sergeant Doughty pressed home his
attack with great resolution, obtaining many hits with cannon fire
and releasing two depth charges. He set an example of a high
order.

Les Doughty:

The postscript to this story came 51 years later. I attended a
reunion of the U boat crew and met its commander and surviving
crew members. A small aeroplane was chartered and my wife,
son, myself and two friends plus the pilot, were welcomed and
treated like Royalty, not just by the U boat commander, Johannes
Rudolph and his wife but by the whole crew, and the townspeople
of Ottenhäffen, where special events were laid on in our honour.
   Apparently, my observer and I had been lucky to escape further
damage as the Commander told me there were over 100 anti-
aircraft guns situated on the harbour mouth alone. He told me
that U 155 had been damaged by our attack and that the war in
Europe was happily over before it could be repaired satisfactorily
in order to put to sea again on a war cruise.

Submarine U 867 was another boat to feel the Mosquito's 'caress'.

A type IXC-40 from the Deschimag AG works she was commissioned in December 1943, command going to Kapitän zur See Arved von Mühlendahl, who had celebrated his 39th birthday the previous month.

However, it was nine months before she was ready for her first war cruise, which began on 9 September 1944 from Kiel. After a brief visit to Kristiansand, she sailed on the 12th, one report saying she was destined for the Far East, another saying her task was to put an automatic weather station ashore in Canada.

However, five days later she reported a technical defect, empty batteries, engine trouble, and being unable to dive, sent out distress signals. Shore-based HF/DF picked up a good fix on these and Coastal Command were on the scent. Six Mosquito aircraft of 248 Squadron were sent out to patrol off the Norwegian coast soon after dawn on the 18th, led by Wing Commander D G Sise RNZAF, with two 235 Squadron aircraft acting as fighter cover. One of the crews was non other than Hilly Hilliard and Jim Hoyle who had been involved in the Tsetse gun attacks on U 976 and U 960 referred to in the previous chapter.

Pilot	Navigator	A/C
WC G D Sise RNZAF	FO R G Price	'J' Mk VI
FO A McLeod	FS N Wheeley	'V' „
WO H A Corbin CGM	FS M J Webb DFM	'B' „
FO R G Jefferson	FO J H Jamieson	'U' „
PO W N Cosman RCAF	FO L M Freedman	'O' Mk XVIII
FO A H Hilliard	WO J B Hoyle	'E1' „

The aircraft made landfall, from over a rough sea and under 10/10th cloud (base 500 feet) just north of Ylteroene Light, then turned to starboard and followed the coast, keeping about one mile off-shore. The original plan had been for the anti-flak/DC aircraft to fly at 1,000 feet and the Tsetse aircraft at 1,500 feet, the fighter escort keeping to seaward at 2,000, but the low cloud forced an alteration, all aircraft staying at 500 feet or below. Sise was at 300 feet, at 0820, and spotted the surfaced U boat two miles ahead. Bill Sise ordered an immediate attack and each Mossie wheeled to port and attacked with cannon and machine-gun fire, Hilly firing five rounds from his Molins gun. Mosquitos 'B' and 'U' also carried depth charges which were dropped, but a third D/C carrying aircraft failed to get its bomb doors to open on the first run.

Aircraft 'U' had its D/Cs fall astern but the crew of 'B' saw its D/Cs enter the water 20 feet from the boat's port beam, exploding some 5-10 feet from its conning tower, and along the water line fore and aft of it. Hilliard recalls:

It was our second trip from Banff (Strike Wing), our last from down at Portreath having been flown on 23 August. We registered five hits but there were many Mossies milling around and lining-up to 'have a go'. I did see the depth charge chaps attack and there was too much spray and columns of water splashes to get a good aim. But I do remember the shells I fired were pretty good according to the tracer they emitted.

The U boat appeared to be lifted by the exploding D/Cs and later commenced to settle, listing 10-15 degrees to port. Photos later showed the boat with a heavy list and making for Utvaer, seemingly badly damaged. Mosquito 'B' was crewed by Warrant Officer H A Corbin CGM and Flight Sergeant M J Webb DFM. In his diary, Harold Corbin later wrote:

Went on U boat hunt near Bergen. Sighted U boat on surface. Strafed it with cannon (20 mm), also straddled it with my two depth charges. Claimed as sunk. I hope this is kept out of the newspapers.

Today Harold Corbin recalls:

I do have a memory of U 867 being very close to a rocky shore and half submerged so that at first it appeared to be almost beached. The last sentence in my diary was written as my wife and parents had had so much worry with me being reported missing back in August.

Maurice Webb, Harold's navigator, remembers:

We dropped two depth charges close to the target, and assessed it as 'damaged'. My only other observation was this was one of the few times we returned from an 'op' without sustaining damage to the Mossie.

U 867 had indeed been heavily damaged and this, added to her earlier problems, put her in even graver peril. Von Mühlendahl struggled on until the next afternoon but was then found by a Liberator of 224 Squadron. Still on the surface and unable to submerge, the Lib crew headed in despite flak fire from the boat, but the sun was behind them which could not have helped the gun crews. Later photos showed two dingies by the boat, so perhaps her crew had already decided to abandon her. The D/Cs mostly overshot and if the U boat captain had indeed decided to abandon, he now continued to do so, knowing that this further sighting and attack would only bring more aircraft to his position. After the D/Cs exploded, the boat remained afloat for a few minutes, then sank. As the Liberator circled, the crew saw one large and several small dinghies, containing an estimated 50 men, floating in the pool of oil left by the sinking submarine. Pieces of timber and other debris could be seen too.

The attack position was 6215/1050, west of Stadlandet. This was not that far off the coast of Norway yet in the event, none of the 61 crewmen survived. The Liberator crew consisted of:

FL H J Rayner	Pilot	FS S H Whiter
WO E C Browning		FS W Robinson
PO M H Evans RAAF		Sgt R J Munro
WO L C Kenney RAAF		FS W S Newlands
FO H Lord		FS A M Bell

When Harold Corbin wrote in his diary about hoping the press did not mention his attack on U 867, explaining that he did not want to worry his wife and parents, he had good reason.

Just over a month earlier, on 14 August 1944, he and Maurice Webb had flown a sortie that had resulted in Corbin being awarded the Conspicuous Gallantry Medal (Flying), one of only 109 awarded during WW2. It was the NCO's DSO, and considering well over a thousand DSOs and 85 bars were awarded to officers, the CGM is pretty rare.

Harold Corbin, of course, was not a Warrant Officer in August, but still only a Flight Sergeant. Having joined the RAF in November 1940, four days following his 17th birthday, he was eventually to join 235 Squadron, flying Beaufighters on anti-shipping sorties, later 248 Squadron, with Mosquitos.

On 14 August, Corbin and Webb, in HP866, took part in a shipping strike to the Gironde river, which led to the port of Bordeaux, situated on the west coast of France. They attacked and damaged a Seetier Class destroyer but return fire damaged three of the Mossie's fuel tanks. Corbin set course for Vannes airfield, now occupied by invading Allied forces in Brittany, trailing fuel from his punctured tanks, the port engine knocked out and the other damaged. Knowing they were not going to make it, they decided to bale out. They were picked up by American troops the next day. Maurice Webb tells a sequel to the story:

> In April 1995, accompanied by my son, a fluent linguist, I returned to St Brieuc on the invitation of a local historian. This was my first visit to France since baling out in August 1944.

I was shown the point where our Mosquito crashed and the spot where Harold Corbin landed. The high-spot though was when I was taken to a farmhouse in Treguidel and re-united with the lady to whom I had given my parachute. At that time she was aged 20, as I had been, and in 1945 she married and her mother made her wedding dress from the parachute silk. Remarkably she still retained the bodice of this dress, fifty years on, and in a traumatic ceremony it was presented to me.

I also met a member of the local unit of the Maquis who looked after me until I was re-united with Harold, and then the Americans arrived.

In being awarded the CGM – Maurice received the DFM – Corbin's award recommendation had also mentioned an attack upon an M-class minesweeper on 30 June and an attack on a convoy off the French coast on 27 July. On that occasion their aircraft had been hit and they had to return on one engine and landed with a punctured tyre.

Not that their attack on U 867 was an end to their adventures, as Harold Corbin relates:

On 26 December 1944, in company with four aircraft of 235 and four of 143 Squadrons, and outriders of 333 (Norwegian) Squadron, led a formation into Leirvik harbour where two Motor Vessels were attacked. One was left on fire, the other smoking heavily. Light (?!!) flak was experienced from ships, and heavy flak from the harbour area. Leaving the entrance to Bomba Fjord the formation was met by a mixed force of 24 Me109s and FW190s. In the resulting melée, one enemy aircraft was destroyed and another damaged. One aircraft of 235 was lost but the enemy fighters later left us once we were well out to sea.

Maurice and I, in Mosquito 'N', had been hit by flak which had damaged one engine, causing a loss of glycol coolant. Seeing the German fighters waiting for us as we came out of the fjord I risked full throttle, got down on the deck and hoped the damaged engine would last until we were out of danger and that no German would pick on us.

We were lucky, and finally out of danger, but the damaged motor, having done what was necessary, was finished, so I feathered the prop and once again headed for home on one motor. Having got safely back to Banff I then misjudged the approach and realised that I was going to touch down in a field some 100 yards short of the aerodrome boundary and runway.

I was not unduly worried until just after touch down. I saw a stone wall at the aerodrome edge. Just as we hit this I switched off to avoid possible fire and selected 'wheels up' on the under-carriage to allow the wall to knock the wheels back up. I felt we might somersault otherwise, and end upside-down.

Well, dear old 'N' hit the wall with the result that can be seen in photographs; flat on our belly, both props and wheels torn off but otherwise on an even keel. Maurice and I were trapped in the wreckage but within seconds, Max Aitken [leader of the Banff Strike Wing] had raced around the perimeter track in his station wagon and dragged us out, then took us to the station hospital.

We were only slightly injured and soon recovered, but when 248's CO, Bill Sise DSO DFC, came to see us he said: 'I'm giving you a rest. No more ops, but I want you to stay with the Squadron to help newcomers.' We then went off to an aircrew officer's course at Hereford. After a month or so we returned to find the Squadron had suffered many losses during our absence. Bill Sise had been posted to 143 Squadron, many friends were gone and the biggest blow of all was that our dear, our beloved, Wing Commander Maurice Geudj had been lost to FW190s.

We were posted to Air Sea Rescue work at Thorney Island, so that at long last I was back on the type of aeroplane I had been trained to fly at Pensacola, Florida – a flying boat, the Walrus.

EPILOGUE

'LOVE EASY'

Not long after the updated second edition of my book *Search, Find and Kill* (Grub Street, 1995) was published, I received a letter from a John Davenport:

6 January 1996

Dear Mr Franks,

My son sent me a present of *Search, Find & Kill* – I had a particular interest as I was a pilot in 502 Squadron flying Halifaxes from St Davids and later from Stornoway.

I have been doing a bit of research myself about a U boat attack we made in T/502, on 8/9 July 1944. I was at the controls and stayed there to do the attack while the captain, Lieutenant C D Kramis USAAF, watched with binoculars on my right. Bright moonlight, some flak, dropped five 600-lb AS bombs very close. U boat appeared to turn 180 degrees and stop. Attack then assessed: 'Good attack, insufficient evidence of damage.' Place – approaching Lorient near Ile de Groix.

I wrote to the Air Historical Branch in late 1993 quoting the details, suggesting that they often knew the whereabouts of U boats, particularly in 1944-45. They replied in November 1993, saying that this was U 802, enclosed a copy of its log and confirmed the attack could now be re-assessed as 'Damaged', as the U boat reported damage; rudder jammed and gyro compass out of action.

John, of course, had been referring to the first edition of my book, but had been informed that in the second version, the name of Karl Wahnig, former crewman in U 802, had been noted in the acknowledgements. John quite naturally wondered if he could be put in touch with him.

I immediately telephoned Karl Wahnig, who lived in London then, and he could not believe it. He is something of a U boat historian himself and had often wondered who had attacked his boat that July day, for, as he explained, that had been the nearest he had come to being killed during the war.

U 802, commanded by Kapitänleutnant Helmut Schmückel, had been returning to port after a war patrol and searching for her expected escort vessels. Her log reads:

0000 Quadrant BF6177

0231 A few small clouds, bright moonlight. Very good visibility. On surface, distance to go, 14 nautical miles, course 055 degrees.

0225 Three contacts bearing 320 degrees. On the assumption that this is the escort, we moved towards it. No navigational aids (radio aerials not clear, light beacons not switched on).

0240 Radar images revealed as Iles de Glénan. Course 110 degrees. Our escort vessels now in sight. Distance 6 nautical miles.

0255 Radar reports approaching aircraft, height about 6,000 metres.

0305 No point in diving. At full readiness, making zig-zag course sailing to meet escort. Aircraft standing off at about 2-4,000 metres in height. No visual sighting.

0314 Aircraft approaching at 5-600 metres. First sighted crossing the boat. It flies across almost athwart the boat. Make avoiding manoeuvre with rudder hard over. Aircraft dropped six bombs, three to port, three to starboard, about ten metres astern, together with a light buoy.

Aircraft flying over, the aircraft (a large sluggish machine) is driven off by flak, flew into a bank of cloud and stayed 2-4,000 metres in height. Rudder malfunction, jammed hard to port. Boat turned in circle around the light buoy [flame-float]. Apart from the gyro compass – out of action – apparently no other damage. My short signal about the aircraft is not acknowledged inspite of two transmissions. No further approach from aircraft.

0320 Alarm! Dived to 40 metres (water depth 60 metres). Closed up to periscope depth. As escort is only about four nautical miles distant I hope it will come to me. Escort, however, remains at Leben point.

0340 Surfaced. Sailed at top speed towards escort.

0355 Closed up to escort.

0528 Tied up at Lorient.

Schmückel, Commander

John Davenport recalls:

Halifax T/502 took off from St Davids at dusk on 8 July with orders to carry out a 'Ranger' patrol in the Bay of Biscay to search, find and attack German U boats leaving or approaching French west coast bases. Bomb load consisted of 600 lb anti-submarine bombs, flares; extra fuel tanks in the bomb bays provided for an endurance of twelve hours.

Modern equipment included the Mark XIV automatic bomb sight which only required a wind to be set on it and thereafter, could automatically take into account the speed, height and attitude of the aircraft.

The other item, vital in night patrols to detect surfaced U boats, was the latest Mark III centimetric radar, which worked by transmitting and receiving pulses via the rotating antenna in a blister under the rear of the fuselage. The signals were then displayed on a Plan Position Indicator, a circular cathode ray tube on which a line moving around a centre point (the aircraft) rotated once every four or five seconds with contacts of land, surface shipping or other aircraft appearing as brighter 'blips'. Bearings and distances could be read off quite simply and reported on the intercom.

For night attacks the aircraft were supplied with two types of flares – High Intensity (HI), very bright instantaneous parachute flares for low level approaches and less bright but longer lasting parachute flares, with a 1½ minute delay, for high level attacks. These were to prove ideal for later anti-shipping operations.

Flame-floats were dropped with the bombs for marking position. Others were manually fed down a flare chute for wind finding when the rear gunner sighting the flame-float, could read the drift off a gauge in the turret on each of a series of three courses. These drifts were plotted on a [manual] computer by the navigator. In Dead Reckoning (DR) navigation at night, this method of wind finding was frequently used when other aids like GEE were not available.

The Ranger patrol in this case covered a rectangle about 80 miles long, 15 miles wide, angled slightly to correspond with the coastline, on average, ten miles away. Similar rectangles had been swamped by aircraft before and after D-Day in the Cork Patrol configuration where every area of water from Land's End to Bordeaux was covered by radar every 20-30 minutes.

On patrol, at 0030 hours in full moonlight, clear visibility, small amounts of low cloud. The radar could also be used for map reading with bearings and distances of prominent points or islands being reported to the navigator at intervals.

As we started a second time round the patrol area, with me as second pilot at the controls, the Glénan Isles and the Ile de Groix were picked up on radar. Further smaller contacts were obtained at 45 degrees to starboard. Our attack report takes up the action:

'Aircraft was flying on track 090 degrees at 4,500 feet, when several radar contacts were obtained bearing Green 045, range 6½ miles. Aircraft turned on to a course of 120 degrees and contacts were maintained, a further blip also appeared on the screen bearing Green 030, range five miles.

'Aircraft homed on to this last blip and then mid-upper gunner sighted a U boat on the surface, bearing Green 030, distance four miles. Pilot made a 330 degree descending turn to port down to 3,000 feet.

'U boat was now well silhouetted in moonpath, bearing dead ahead. Navigator/Bomb Aimer then took over and gave the necessary slight corrections in order to line up the target in the Mark XIV bombsight.

'Five 600-lb Mark I A/S bombs, tail fused chambers anti-count mining, spaced 120 feet apart, were released from a height of 1,400 feet, using the Mark XIV bombsight. U boat was still on the surface and aircraft tracked over the U boat just forward of bows.

'A short accurate burst of flak was encountered on run-in followed by slight inaccurate fire, ceasing altogether when bombs were released. Navigator/Bomb Aimer saw two explosion plumes to starboard of U boat just aft of conning tower followed by a wall of water enveloping the target. Rear gunner only had a glimpse of the U boat which then became completely obscured by water flung up by the explosions.

'Flight Engineer from astrodome saw, as co-pilot made a rate two climbing turn to starboard, a steady brilliant red/yellow glow for approximately 12 seconds from positions of explosions. Mid-upper gunner also saw this glow for a few seconds; the low drifting cloud had closed in from the west and made further immediate observation impossible.

'When aircraft had completed turn and came out of cloud over the position some four minutes after the attack, it was seen again in the moonpath heading on a reciprocal course and from visible wake, had made a complete and very tight about turn, almost on its own axis, making very little way and when last seen by Captain, appeared to be still circling to port.

'Second pilot also saw oil or scum residue on the original track of the target, 250 to 300 feet in length and about 100 feet wide, approximately 300 feet from the U boat on its starboard side. No flak was encountered in spite of aircraft passing fairly close.

'Three possible escort vessels had been seen approaching . . . . [but they] did not open fire, but were seen to be signalling each other with Aldis, and appeared to be going faster when last seen.'

John Davenport:

0330 – left area, the intercom buzzing with crew comments on what had been seen. The question arose about failing to pick up a contact on the third pass – this could be explained by the U boat diving at 0320 in U 802's subsequent log, but at the time led us to hope that we'd sunk it!

Diverted to RAF Chivenor during return trip owing to low cloud and drizzle at St Davids. Landed Chivenor at 0530.

John O'Kane was the navigator, and remembers:

I obviously gave the attack a lot of thought afterwards, wondering if it could have been carried out more efficiently. This was the first sighting of a U boat we had experienced as a crew and that in itself made it an event.

When the sighting was made the Captain decided to attack immediately in the moonpath at 1,400 feet. We were flying at 4,000 feet and the wind on the bomb sight would be the one I had found and was using for navigation purposes at that height. It was quite likely that the wind at the lower level was different from this and some error would be caused by that. This, coupled with the action of the U boat, may have resulted in a very close but unsuccessful attack.

I must add that with more experience we became a most efficient crew as was evidenced by attacks on shipping in the Skaggerak and off the Norwegian coast. We found that accuracy of the wind factor on the bombsight was the crucial factor in bombing accuracy, assuming that we could get a straight and level run-in.

As John Davenport also asserts:

I think we missed because we had no chance of finding a wind at our intended bombing height like we could do for ships, evasive action by U 802, and also that we had not yet learnt then of relative drift radar homing. We employed this later in attacking moving targets when we specialised on ships, and developed remarkable accuracy.

The Halifax crew consisted of:

Lt C D Kramis USAAF	Pilot
FO J K Davenport	2nd pilot
FS J H O'Kane	Navigator
Sgt J A Leavy	Engineer
WO W J Watson RCAF	Radar
FS R A Ovenden RCAF	Rear gunner
Sgt J Robinson WOP	
FS W Stetsko RCAF	M/Upper
WO Gallacher	WOP/AG

It had been a near thing for U 802. Perhaps if John O'Kane had had those few extra seconds to check the wind, perhaps if the bombs had fallen a second earlier, or later; if Schmückel had changed course a moment earlier, or a moment later . . . The possibilities are endless.

What was important 52 years later was that two men who had been oblivious to each other since that night, were about to meet. Having checked with Karl that I could give John his address and telephone number the next thing I knew was when John wrote to say he had talked to Karl on the telephone, and Karl had admitted to: '. . . never having been so scared in his life and was glad we had missed.'

When 'Cap' Kramis, John's former skipper heard they were going to meet he commented from his Boise, Idaho home: '. . . it should be enlightening and interesting. I hope the German is not still mad at John over that sneak attack, and at night yet!'

I managed to horn-in on the reunion of the two men which took place in the time honoured fashion, under the clock at Waterloo Railway Station, at 1030 am on Thursday, 15 February 1996. We then relocated to Karl's flat where the three of us, but especially John and Karl, had a good long chat over old times and their respective activities during WW2. It was quite a morning and has to prove something about fighting men in later life, having learnt to live with their moments of fear, anguish, anger, and developing some degree of forgiveness, or at least tolerance.

U 802's minor damage was repaired, she was converted to a schnorkel boat and sailed again, this time to Canada. She had a pretty hectic time being hunted by surface ships near Newfoundland and in the St Lawrence Estuary in the autumn of 1944. She eventually surrendered in May 1945 having sunk one ship.

John Davenport went on to command his own crew, including John O'Kane as navigator, and both were decorated with the DFC and DFM respectively, sinking two ships in 1945. John had a twin brother who was also a pilot and also with 502 Squadron.

After capture, Karl Wahnig was a prisoner in England, later met and married an English girl and remained in this country. Seeing these two meet that February day at Waterloo Station was quite an event. Fifty-odd years ago they would quite happily have tried to kill each other but now they are developing friendship. Perhaps there is hope for the future of mankind after all, if people can resolve their differences without resorting to war, and dictators are not allowed to prosper.

And why is this Epilogue given such a title? The code name given to U 802 by Allied intelligence was LE – Love Easy. John and Karl will obviously not go that far, but having each shared their own glimpses of the anti-U boat war, making a new friendship *was* easy.

INDEX OF PERSONNEL

(See page 218 for US Navy and AAF Personnel)

Abbey, WO J E 179
Acourt, Sgt V 141
Aitken, GC M 209
Akers, Sgt F 34
Aldridge Sgt N J 56
Allwood, Sgt A 17, 93
Altmeier, Oblt F 202
Altmeier, Oblt J 174
Anderson, FS R 156
Angelo, Sgt S 156
Antoniewicz, FO L 135
Archibald, Sgt D W 4
Armstrong, Sgt R P 92
Atkinson, SL R A 200
Aubrey, Lt Cdr R M 53
Auld, Sgt D H 57
Austin, FO 15, 28

Bach, FO T E 96, 97, 101, 103, 104, 105
Baird, FO R D J 72, 74
Ball, Sgt J 152-3, 156
Bamber, Sgt F 54, 73, 76, 77, 79-80, 81, 87, 90
Bamford, FO R D 159, 160, 163
Barber, PO A F H 169
Barden, FS D A 199
Barnes, FS L 183
Barnett, FL L O 147, 149, 150-4, 156
Barrow, Sgt J 172
Bartels, KptLtn R 149
Baty, Sgt D 156
Bathurst, FS A L 43
Baylies, WC N M 138
Beal, FS A 34
Beaton, WO S 137
Beaudry, Sgt E 65-66
Bedford, FO H M 18, 21
Bedford, FS R T 17, 93
Belcher, FO W R M 200
Bell, FS A M 207
Bell, FL D A 132, 133
Bell, FO R K 169
Bemister, Sgt J 92
Benker, KptLtn 180
Bennett, Sgt B J 57
Bennett, Sgt H J 57
Bertram, Sgt D W 29
Bertram, FS S 193
Biggar, FO W S 46
Bisdee, WC W N 147
Bishop, FO A A 66-71
Blackmore, PO F 3, 4
Blanchard, FO R 193, 194
Bland, FS B J 200
Bonnett, FO A J L 185
Borchert, Obfrn 190
Borland, Sgt Y T 65
Botsford, FS I N 137
Brame, FS E L J 65-66
Braun, Ltn G 61
Braun, Ltn K 139
Brignall, Sgt C V 19, 21
Brins, Obstm 176, 177
Brown, FS A W G 133
Browning, WO E C 207
Bruton, Sgt E B 171
Buchan-Hepburn, FO R H 183
Buchholz, Kvtkpt H 124, 125
Budd, FO H R 60, 61
Bugs, Oblt H-H 21
Bulloch, SL T M 93, 94
Bunce, Sgt A W 56
Burden, FO A D 193
Burns, FO A R 34-35
Burton, Sgt E F 56
Butler, FS A H 141
Buxton, FS J W 42

Caligari, FS K V S 147-8, 152-3, 155, 156
Carter, Sgt J 156
Celdart, FO D E 137

Chadwick, FS F 181
Christie, FL I J M 181
Churchman, Sgt J W 132
Ciano, Count G 10
Clegg, FS F 133
Clifton, FO M A 168
Clutterbuck, FO A R D 32-35
Collett, PO 28
Collins, Sgt A 183
Collins, Sgt L S 171
Colquohoun, FO L A 159, 162
Cobbledick, FL L T 200
Cole, Sgt W W A 35
Compton, FS L A 189, 193, 194
Conacher, Sgt D I 60-64
Conner, FL G L 139
Cook, FS B E 60, 62
Cook, Sgt W 14
Cooke, PO H G 56
Cooper, FS T K 29
Corbin, WO H A 205-6, 207-9
Cordes, KptLtn E 130, 131-9, 141
Cosman, PO W W 205
Coulson, FO J A 84
Cox, Sgt L W 172
Criddle, Sgt P R 73, 80
Critcher, PO E R 172
Crompton, FS R J 133
Cruickshank, Sgt G 84
Cruickshank, FO J A 84-5
Crumpton, FO R A 17, 93
Culling-Mannix, FO F T 137
Cundy, FL P J 14
Curtis, FO D 185-8
Curtis, FO J M 60, 62
Cutbush, Sgt L T 168

D'Allessandro, ten. 4
Dadson, Sgt J V 168
Dale, Sgt L J 35
Davenport, FO J K 210-2, 213-5
Davey, PO A M 178
Davidson, WO E 26
Davidson, FO W F Mc 168-9
Davies, FO M N 199
Davis, Capt D M S 44
Dawson, PO C J 172
Dennehay, Sgt B 173
Dewar, FS W D 139
Dewhurst, Sgt 15
Dickinson, FS M 183
Dickson, FO J C 84
Dickson, FO W J 43
Dimmock, Sgt G F 38
Dobson, FL L S 189, 200, 201
Dobson, FO J S B 73
Dönitz, Adm K 30, 110, 173, 191
Done, PO W G 73, 75, 78-80, 82, 85-90
Doughty, WO L C 200-4
Downey, SL J C T 140-1
Drought, Lt Cdr E A F 101
Duckworth, Sgt G J 57

Earl, FS H 183
Earnshaw, FS N 172-3
Eccles, FO L W 142-7, 149-150, 151-2, 153-4, 156
Eckermann, Kvtkpt 170
Edelman, Sgt T 182
Edwards, WC H R A 85
Ehrlicher, 176
Elder, Sgt R W 93
Elliott, Sgt S J 139
Ellison, Sgt T W 133
Elisha, PO F C 14
Elworthy, FL M J 39
Eminsang, Sgt R S 168
Emmermann, KptLtn 117
Erskine-Crum, SL W D C 139
Esche, Kptltn D von der 127
Eshelby, Sgt J T 73, 81

Esler, PO L L 133
Esler, FO S 94-5
Evans, PO M H 207
Evans, Sgt P 56
Excell, Sgt A N 171

Facey, FO H 20
Fahey, A C C 138
Fahey, WO M J 137-8
Fahey, Maureen 137
Fairs, FS G J 183
Fantoni, Adm G 5, 6-7
Finch, FL J 169
Finley, FS H 181
Finn, Sgt H E 69, 71
Fisher, FO A 43
Foster, WO W P 26
Fowler, FS E J 132
Fox, Sgt A S 96, 97, 98, 103
Foxon, FS F S 163, 164
Franco, Gen 10
Franke, Ltn 19
Franzel, 176
Frewin, FS J H 57
Friedeberg, Oblt L von 202
Frost, FO L J 168
Fry, FL K G 58, 60, 61-62
Fryer, Sgt J E 60, 62
Fuller, Sgt A G 168
Fuller, Sgt E A 56

Gallacher, WO 214
Gamble, FS J 172
Gascoigne, FL F B 172
Gassauer, Ltn F 35
Geils, F 19-21, 24-25
Gerrard, PO N C 28
Gibb, PO A P 23-24, 26
Gilardone, KptLtn H 94
Gillies, WC R 64
Glaser, Ltn J 18, 19, 22, 24-25
Glasgow, Sgt A D 65
Gneuss, Ltn G 189
Goodall, Sgt G M 95
Goodhew, FO B J 169
Goodman, Sgt E C 14
Goss, Chris 90
Gossip, Sgt H 71
Grainger, K 143
Green, PO L R 176
Greenaway, FO 176
Greise, WO D H 23
Greswell, WC J H 3-8, 12, 158, 168
Griffin, Sgt R H 141
Griffiths, Sgt L 181
Griffiths, Sgt M 96, 97, 103
Grime, FS R 200-202
Guedj, WC M 209
Gutermann, Ltn W 90
Gwinner, Lt Cdr G 53
Gysae, Kvtkpt R 122-124

Häcklander, KptLtn B 55, 61
Hadcroft, Sgt F 70, 71
Hall, Sgt B H 178
Hall, Sgt E J 156
Hamer, Sgt J 26
Hanbury, FO R D 32-34
Hands, FS B 183
Harbison, Sgt S B 84
Hardy, FO C 189, 200
Harrop, FS L 42
Hart, Sgt R 92
Hartenstein, KptLtn W 110
Hartley, FO E L 96-105
Hascoet, Capt J 25, 26
Haslam, Sgt J 60
Haye, SL A L A L de la 65
Heinrich, KptLtn G 194-6
Henderson, Cpl 156
Henderson, Sgt 109

Herman, Sgt A 182
Heron, Sgt W 181
Herwartz, KptLtn O 126
Hill, FS S G 132
Hill FL 183
Hilliard, FO A H 185, 187, 188, 190-3, 196, 200, 205-6
Hodson, FO G H 139
Holden, Sgt D M 133
Holton, FS R N 163, 164, 166
Holtorf, KptLtn G 115
Hötring, KptLtn O 126
Horgan, Sgt G F 15, 16
Horsburgh, FS J B 71
Horsemann, Ltn E 35
House, FS E 34
Houston, FO R 171
Howard, Sgt R D 132
Hoyle, WO J B 185, 187, 188, 191-3, 200, 205
Hugonin, Lt Cdr R E S 53
Hutton, FO J T 163, 164, 166

Irving, FO W J 45, 47
Irwin, Lt 60
Isted, SL D J 16-17, 93-4

James, Sgt T J N 35
Jamieson, FO J H 205
Jantzen, M.obgfr V 35
Jennings, FO W H T 39, 42
Jensen, PO P T 46, 54, 73-83, 84, 86
Jeschonneck, Gen H 27, 36
Jeschonneck, Oblt W 27, 29-31, 33-35, 36
Jefferson, FO R G 205
Jeffreys, FL E H 192
Jewell, FL J 63
Johnson, FO J 42
Jones, Sgt S R 178

Kammelard, Sgt J 95
Kämper, Oblt K 39
Kawalchuk, FO M 141
Keeble, PO N 147
Keech, FS A R 139
Kelly, FS J B 71
Kempton, FST H 95
Kennedy, FS A 183
Kennedy, PO D H 56
Kenney, WO L C 207
Kershaw, Sgt J 171
Ketcherson, FO J M 26
Kiln, FS P C 163, 166
Kinsman, WO W R 133
Kirby, Sgt L H 34
Klimaschewski, Obstm 47
Knight, PO J L 133
Knights, PO K W 34
Köppe, KptLtn H 31
Korger, Ltn 25
Koroby, Sgt W 92
Kramis, Lt C D 214-5
Krieger, A 177
Krüger, Oblt H 48
Kuhnke, Kvtkpt 203
Kurnik, FS K 182

Lacey, FS B 34
Ladd, Sgt F 35
Ladds, FS K E 96, 97, 102, 103, 105
Lanedziewitz, Matr. K 35
Lawrence, Sgt R B 179
Layson, FS C T 163, 166-7
Layzell, FS S W 160, 161-3
Leavy, Sgt J A 214
Lehsten, KptLtn D von 18, 21, 22, 25
Leigh, FO P C 54, 73, 77, 78
Leigh, WC H de V 1, 3, 12
Lender, Sgt Z 182
Lewis, FS J O 132
Liddell, Sgt W S 29
Lidgett, Sgt C 132
Lloyd, AVM H P 157, 158, 166
Lococco, G 112
Loeser, KptLtn P 13, 15-18
Lorains, Capt 44
Lorbeer, CPO 25

Lord, FO H 207
Loveday, FO G B 139
Lowe, FO R W 141
Luis, KptLtn W 43
Lydeamore, Sgt H B 60, 62
Lynn, Sgt G 156

MacDonald, Sgt R 172
MacGregor, FO D 14
Mackenzie, PO 15
McAndrews, Sgt J J 29
McComb, WC W T 23
McCormack, FO J G 42
McCubben, FS J M 181
McDonnell, Sgt P 71
McDougall, Sgt M G 35
McDowell, PO L 171
McDowell, WO T J 23, 26
McFarlane, Sgt A 34
McInnes, Sgt M 168
McKenzie, Sgt V B 57
McLeod, FO A 205
McNicol, FO A M 185
McQuiston, Sgt L J 173
McRae, Sgn Lt 101

Mainprize, PO M S 8
Manger, FL F V 72
Manson, Sgt 175
Marrows, FL D 46-54, 72-90, 91
Martin, Sgt J F 156
Martin, Sgt R 149, 156
Mason, FO A 134
Masters, FO T J 159, 160, 163, 169
Maton, SL C A 138
Maus, KptLtn 117
May, FO J T A 21
Mead, GC R C 96, 97, 102, 104, 105
Mealin, Sgt A H 95
Medcalf, FO W L 160, 161-2
Meder, Funkgfr 19
Mengerson, KptLtn E 27, 29
Migliorini, ten. Count A 4-5, 8-11
Miles, FS W 56
Millard, Sgt M G 173
Mills, FS J L 139
Milne, Sgt E C E 56
Mitchell, Sgt C A 84
Moore, FO K O 22-26
Moore, LAC 15
Morgan, FS H H 54
Mountford, FO A E 68-71
Mude, Oblt H 71
Mühlendahl, Kpt A von 205
Muldowney, Sgt J A 199
Müller, K 196
Mundy, Sgt J F 29
Munro, Sgt R J 207
Mussolini, B 10

Neide, KptLtn K 170, 173, 176, 177, 180-2
Neumann, KptLtn H 39
Newlands, FS W S 207
Newman, FS A P 169
Nielson, Btsmt 24-5
Norrie, FO K 200

Oehring, Obgfr 25
Oliver, Sgt E 134
O'Hara, Sgt M M 168
O'Kane, FS J H 213-4
Osborne, PO H L 56
Ostler, Sgt C 137
Ovenden, FS R A 214
Ovens, Sgt H R 56
Oxley, Sgt S 156

Pakula, Sgt K 182
Parker, Sgt C 168
Parliament, PO H 71
Passey, FO F R 193
Patey, Sgt T A 132
Pearce, Sgt A N 54, 73, 76, 79, 90
Pearce, Sgt N 148, 150, 154-5, 156
Pearson, PO T 34
Peatty, PO I V R 73, 78

Perry, Cpl 15
Peterman, Sgt A L 199
Peters, Sgt A D 189, 193, 194
Peters, Sgt W M 149-152, 156
Petterson, Sgt F O 60, 61
Phimister, WO G 193, 194
Piening, KptLtn A C 197, 199
Pincott, Sgt F B 57
Pledger, FS D R 134
Pledger, FS 85
Pooley, PO S J 4
Pope, Sgt J S 171
Portus, FO J H 60, 62, 63
Prescott, FST R 108
Price, FO R G 205
Price, Sgt 15

Rabig, FS W A 181
Radcliffe, FS L 169
Rahn, Oblt W 158, 169
Ranson, Sgt R A 141
Rautenberg, G 170 et al
Rayner, FL H J 207
Reckordt, Mat. 189
Rentop, Oblt 197
Rice, Sgt J D 35
Richardson, Sgt A 17, 93
Richardson, FS J A V 69, 71
Richardson, Sgt J 92
Ricketts, WO I G 163, 165, 167
Roberts, Sgt E 4
Robertson, Sgt G R 96, 101, 102-5
Robin, FL C E 155-6
Robinson, FL A S L 23
Robinson, Sgt J 214
Robinson, FO R E 139
Robinson, FS W 207
Rochinski, Matros H 47-8
Rolland, FO J S 46, 54
Rollmanm, Kvtkpt W 120
Rosin, MtObgfr 190
Rossom, FO A van 46
Rowland, FO C S 134
Russell, WC J B 4, 18-19, 20-22
Russell, PO R A 38

Saccadro, ten. G 112
Schacht, Kvtpkt H 108-9, 111
Scheer, FO V R 189
Schindler, Bootsmt 176, 177
Schmandt, Oblt A 64
Schontaube, 176
Schötter, Oblt K H 141
Schötter, KptLtn H von 195
Schmückel, KptLtn H 211, 215
Schulemson, FO S S 65
Schultze, KptLtn H-O 121
Schultze, FO J D 176
Schwinge, Sgt G B 134
Scott, FS J J 179
Segrave, Lt Cdr W F R 53
Sennett, Sgt M T 199
Shaw, Sgt L 173
Sheridan, FS V 169
Shuck, Sgt I M 199
Sidney, Sgt D C 54
Sills, Sgt W F 178
Simpson, FS L G 43
Sinclair, PO D A 172
Sise, WC D G 205, 209
Skyrme Obs 21
Slade, Sgt L 38
Sladen, FL A I 179
Smedley, FS H 172
Smith, FS C A 65
Smith, FL E C 171-2
Smith FS J 84
Southall, FO A W 3, 4, 14-15
Starr, FO A J 179
Stiebler, Kvtkpt W-H 39, 43, 45, 47, 48, 50, 54, 96
Stetsko, FS W 214
Stewart, Sgt R V 172
Stobel, FS C C 92-3
Stockden, Sgt R D 84
Stokes, Sgt 109

Stoddart, FS L D 189
Styring, FS W 65
Sugden, FS A D S 169
Sumner, SL J R 66
Sutton, FO H 141
Swain, FL A 181
Szablowski, SL S 174

Tainer, J 54
Taplin, FS P E 54
Tennant, FO W 143
Teschke, Obfän G 35
Thiele, Dr 18
Thomas, Sgt W R 14
Thomas, Sgt 109
Thrower, FO P 159
Tiesler, Oblt R 189-190, 195
Timoney, FS T 17
Tomolin, FS C R 193, 194
Treuberg, Oblt R von 31, 36
Triggol, Sgt R K 96, 97, 103-4
Triggs, PO A W R 4, 5
Trojer, KptLtn H 91, 94, 95
Tunnell, Lt R A 179-80
Turner, Sgt A A 41-2, 43
Turner, FO D J 185, 186-8, 190-1
Turner, FS O H 179
Twallen, FO R W 189

Underhill, Sgt G H 19, 21
Unterhollenberg, Mat. G 35
Upton, FO V C 200

Urquhart, Sgt 109

Vines, Sgt G W 38
Vöwe, KptLtn B 43, 44

Wahnig, K 210, 215
Walker, Sgt E A 4
Walker, Capt F J 45, 53, 55, 58, 61, 74, 77-8, 83, 89
Walker AC 15
Wallace, Sgt C J 84
Wallace, Sgt F W 95
Wass, Sgt E 169
Watson, FS C 189
Watson, Sgt G M 54, 72-3, 80, 83-4
Watson, WO W J 214
Watts, FL R S 73
Webb, FS I C 26
Webb, FS M J 205-6, 207-8
Weber, FO D C L 95
Webster, Sgt D E 84
Webster, Sgt R L 54, 73, 80, 83-4
Welch, PO A M 60, 62
Welfare, FS R G 60, 62, 63
Wemyss, Lt Cdr D E G 53
Werbiski, WO W N 23, 26
Werakso, SL J 182
Werner, Oblt H 182
Wettlaufer, FO D M 67-71
Wheeler, Sgt C A 29
Wheeley, FS N 205
Whitby, FS J D 183

White, FO S 45
Whiter, FS S H 207
Whitley, Cpl C A 15
Whitteron, Sgt A 92
Whyte, FO J 43
Wicks, Sgt W F 38
Wieser, R 132, 136, 140-1
Wilamowitz-Möllendorff, Kvtkpt G von 37-43
Wilkinson, FS P T 193
Williams, FO D G 193
Williams, WC G 157-8
Williams, FO N J 132
Williamson, FO D J 137
Williamson, FS J 166, 168
Wilmer, WO J F 134
Wilson, Sgt A R 141
Wilson, SL M 23
Wilson, FS N 34
Wilson, Sgt R W 179
Wilson, FO W 178
Wilson, PO W 156
Wood, FL S R C 15-16, 28
Wood, Sgt W J 38
Woodhouse, PO 156
Woodland, Sgt L 81
Woolcott, FO L 137

Yarston, R 129-130
Yeadon, PO R S 178
Yeomans, FL E StC 9, 16

US Navy and Army Air Force Personnel – Chapter 8

Akins, Maj 119
Anderson, AMM3c H L 126
Arnold, Ens L 120

Baldwin, Lt C A 113-5, 118, 120, 126
Bamber, AMM J 112, 113
Bennett, AMM2c J F 120
Bergstrom, ACRM L M 120
Besmehn, Ens D R 114
Blair, AOM2c J A 120
Bohon, S1c R L 115
Bofenkamp, Lt W 120
Bradford, Lt G 112
Branden, ACRM H C 117
Brownlee Jr, AMM1c G 122
Burggraff, S2c A P 113
Burton, Lt J T 113, 115, 126-7
Buskirk, AMM3c C N von 113
Butler, Ens N F P 115

Carpenter, S1c D W 115
Carpenter, Lt 119
Chapman, ACRM E L 114
Clark, Ens H C 120
Clark, Lt Cdr R S 106
Cook, Ens J D 126
Coupe, Ens E L 117
Cowdery, ARM1c T W 113

Damiano, AMM1c R L 114, 115, 120
Davis, Lt D 115
Dawkins, Lt M V 107, 121-2
Deutsch, Lt M M 128
Dickinson, AMM1c W J 120, 128
Dugan, Ens W 120
Dupree, ARM2c D W 107, 115, 120

Edwards, ARM2c J D 114
Eide, Ens M E 121-2
Ellis, ARM3c W E 120
Ernst, AMM2c G 115, 120

Feckoury, Ens N 120
Fisher, AOM3c E J 120
Ford, ARM2c D J 114
Ford, Lt W R 106, 113-5, 118-8, 120

Gallagher, Ens P W 128
Gardner, ARM2c D W 117
Geer, AMM3c R 120

Gilpin, AOM3c R D 122
Goodall, AMM3c B 107
Greenberg, ARM2c S 113, 115
Grimm, Ens W A 122

Hale, ARM2c S B 107
Hamilton, AMM1c W T 113
Hammer, AMM2c T S 120
Hannever, Lt G C 117
Helfenbein, Ens G H 128
Hilgeman, ARM2c C W 128
Hill, Lt W E 119, 120
Holt, Ens 108
Houchin, Ens G A 112

Jenkins, ARCM J C 113
Jorgensen, ARM2c M I 113, 128

Kiefler, Ens J C 120
Kloss, S2c E J 111, 113, 122
Krug Jr, Lt E A 126, 127-8

Lacey, Lt 110
Laux, AMM2c D M R 128
Leonard, Ens J M 120, 126
Loomis, Lt Cdr A E 106
Ludwig, Lt 108

McCoy, Ens B S 112
McKernan, ARM3c R L 126
McLatchie, S2c D W 114
Mairhofer, Ens W G 114
Main, Capt 119
Mangano, S1c G B 128
Merrick, AOM1c G G 117
Meyer, ARM3c G E 115, 120
Milhalsky, S2c J 117
Morrison, Ens E C 111, 112
Mosher, AOM2c W H 128

Nicpon, AMM2c E A 128
Nix, AM2c S E 115

Orr, Maj 119

Petaccio, ARM2c A J 114
Phelps, AOM3c W H 126
Pinnell, Lt C I 112, 125-6
Pittman Jr, ARM2c J W 113
Prueher, Lt Cdr B J 111, 113, 116-7

Rackley, S2c F J 115
Ratka, ARM3c L G 120
Renda, AMM2c F S 122
Resner, AMM3c F E 128
Richards, AMM1c C W 128
Richter, ARM1c P G 115
Riley, Lt R A 128
Riggs, Ens R M 113, 115
Roberg, ARM1c V C 122
Robertson, Ens T E 111, 112
Roewer, Lt 126-7

Schneider, ARM1c H A 115, 120
Scholer, Ens W 120
Schoolfield, AMM3c J E 120
Scott, ARM3c R M 113
Seidel, ARM3c W G 114
Seymour, ARM2c S F 114
Shannon, Ens R M 115
Shedaker, AMM1c S S 115, 120, 126
Simpson, ARM3c J 122
Slusher, ARM2c H L 113
Smith, ACMM C A 117
Stamps, ACMM R B 107
Stern, S2c F W 115, 120
Striano, AOM3c M 115, 120
Swan, Lt R S 107, 114
Swanson, Ens R S 126

Taylor, AOM3c C B 128
Taylor, Lt M G 108
Taylor, Lt S K 119, 120
Tehan, Ens R 117
Tettlinen, AMM3c L N 120
Thomas, Lt Cdr T D 116
Turner Jr, Lt Cdr J R 113, 118

Valentine, Ens G H 122
Van Horn, AMM1c J R 117
Verity, ARM3c A H 128

Waugh, Lt G E 114
Whyte, Ens E G 120
Wilson, ARM3c R A 120

Zudrell, ARM1c W R 126
Zukiewicz, ARM3c G J 114